The Labour Party and Electoral Reform

The Labour Party and Electoral Reform

Jasper Miles

BLOOMSBURY ACADEMIC
LONDON • NEW YORK • OXFORD • NEW DELHI • SYDNEY

BLOOMSBURY ACADEMIC
Bloomsbury Publishing Plc
50 Bedford Square, London, WC1B 3DP, UK
1385 Broadway, New York, NY 10018, USA
29 Earlsfort Terrace, Dublin 2, Ireland

BLOOMSBURY, BLOOMSBURY ACADEMIC and the Diana logo are trademarks of
Bloomsbury Publishing Plc

First published in Great Britain 2023

For legal purposes the Acknowledgements on p. viii constitute
an extension of this copyright page.

Series Design: Adriana Brioso
Cover image © PA Images / Alamy Stock Photo

A catalogue record for this book is available from the British Library.

Library of Congress Cataloging-in-Publication Data
Names: Miles, Jasper, author.
Title: The Labour Party and electoral reform / Jasper Miles.
Description: London ; New York : Bloomsbury Academic, 2023. |
Includes bibliographical references and index.
Identifiers: LCCN 2022038676 (print) | LCCN 2022038677 (ebook) |
ISBN 9780755640683 (hardback) | ISBN 9780755640690 (epub) |
ISBN 9780755640706 (pdf) | ISBN 9780755640713
Subjects: LCSH: Labour Party (Great Britain)–History. | Elections–Great
Britain–History. | Great Britain–Politics and government–20th century. |
Great Britain–Politicsl and government–21st century.
Classification: LCC JN1129.L32 M49 2023 (print) | LCC JN1129.L32 (ebook)
| DDC 324.24107–dc23/eng/20221021
LC record available at https://lccn.loc.gov/2022038676
LC ebook record available at https://lccn.loc.gov/2022038677

ISBN: HB: 978-0-7556-4068-3
ePDF: 978-0-7556-4070-6
eBook: 978-0-7556-4069-0

Typeset by Newgen KnowledgeWorks Pvt. Ltd., Chennai, India

To find out more about our authors and books visit www.bloomsbury.com
and sign up for our newsletters.

Written in loving memory of
Doreen Ann Coates

Contents

Acknowledgements

This book emerged out of my PhD studies on the same subject. The topic came to mind during the Alternative Vote (AV) Referendum, 2011. The Labour Party split between supporters of First-Past-the-Post (FPTP) and electoral reformers, some genuinely convinced by AV, others hoping for something else but realized this was as good as it was going to get. From there, the research developed, first as a PhD thesis and now as my first sole-authored manuscript.

As such, I'd like to thank my PhD supervisory team and the wider community at the University of Liverpool. A particular note of thanks goes to my primary supervisor, Dr Kevin Hickson. He has been a constant source of encouragement during my doctoral research and subsequently, and his knowledge and expertise have proved invaluable. At Liverpool, I also had the pleasure of meeting Dr Tony Williams, now doing meaningful work with the Barnabas Fund. Both spent far too long indulging me with the ins and outs of the electoral reform debate. However, both remained interested and good-humoured about a matter that is popularly (and perhaps accurately) characterized as of interest only to anoraks and obsessives.

I'd also like to thank the team at Bloomsbury. Particularly Nayiri Kendir, the assistant editor (Politics) and Atifa Jiwa, the senior commissioning editor, for supporting the project and the two anonymous reviewers for their helpful comments. Elsewhere, the research would not have been possible without those within and without the Labour Party, who gave up their time to meet and discuss the topic. Their generosity helped the research come alive. While I have made every attempt to make sure the manuscript is accurate, any remaining errors are, of course, my own.

Lastly, such things are only possible through the continued love and support of family, friends and loved ones. My parents, Vivienne and Graham, my sister, Alice, and my wife, Katy, have been a constant source of encouragement as I have navigated the challenging terrain of an early career researcher.

JM

Brough, East Riding of Yorkshire

Introduction

A study of the Labour Party and electoral reform is valuable at a time when the Labour Party has lost four successive general elections, the most recent of which was the worst electoral result since 1935. As the Labour Party considers how it can win a general election and return to government, thoughts will turn to electoral reforms, electoral pacts and coalition government. Indeed, after the 1987 general election defeat, which was the third successive general election defeat, interest within Labour in constitutional and electoral reform grew. While history never repeats itself, it does rhyme. Those within the Labour movement will likely entertain similar thoughts and arguments as the previous generation did when facing similar electoral and political problems.

The considerable two-to-one margin of defeat for the Alternative Vote (AV) in the referendum in May 2011 has, at least for some within the Labour Party and the broader Labour movement, failed to settle the question of electoral reform at Westminster. Immediately before the May 2015 general election, reports emerged of senior trade union leaders urging the then Labour Party leader Ed Miliband to offer the Liberal Democrats electoral reform to support a Labour government.[1] In the 2019 general election campaign, thirty individuals associated with the Labour Party – MPs, peers, Welsh assembly members, and supporters from across media and culture – signed a letter in the *Guardian* supporting a Make Votes Count campaign to introduce proportional representation (PR). The signatories argued that it would show Labour is serious about democratizing the UK, win votes to defeat the Conservatives and offer an exciting opportunity for citizens to decide how the House of Commons is elected.[2] Constitutional reform, including electoral reform, featured in the 2020 Labour leadership contest. Clive Lewis was the most vocal supporter. The eventual winner, Sir Keir Starmer, remained non-committal.

As this book will show, there is nothing new to Labour's divisions over electoral reform. At times in the Party's history, the matter has been prominent. For instance, the early years of the Party, the 1920s, the second minority Labour government during 1929–31, the 1980s and 1990s. However, only briefly has Labour collectively been committed to electoral reform at Westminster. Importantly, this study will show how Labour has approached the topic of electoral reform, offering the reader an in-depth study of how and why the issue has divided the Party since its inception in 1900. As such, *The Labour Party and Electoral Reform* is of interest not just because of the flurry of recent attention to the topic and the electoral and political problems facing the Party, but also because of the longer historical view and theoretical aspects that are under-researched. The Labour Party's role in maintaining First-Past-the-Post (FPTP) for British general elections warrants research.

Moreover, critics argue that Labour has accepted an electoral system that is not in its electoral and political interests. The Conservative Party spent most of the twentieth century in office, either as a single party or in coalition, enjoying prolonged periods in office. Interestingly, Labour lost the 1951 general election despite polling more votes, a defeat that led to thirteen years in opposition. In the latter half of the twentieth century, FPTP facilitated eighteen years of Thatcherism, undermining the planks of social democracy, achieved even at the height of Conservative popularity on a vote share in the low to mid-forties. Most recently, the formation of the Conservative–Liberal Democratic coalition in 2010 challenged the 'progressive left' thesis, and while Labour polled surprisingly well in the 2017 general election, the 2019 general election saw Labour's 'red wall' turn Conservative.

The electoral reform debate relates to wider discussions concerning the nature of the British constitution, political tradition and British state. Once Labour had replaced the Liberals as the main opposition to the Conservative Party, vying to form a single-party government, constitutional issues were of secondary importance to the far more critical social and economic issues facing the country and, therefore, the Party. Hanson claimed in 1956, 'We appear, then, to be at the end of an epoch in the history of British Socialist controversy about parliamentary procedure.'[3] Consequently, accusations of 'constitutional conservatism' were levelled at the Labour Party, as it displayed a general satisfaction with the workings of the British constitution and the Westminster model.[4] It is important to note how a lack of action on the constitution does not entail a lack of discussion on the constitution.

Prior to New Labour's constitutional reform agenda, the accusation of 'constitutional conservatism' appeared sound. The Attlee governments displayed little interest in the constitution. The notable exception was the reduction in the House of Lords delaying powers, designed to ease the passage of nationalization through the Lords. Therefore, politics motivated the reform intending to defeat a political opponent rather than a deep-seated commitment to constitutional reform. The Wilson and Callaghan governments displayed more interest in the British constitution – Wilson governments primarily over House of Lords reform and other aspects, including the House of Commons and the Civil Service with the intention of 'institutional streamlining'. The Callaghan government brought forward legislation on devolution to counteract the rise of Scottish nationalism, an attempt to defeat the political and electoral threat of the nationalists. Wilson and Callaghan's key constitutional reforms failed to materialize and the core planks of the Westminster model remained intact.[5]

The Labour Party abandoned its constitutional orthodoxy as it modernized in the 1980s and 1990s, culminating in New Labour's constitutional reform agenda. This included devolution to Scotland, Wales, London and power-sharing in Northern Ireland; House of Commons reform; Freedom of Information; Independence for the Bank of England; and the incorporation of the European Convention on Human Right into British law. The extent to which those at the top of New Labour were fully committed to constitutional modernization is debatable. Constitutional reformers accused New Labour of piecemeal reform and not seeing the constitutional reform agenda through to its end point. As such, it was an incomplete constitutional revolution, leaving much of the Westminster model intact. David Marquand lamented that 'the old constitution is dissolving beneath our eyes. The only question is what will replace it. To that question the authors of the revolution have no answer'.[6] Anecdotally it was often said that Blair's eyes glazed over when the topic of constitutional reform was raised. For him, it was not of concern to the 'man and woman' on the street, far removed from the 'bread-and-butter' issues and lacking saliency with the British electorate. Indeed, this was a position shared, according to the journalist Andrew Rawnsley, by Blair's closest aides, who dismissed it as 'an anal obsession of *Guardian* and *Observer* readers'.[7]

Regardless, there was one vital omission from the list of reforms – the Westminster electoral system – and although the Jenkins Commission drew up an alternative electoral system, the manifesto pledge remained unfulfilled. However, whilst FPTP remained untouched by New Labour, the devolved institutions adopted systems other than FPTP; the Additional Member System (AMS) in Scotland and Wales, the Single Transferable Vote (STV) in Northern Ireland and the Supplementary Vote (SV) for the London Mayoralty and the Party list system for election to the European Parliament. Later, the Labour–Liberal Democrat coalition at Holyrood introduced STV for local government in Scotland.

The argument in brief

The primary focus of this study is the House of Commons, supplemented when appropriate by events within the devolved assemblies. In addition, this study differs from much of the literature as it does not set out to be a work of advocacy. The book does not attempt to argue that the principles of reform are stronger than retaining the status quo, or vice versa, nor is one system necessarily preferable. Instead, its primary objective is to investigate the approaches and arguments expressed within the Labour Party towards electoral reform. Only at the end of the conclusion does the author present their perspective.

Some like to view Labour's commitment to FPTP as little more than crude self-interest, supporting a system that maintains its position as one of the two major parties of British politics. Martin Linton told the Labour Campaign for Electoral Reform (LCER) that MPs were unreceptive to reform as 'they have a vested interest in the system that elected them. Deep down they are thinking, this is the best system because it elected me.'[8] The historian Ross McKibbin wrote that Labour MPs adhered to a system based on a secret that they rarely admitted to themselves: 'that strictly proportional representation would in ordinary circumstances probably return an anti-socialist majority to the House of Commons. That is, the democratic electorate was undependable.'[9] Others resort to unhelpful language and imagery, which masks much more than it reveals about the complexity of voting reform and electoral systems.

For instance, a popular claim amongst reform-minded journalists writing for the liberal broadsheets is that FPTP supporters are 'dinosaurs', clinging to an 'out-of-date electoral system'. On the other hand, they believe in 'fairness', 'progress' and 'modernization'.

While it would be a mistake to dismiss self-interest completely, this book reveals that within the Labour Party and the broader Labour movement, a much richer and more politically profound divide is present. Differing views of electoral reform have prompted a diverse range of arguments – as well as a consistency of argument from both reformers and supporters of the status quo throughout the period assessed – based on competing beliefs about the purpose of elections, ideas of democracy and the day-to-day experience of politics at both a local and national level. Consequently, the study has a solid historical foundation, as it charts the debate from the foundation of the Party to the present. Yet, the matter is also approached from a political perspective, locating the arguments in broader frameworks to give the reader a more systematic view of the topic. The historian H. J. Hanham understood the twofold nature of the electoral reform, acknowledging the position of both the historical and theoretical, writing:

> It is impossible to carry on a debate about electoral reform without raising a number of theoretical issues. As a result, the history of electoral reform has always had a dual character, since it consists both of the history of certain measures and the history of certain ideas.[10]

Here, it is worth fleshing out the key elements of each theoretical approach. We begin with pluralism, a tradition with a rich heritage within the Labour movement. At its most basic, pluralism is about the dispersal of power, whether that be political or social. The belief that political institutions should be more reflective of society as a whole had support in the early twentieth century from leading intellectual figures like G. D. H. Cole, who deemed that parliament claimed to represent all the citizens in all things, but in practice represented none.[11] However, the positive perception of the reforming Attlee government gave credence to the belief that all required to enact social reforms is a Labour majority at Westminster, aided through FPTP. Consequently, FPTP was accepted as the best electoral system to deliver strong, effective, single-party governments.

For Tony Wright, the former Labour MP and academic, the rationale and purpose within the Labour and Conservative parties differed, but the effect was the same. 'A Tory governing tradition and socialist collective tradition found common ground in applauding the merits of the top-down and flexible constitution and in resisting proposals which would imperil its unity, discipline and cohesion.'[12] Elections were no longer about representing individual interests but creating governing majorities, tying representatives to parties. Competition was limited, and given the winner-takes-all system prioritizing the mandate and the manifesto, the imperative was to become the winner. This harmed politics.

> Citizens are reduced to voters, multiple arenas of citizenship narrowed to the periodic visit to the polling booth, professional party machines substituting for the authentic activity of democratic politics, a politics of observation rather than of engagement.[13]

Elsewhere, Henry Drucker elaborated on what he termed manifestoism and its role in the Labour Party. In place of a theory of politics, the Party had a theory about elections, accepting 'the radical liberal view of the constitution and of the respective roles of elections, party, Parliament and government contained in that view' adapting it to the ethos of the working class. Manifestoism fits neatly into a constitution that emphasizes Parliament's sovereignty and grounds that sovereignty on democratic election. 'It is about representation first of all and only secondarily, and indirectly, about governing.' Drucker continues, arguing that manifestoism is widespread in the Party and offers additional benefits. For instance, attempts to control the Labour leadership, protect the ideology from any blame if it is unfulfilled and protects constituency activists from having to accept any responsibility for the acts of their leaders.[14]

Consequently, pluralists within and without of the Party are generally critical of Westminster's adversarial style and single-party government. Specifically, they are critical of the Labour Party's aversion to electoral pacts, coalition government, proportional representation and its broad acceptance of the Westminster model. For much of its history, the Labour Party has abided by, if not celebrated, Britain's existing political institutions, believing them to be benign. As long as the Party could gain a majority of seats in the House of Commons, it could govern free from constraints and implement its agenda.

Yet, single-party government, even Labour governments, fail to represent the diverse interests found within society. As such, a reformed electoral system would better represent those groups and factions currently excluded from the decision-making process, leading to a new collegiate and consensus-based politics. In turn, this would force the Labour Party to move beyond its working-class base, to a broad-base social movement, representing in agreement all the anti-Conservative forces in the country. In sum, a more accurate representation of pluralistic Britain.

Indeed, a truly 'progressive' government can materialize only through realigning the British left – a rapprochement between Labour and the Liberal Democrats – and a coalition government. Realignment, according to its proponents, serves four main purposes. Firstly, it heals the historic schisms on the British left between liberalism and socialism. Secondly, and electorally, it would see a joining of the 'progressive forces' against the Conservatives. Thirdly, a key policy would be the introduction of proportional representation, resulting in greater citizen participation, binding the progressive forces together and supposedly locking out the Conservatives from office. Fourthly, progressive intellectuals would no longer face the dilemma of choosing between Labour and the Liberal Democrats. Currently, the Labour Party is 'dominated by a class and an ethos which was not their own, and which they would often find irksome and uncomfortable'.[15]

Briefly, it is worth reflecting on Labour's ethos. Drucker distinguished two elements of Labour's ideology. Firstly, doctrine, by which he meant the more or less settled ideas about social, economic and political reality, something accepted by a large group of people. Within the Labour Party, it is derived from a diverse body of sources, but there is common doctrinal ground centring on equality. In turn, the common doctrinal ground encourages policies that strive to bring about an equal Britain. Secondly, ethos. For Drucker, this element had been overshadowed and neglected in studies on the Labour Party, but it was no less important. The Labour Party's ethos reflected the dominant group, organized labour. The experiences of the working class, which have predominantly been exploitation and the slow, painful building of its own defensive organizations, have shaped the Labour Party giving rise to distinctive practices and institutions. This has resulted in a 'defensive' character, evident in various ways, including manifestoism. Drucker identified how this distinction posed a problem for progressive intellectuals. While doctrine is open to recruitment by agreement, ethos and its meanings are readily available 'to those for whom it arises naturally out of experience'.[16]

Consequently, we can start to see how ethos relates to the debate over electoral reform and proportional representation. The Labour Party, as the political wing of the trade union movement, has sought to defend the working class in parliament. At times, the Labour Party has won enough support to win a parliamentary majority to implement policies for the betterment of the working class. A realigned left, bound together through proportional representation and open to different perspectives, positions and attitudes, would be a more attractive option to progressive intellectuals. However, sceptics point to this impact on the Party's ethos, conceivably challenging the traditionally dominant group, the trade unions. Therefore, if this group were to be replaced by other groups with different experiences, identities and traditions, it would transform the Party's ethos. Depending on one's view, the Party would shed what's left of its labourism and working class identity, or become a modern social-democratic party fit for the twenty-first century.

The second approach is 'elitist'. Adopting this term does have its limitations. For instance, few in the Labour Party, given its commitment to equality, would refer to themselves in such a way. After all, it conjures up images of hierarchy, inequality and privilege. Moreover, within this approach we see elements of conservatism and agnosticism. For instance, Herbert Morrison told the Liberal leader Clement Davies that rather than reform the House of Lords 'we should try to maintain continuity and not set up something new and different from the past'.[17] Clement Attlee thought 'the British have the distinction above all other nations of being able to put new wine into old bottles without bursting them'. The agnostics deem constitutional and electoral reform unimportant or a distraction from 'bread-and-butter' issues. When confronted by such issues, they tend to side with the leadership which, as we will see, has teated calls for reform with caution. Therefore, they lack the zeal of reformers and defenders of the status quo.

However, the term's relevance is threefold. Firstly, Labour has predominantly conceived of social democracy as being top-down, something done *for* the working class, not *by* the working class. The leadership of the Labour Party seeks to represent workers within the confines of Westminster, locating the class conflict in Westminster by having working people and those sympathetic to the working class and socialism elected to Parliament. This has rested on a 'centralist tradition in which strong executive government was viewed to be the key instrument of statecraft for achieving and promoting greater social equality'.[18] Consequently, socialism could emerge from having the right people controlling the levers of power at Westminster, thus negating the need for popular involvement. Richard Crossman, the former Labour Cabinet minister considered that few of his colleagues believed in participation.

> The notion of creating the extra burden of a live and articulate public opinion able to criticise actively and make its own choices is something which most socialist politicians keenly resent.[19]

Secondly, the Westminster model of politics and the classical view of the British political tradition is elitist, generally conducted by a narrow group of politicians and officials through a particular set of institutions. For instance, the core tenets of the British political tradition include a limited, liberal notion of representative democracy, encapsulating the view that the government governs in the nation's interests and that power should rest with the central government. In addition, responsibility for decision-making is in the hands of Cabinet ministers, and government must be willing and able to take strong, decisive and necessary action.[20] For much of the Labour Party's history, it has defended and promoted Britain's parliamentary traditions. Indeed, critics of New Labour's constitutional reforms argued that the central planks of the 'old' constitution remained in place, partly due to the ideational tension between pluralism and elitism.

Thirdly, Labour's *elitists* share a similar view of the nature of democracy and the purpose of elections with leading democratic elitist thinkers. Here, we need to look outside of the Labour Party. Clearly, Labour's supporters of FPTP do not directly reference Joseph Schumpeter and his claim that 'we now take the view that the role of the people is to produce a government, or else an intermediary body which in turn will produce a national executive or government'.[21] Nor do they reference other democratic elitist thinkers such as Giovanni Sartori, Max Weber or Karl Popper, whose works do not belong in the canon of Labour Party thinking. Regardless, there is an interesting overlap in rationale. Labour's FPTP supporters regularly state that a general election's purpose is not just to elect a representative or parliament but to create a government. In addition, both see a passive role for the masses beyond a role in the electoral and political process. Rodney Barker considered this approach as 'socialist elitist', a tradition of democratic oligarchy, primarily viewing citizens as consumers and popular government approved as it permitted the extension of state function, which they believed went with it.[22]

The third approach, Marxism, has rarely held much influence within the Labour Party and movement. Nevertheless, 'it has served as a constant point of reference'[23] and is a valuable framework when considering Labour's acceptance of the British state, parliamentary method and FPTP. Such continuity, respect and unwavering faith in the British Parliamentary system led Ralph Miliband to state, 'Of all political parties claiming socialism to be their aim, the Labour Party has always been one of the most dogmatic – not about Socialism but about the Parliamentary System.'[24] As such the Labour Party has been concerned about winning the levers of power, not the transformation of society. Miliband says, 'The Labour Party has not only been a parliamentary party: it has been deeply imbued by parliamentarianism.'[25]

Consequently, extra-parliamentary activity is secondary to the primary task of gaining representation. After all, a majority in the House of Commons committed to socialism can deliver a socialist Britain. The influence of Fabian 'gradualism' can be observed, as can the role and influence of the early leaders of the Labour Party. Keir Hardie and James Ramsay MacDonald placed their faith in society evolving towards socialism, draining British socialism of a scientific analysis, instead adhering to an ethical creed. People it was deemed were bound together through a common identity, synthesizing elements of class and nation. This has taken the Labour Party down the road of moderation, electoral politics and constitutionalism. According to the Party's critics, this has been to its advantage, allowing Labour to channel the class struggle through political institutions. 'Since the birth of the Labour Party there had been a link, albeit indirect and tenuous, but real nevertheless, between the class struggle and voting Labour' meaning 'politics is about elections and which party forms the government.'[26]

Andrew Gamble, in the first edition of *Britain in Decline*, noted that the method of the Labour Party under FPTP and the policies it pursues were not designed to challenge the existing state and the social relations it upholds.

Instead, they promoted policies to administer it. This had encouraged some on the left to embrace PR, as it mattered not whether the Labour Party was in government with a majority if it had not won 'the wider battle for ideological and political hegemony'.[27] For Gamble, it was regrettable that PR had not been introduced at the beginning of the twentieth century, as this would have prevented the Labour leadership from seeking to manage the economy and state. Introducing PR would end the 'dishonest association between social democrats and socialists in the Labour party', and allow a more open debate about policies and strategies'. FPTP masked the disunity within the Party and the 'extent to which the movement is dominated by leaders and perspectives that do not seek any socialist transformation of society at all'.[28]

Consequently, Marxists contend that the Labour Party's faith in the reforming capabilities of Westminster has been erroneous. The state that the Labour Party seeks to govern through is not neutral but a capitalist state, and therefore the emancipation of the working class – the alleged historic mission of the Labour Party – is futile. Political power finds its organized expression in the liberal-democratic state, which is a capitalist state and exists to defend and maintain the dominant class's economic and social power. Moreover, the Labour Party is not the vehicle to introduce socialism and emancipate the working class as it is wedded to parliamentary politics in a capitalist democracy. Whilst PR would be secondary to the pressure from society, it could result in a socialist challenger to the Labour Party, providing 'a beacon spreading light on needs, initiatives and ideas that up till now have existed only in Labour's shadow'.[29]

Structure and content

Combining the historical and theoretical elements of the debate offers the reader a full explanation of the cause of the division and how it has played out. The monograph follows a hermeneutic methodology, 'seeking to recover the meaning of concepts, arguments and ideas in their historical context'[30] and is structured chronologically. The first chapter covers the period 1900–31. Here, the narrative charts the debate from the inception of the Labour Party, through the pre–First World War debates, the displacing of the Liberals in the

1920s and minority government from 1929–31. Chapter 2 covers the period 1931–87, including the lack of interest pre– and post–Second World War and then the increasing interest in the 1970s and 1980s. The study then moves on to the 'case study' chapters. Each case study and timeframe has been chosen due to its explicit connection with Labour's attitude towards electoral reform at Westminster, revealing something of the division, its depth and significance within the Party. Moreover, each event is important, individually and collectively, as they all form the broader narrative found within the Labour Party, with the arguments professed, the processes and decisions made all impacting Labour's place within the British political system.

The Plant Report met for three years from 1990 to 1993. It was Labour's first internal enquiry into electoral reform since Ramsay MacDonald, George Roberts and William Anderson discussed the topic in *The Labour Party and Electoral Reform: Proportional Representation and the Alternative Vote* in 1913. During the 1980s, there was a burgeoning interest in constitutional reform within the Labour Party and wider society. The inability of Labour to counter Conservative statecraft led the Party to consider different methods and ideas to broaden its appeal, and through the Plant Report, such ideas on constitutional reform were fleshed out in detail.

The Jenkins Commission met for eight months in 1998 and put forward an alternative to FPTP that they hoped would be placed in front of the electorate in the form of a referendum. It was a key element of 'the project', an elite-level attempt by a handful of individuals within the Labour Party and Liberal Democrats to realign the 'progressive' forces in British politics. Neither 'the project' nor the Jenkins Commission proposals came to fruition. Initially, New Labour displayed its radicalism by transforming the British constitution but gradually lost interest once the major alterations, such as devolution, had passed. As such, the chapter begins with Blair assuming the leadership and ends with the declining interest in electoral reform after Labour's second landslide victory in 2001.

Chapter 5 charts New Labour's declining interest, the drifting apart of New Labour and the Liberal Democrats, and the end of 'the project'. Interestingly, electoral reform at Westminster rose to prominence under Gordon Brown's premiership. Brown, often thought to be opposed to electoral reform at Westminster, was sceptical of coalition with the Liberal Democrats. However, it was raised alongside other constitutional reforms and was a commitment designed to appeal to the Liberal Democrats. This chapter also assesses how electoral reform was one of the key policy areas in the five days following the 2010 general election, revealing the extent of Labour's division and the antipathy towards entering a coalition with the Liberal Democrats at Westminster.

The final chapter examines how the Labour Party has thought about the electoral system in opposition. The discussion begins with the AV Referendum 2011, which occurred as the Labour Party attempted to move on from 'New Labour' in opposition, having been defeated in May 2010 and forced from office through the formation of the Conservative–Liberal Democrat coalition. Indeed, we will consider how the Conservative–Liberal Democrat coalition has impacted the notion of the 'progressive majority' and the 'progressive left'. The referendum campaign pitted Labour politicians against one another. In addition, the period from 2010 to 2021 has been a turbulent time for the Labour Party, losing despite the Conservative Party pursuing austerity and the majority of the Labour movement being on the losing side of the EU Referendum. The Party has experienced four successive general election defeats, the most recent of which witnessed the Party suffering its worst result since 1935. Consequently, winning a parliamentary majority appears remote. Therefore, as Labour reconsiders its electoral strategy, ideas around electoral reform, electoral pacts and coalition will return to the agenda as those within and without Labour question the Party's satisfaction with FPTP. Lastly, the chapter will explore the candidates' views on electoral reform and proportional representation in the 2020 Labour leadership contest.

The conclusion will characterize the division within Labour as a split between elitists and pluralists, the former being dominant but the latter experiencing fluctuating influence, particularly in recent years. Indeed, since the late 1980s, the pluralists have enjoyed some success – devolution and the alternative electoral systems used for the devolved levels of government. However, the dominant view within the Party has continued to view Westminster as a different type of institution, where the government of the United Kingdom sits. As such, it entails different understandings of the purpose of voting and, more broadly, democracy which is primarily concerned with the election of a government. Moreover, there is concern about how a movement away from FPTP at Westminster would impact the Labour Party's historic mission to defend and promote working-class interests. Consequently, the arguments put forward by the pluralists around proportional representation, realigning the British left and coalition government, have been treated with the utmost caution.

The arguments surrounding electoral reform within the Labour Party have continuing relevance in the face of the Party's political and electoral challenges. They, therefore, deserve to be brought back to the fore to survey the road travelled and the direction it should take in the future.

1

Labour and the electoral system in historical perspective, 1900–31

The notion that constituencies elect their representatives based on the simple plurality 'of the person with the most votes wins' can be dated back to 1265 when Simon de Montfort summoned Parliament to Lewes. Consequently, territorial constituencies using First-Past-the-Post (FPTP) predate the rise of modern political parties. Focusing on the attitude of the Labour Party from the beginning of the twentieth century to the end of the second minority Labour government in 1931, the chapter will discuss the key events and arguments used by Labour politicians. The period analysed includes the pre–First World War debates and the electoral dilemma facing the Party, the inter-war years in which Labour experienced minority government and Ramsay MacDonald's 'great betrayal'.

1900–18

The Labour Representation Committee (LRC), as latecomers to the political system having entered at the beginning of the twentieth century, sought 'to promote and co-ordinate plans for labour representation.'[1] However, the problem facing the LRC was gaining representation to the House of Commons when fighting in three-cornered contests, with a lack of funds, against the two established parties of British politics; the Liberal Party and the Conservative Party. In secret, James Ramsay MacDonald arranged a meeting with Herbert Gladstone, the Liberal election agent. It was agreed LRC candidates would have a free run in specific constituencies if they left the Liberals an open field elsewhere. The Gladstone–MacDonald Pact of 1903 was born out of fear of splitting the anti-conservative vote.

The pact did have some success in both 1906 and 1910, allowing the LRC to gain representation. In 1906, of the twenty-nine seats won by the LRC, eleven were in double-member constituencies; of the fifty LRC candidates, eighteen enjoyed a straight contest with a Conservative opponent; and only three LRC MPs elected in England and Wales faced Liberal opposition. In January 1910, Labour fought just twenty-seven seats against Liberal opposition; in December 1910, a mere eleven.[2] By 1914, only nine out of its thirty-nine seats had been won against Liberal competition. Whilst the Liberals and Labour reaped the pact's benefits, at the constituency level, Labour activists resented standing down in favour of the Liberal candidate, despite the pact's electoral benefits. After all, the Party was building up its political organizations across Britain.

In 1908, a Royal Commission on Electoral Systems claimed there were over 300 different electoral systems. The report recommended – with one dissentient, who supported the Single Transferable Vote (STV) – the introduction of the Alternative Vote (AV), arguing it was 'the best method of remedying the most serious defect which a single-member system can possess – the return of minority candidates'. However, according to the historian David Butler, there was a lack of enthusiasm to discuss the Commission's findings which was not debated in Parliament.[3] Although too divided to give evidence to the Royal Commission, the Labour Party remained concerned about its ability to gain greater representation in the House of Commons and the restrictive nature of the Pact with the Liberals, with the Party failing to gain further ground. Duly, interest in electoral systems took hold, and between 1908 and 1914, the Party internally debated the matter.

Arthur Henderson, the then leader of the Labour Party, put forward a proposal at the 1909 Labour Party Conference for several electoral reforms, including 'the prevention of the election of members by a minority of votes'.[4] However, this proposal rode on the back of other reforms to electoral practices, including universal suffrage and one-man-one-vote. During this period, the Trades Union Conference (TUC) also concerned itself with the matter yet was indecisive. In 1908 the TUC called for an inquiry into the Second Ballot method of voting.[5] However, one year later, it defeated by a large majority a resolution moved by Labour Chief Whip, George Roberts that proposed PR as 'the best method of removing electoral anomalies and inequalities'.[6] Therefore, whilst the Labour Party and the TUC expressed reservations about FPTP, they had not yet set upon a clear alternative.

Henderson returned to electoral reform at the 1910 Labour Party Conference, moving a similar motion to that of 1909, although when a delegate from the Battersea Labour Party moved a motion supporting PR, Henderson spoke against it. Mentioning the Royal Commission and urging Conference not to bind the leadership to a particular system whilst the Parliamentary Labour Party (PLP) was considering the Second Ballot and STV, Henderson stated that the Party had 'listened to Lord Courtney (a Liberal peer and the Secretary of the Proportional Representation Society), but in spite of all they heard and the consideration they gave to it, the Party was divided as to whether this was really the best method'.[7] Consequently, the Labour Party was officially committed to an unspecified form of PR, yet divisions existed regarding which electoral system was the way forward.

MacDonald remained unconvinced on the merits of electoral reform, refuting the arguments in favour of PR during the Edwardian debates. Constitutional reform, whilst appearing reasonable, will entice socialists, yet 'will probably not bear examination. They may be but "will-o'-the wisps" leading into bogs those who foolishly follow'.[8] MacDonald's first concern was the expense of multi-member constituencies rather than targeting constituencies which the Labour Party had a genuine chance of winning. Therefore, wealthier parties would be favoured.[9] His second concern centred on the strength of minorities, arguing that small parties did not automatically deserve representation based merely on their existence. He told delegates in 1911 that 'no democratic body like the Labour Party ought to associate itself with the idea (of PR)'.[10] Philip Snowden disagreed, arguing that Labour's dependency on the Liberals resulted from Labour's inability to win three-cornered contests under FPTP. As such, the Labour Party could never be truly socialist. Some form of PR would allow the Labour Party to be truly independent in the House of Commons. MacDonald's stature within the Party was critical in the 1911 conference, which defeated a motion 1,255,000 against and only 97,500 in favour of PR.

In 1913 and 1914 the debate within the Labour Party intensified. At the 1913 Labour Party Conference, a delegate proposed that 'no scheme of redistribution will be satisfactory which does not include a system of Proportional Representation applicable to all parts of the United Kingdom.'

However, another delegate moved that Proportional Representation be replaced by the Alternative Vote hoping that Conference vote on AV rather than PR.[11] In the same year a report was published by the National Executive Committee (NEC), *The Labour Party and Electoral Reform: Proportional Representation and the Alternative Vote*. Roberts, the Chief Whip, and W. C. Anderson, the Labour MP and Chair of the ILP, argued in favour of PR, affirming three-cornered contests led to the election of MPs on a minority of the vote, something regarded as 'undemocratic'. They were conscious of the Labour Party's reliance on the Liberal Party to gain representation. AV would leave the Labour Party open to attack from the Liberals, who could unite with the Conservatives – 'a combination of capitalist forces against Labour' – with the potential to harm the representation of the Party.[12] There could be no guarantee that 'weak-kneed' Liberal electors would put the Labour candidate as a second preference. Consequently, a Labour candidate could be eliminated before second and third preferences were counted.

On the other hand, STV 'would spur into activity many Labour organisations which are now compelled either to remain idle or to support candidates of capitalist parties' giving each Labour MP 'security' and 'independence'.[13] STV would provide both 'freedom' and the elector 'equality in the value of the vote' as under FPTP an 'elector has often no first choice nor even a second choice offered to him. If he votes at all he must often record his vote for some candidate who cannot possibly represent him' and 'thousands of Labour voters would for the first time have the opportunity of voting for a Labour candidate'.[14] The Labour Party would be free to 'act independently and to formulate its own policy and to remain in every sense independent and distinct from the capitalist parties'.[15] Acknowledging that coalition would result under STV, Roberts and Anderson considered 'the character of the government that can be formed will be determined by the public declarations made by the parties and candidates seeing the suffrages of the electors'.[16]

MacDonald led the arguments against PR, utilizing the same rationale used at the 1911 Labour Party Conference. He calculated that Labour would be worse off under PR. 'Today every vital political school of thought finds its champion in the House of Commons, and, in addition, is moulding Parties in the House of Commons'.[17] The PR view is that political opinion in the constituencies should be 'divided into watertight compartments … Socialists should vote for Socialists, Labour Party electors for Labour Party candidates, Liberals for Liberals and so on'.[18] This would not give democratic control as the resulting situation in the House of Commons 'is different in its character and in its policy from the separate groups which appeal to the constituencies and receive separate support at the election'.[19] Under PR, parliamentary problems of 'combination and cooperation are left to be solved by detached groups which have no mandate' appealing to the country 'as though they were to be absolutely separate in their Parliamentary action'.[20]

Consequently, MacDonald attached great importance to what happened in the House of Commons, for this was the institution that mattered most in the democratic process. If PR was adopted, the Commons would have to proceed on the same lines of 'criticism, combination and majority rule'[21] as under FPTP. PR would make the House of Commons less representative as parties would have to be regrouped, 'either by coalition or otherwise ... and then all their boasted party independence vanishes'. This would cause 'an enormous amount of log-rolling and the very separateness of the elections makes the necessary co-operation in Parliament all the more dishonest'.[22] Appeals made to the country in elections would be more misleading and on the matter of independence from the Liberal Party, 'nothing has hampered our Movement in the country more than this false idea of independence', writing damningly, 'it is humbug'.[23] However, MacDonald did back the introduction of AV, albeit in the final paragraph. AV 'would enable us to fight every seat we had a reasonable chance of winning and in doing so we would not be hampered by the cry that we were splitting the Liberal vote'.[24]

MacDonald's influence over the Labour movement was vital in shaping the debate in the early years of the Labour Party, although it was apparent that opposition to FPTP existed. However, the reformers could not find consensus on which alternative to FPTP they wished to adopt. At the 1914 Labour Party Conference, speeches by MacDonald, Roberts and Snowden made their case for the status quo or PR. Conference voted, rejecting PR and AV, 1,387,000 to 704,000 and 1,324,000 to 632,000, respectively, with the power and influence of MacDonald key in defeating STV. It was reported that members were 'always suspicious of anything that came from the middle-class movement'. This was echoed by *Justice*, who wrote 'that had a resolution in favour of the present system been put to the delegates it would have been defeated by a still bigger majority'.[25] The Labour Party had been committed to electoral reform in 1909 and PR in 1910. The indecisiveness over the electoral system reflects the conflicting views over the way to gain representation and the role the Party should play in British politics, impacting the depth of the commitment to replace FPTP, for PR was rejected in 1911 and rejected again in 1914 along with AV.

In return for extending the life of the Parliament during the First World War, a Speaker's Conference was established, with a remit of electoral reform. It recommended abolishing plurality voting with most rural seats using AV in 358 constituencies and the STV for cities (boroughs) in 211, which returned three to seven members. Attending the Speaker's Conference on behalf of the Labour Party was S. Walsh, G. J. Wardle and F. Goldstone, who proceeded to argue and vote in favour of AV despite the 1914 Conference resolutions.[26] Although unknown at the time, this system would have harmed the Labour Party in the long run, as it would not have seen its under-representation in rural areas corrected, unlike the Conservatives who would have benefited in industrial cities.[27]

In the changed political circumstances of the War, Henderson considered that Labour had more to gain than to lose from AV. Henderson, in conversation with C. P. Scott, the editor of the *Manchester Guardian*, claimed that 'for more than 20 years … I had held that a really progressive and democratic policy could only be based on the union of the Labour and Radical parties'. When Scott was asked how a Labour Party intending to run candidates over the whole country could secure cooperation with progressive Liberals, he said that 'he would depend on the Alternative Vote and on a friendly understanding between Liberalism and Labour to give each other their second choice.'[28]

The Bill oscillated between the House of Commons and the House of Lords. The opposition of the House of Commons towards PR had gradually stiffened until it had been practically eliminated from the Bill, apart from two- and three-member University seats. The Conservative-dominated House of Lords reinstated PR thinking it was in the Conservative Party's best interests, based on the premise that AV benefitted the Labour Party, which would receive the second preferences of Liberal voters. When the Bill returned to the House of Commons AV was reinstated. On 6 February 1918, the Bill was in danger of being lost with the end of the session and prorogation ceremony scheduled for later the same day. A compromise was reached; AV was dropped and a Royal Commission would examine setting up PR on a limited basis. It was debated a month later in the House of Commons, and quietly rejected.

The 1920s

The 1920s was a defining decade for the Labour Party. It increased its representation in the House of Commons, formed two minority governments, and along with the Conservatives, encouraged the decline of the Liberal Party. The 1918 'Coupon Election' saw Liberals and Conservatives endorsed by the government receive the 'coupon' letter, refusing to stand against one another, hoping to continue the wartime coalition. The result was a Liberal prime minister, Lloyd George, propped up by a much larger Conservative Party, which dominated the government. However, the Liberal Party had split between 'Coalition Liberals' led by Lloyd George and those favouring political independence led by Herbert Asquith. As such, the political landscape had fundamentally altered and the Labour Party emerged as the strongest opposition party mainly by default, achieving 22 per cent of the vote and fifty-seven MPs.

In February 1921, Sir Thomas Bramsdon, a Liberal MP, secured time for a PR Bill. The Bill was debated on 8 April 1921 with twenty-five Labour MPs voting for and five MPs voting against. At the time, three prominent Labour members were vice-presidents of the Proportional Representation Society: Snowden, Clynes and Lord Parmoor. The Proportional Representation Society claimed sympathizers to the Bill included the Trades Union Congress, based upon a Resolution of Annual Conference in 1918, and the Independent Labour Party based on a Resolution from 1914. The Bill's defeat ensured the question's conclusion for that Parliament. Interestingly, far more Labour MPs attempted to introduce PR for local government elections in February 1923 and a Liberal bill a month later to introduce AV.[29]

David Marquand writes that the effects of PR in the 1920s would have made the political motives of MacDonald very difficult. MacDonald's first objective was to ensure that British politics revolved around a struggle between the Conservative and Labour parties, in which the Liberals could be dismissed as irrelevant. The second was that Labour must present itself as a credible alternative government which could govern single-handedly.[30] MacDonald, in his diary, wrote, 'We shall always tend to return to two great Parties, and that is the position today. The two parties fighting for supremacy are our own and the Tory Party of reaction.' MacDonald had bluntly observed in 1920, the old battles for electoral reform were over and the new question was whether Parliament was suitable for modern social conditions.[31] MacDonald was more interested in the long-term ambitions of the Labour Party commanding the heights of the British State and the practical considerations of government rather than the short-term gains of electoral reform.

Interestingly, MacDonald had made statements to the contrary, suggesting his hostility towards PR was mellowing. In the *Socialist Review* in December 1922 he wrote, 'The changes in election problems that followed the last extensions of the franchise seem to me to have greatly strengthened the case for the adoption of some scheme of PR.' In the *New Leader* in January 1924, whilst PR may result in minority or coalition government under the present situation 'everything points to a continued "stalemate".' The first effect of PR would be to 'loosen party bonds'. Members 'will more frequently than they now do, use their own judgement as to how to vote'. Parties in the House of Commons will rule 'more by their administrative success than by party force, whilst the legislation that will be carried will have to be more in accordance than it now too often is with public desires'. Consequently, 'it will weaken organisation, but strengthen reason; it will make Ministers more the instruments of the general (electorate)'.[32]

MacDonald's objectives were vindicated by the general election results of November 1922 and December 1923, as the Party continued to make electoral advances. In 1922 Labour won 142 seats, on an increased vote share of 29.4 per cent, becoming the official opposition, rooted in several major industrial regions.[33] December 1923, fought on the issue of 'free-trade' and 'protection', saw further Labour advances into the remaining Liberal strongholds in the industrial areas. The three parties were separated only by 100 seats (Conservatives 259, Labour 191 and the Liberal's 159). The Labour Party had announced their readiness, if called upon, to form a government. On 21 January 1924 Baldwin's Conservative government was defeated by seventy-two votes on a Labour amendment to the king's speech. Asquith instructed his Liberal Party to vote with the Labour Party and bring down the Conservative government, rather than form an anti-socialist alliance. The following day Baldwin resigned, and the first Labour government took office.

Labour's NEC in 1923 had called upon the parliamentary leadership 'to accept full responsibility for the government of the country without compromising itself with any form of coalition'.[34] Given the precarious parliamentary arithmetic, the Labour government was likely to be short-lived unless it could ally with one of the parties of 'capital'. Indeed, relations between Labour and the Liberals in the formative weeks of the government appeared cordial: a Liberal candidate did not contest the Burnley by-election, ensuring Henderson could return to Parliament. The Liberal Chief Whip Vivian Phillips stated: 'For the first time for ten years the forces of progress in this country were able to command a majority in the House of Commons' and the Liberals were ready to help the Labour government'.[35] Such optimism proved to be short-lived.

If the Liberals believed that they would receive gratitude for keeping Labour in power, they were mistaken. The historian Trevor Wilson wrote that the principal voices for positive relations with the Liberal Party were the *New Statesman* and Snowden. However, the 'attitude of the Labour party was faithfully reflected by its leader' sharing 'the same petulant rage against the Liberals for continuing to exist'.[36] MacDonald displayed little cordiality and, in conversation with Scott, had 'reverted again and again to his dislike and distrust of the Liberals. He could get on with the Tories. They differed at times openly then forgot all about it and shook hands. They were gentlemen, but the Liberals were cads'.[37] Lloyd George, in April 1924, had protested at Labour's attitude towards the Liberal 'patient oxen' who were keeping them in office. In his first speech as prime minister, MacDonald emphasized that the Labour Party will concern itself with what it considered to be the great national and international matters, setting the tone for how his government would act and their attitude towards any idea of coalition.

> Coalitions are detestable, are dishonest. It is far better, I am perfectly certain, for the political life of our country, and for the respect, in which we desire to be held by colleagues who disagree with us, that we should express our views as an independent political party.[38]

As Marquand notes, the cause of MacDonald's 'lordly, not say cavalier, attitude to the Liberals' was the desire for British politics to revolve around the Labour Party and Conservative Party. Thus, the Liberals had to be marginalized and shown to be ineffectual. Regardless of the threat of Liberal MPs in parliamentary votes bringing down the Labour government at almost any moment, MacDonald refused to allow the 'government to look as though it depended on the Liberals' for this would not only strengthen their credibility but 'would weaken Labour's credibility as well'. Consequently, MacDonald, 'had to prove that he could govern without the Liberals, and he could only do that if he behaved as though he did not care whether they voted against him or not'.[39] Despite being a minority government and the limits it placed on its actions, the Labour government intended to govern as if it were a majority.

MacDonald, speaking at the newly opened Tufton Street Labour Club in May 1924, expressed his doubts about PR and whilst it was 'admirable and unanswerable in theory up to a point', the issue of the purpose of voting remained:

> What we have got to solve in representation is not merely how the House of Commons is going accurately to reflect party opinion outside, but when party opinion outside has been accurately reflect in the relative proportion of parties in the House, how from that representation are you going to form a workable Government?[40]

After failing to abandon FPTP in 1918, the Liberals and Lloyd George were becoming increasingly conscious during the 1920s that they were now the third party in British politics, encouraging thoughts that only PR could save them. In January 1924, a Liberal Committee examined the merits of PR and AV. In May the second reading of a Private Member's Bill containing PR, put forward by a Liberal, was up for debate. On 30 April, a Liberal Party meeting affirmed that cooperation depended on electoral reform, and no election should occur until this was passed into law. The historian Martin Pugh notes that the Liberals had invited Labour to support the Bill two days before the debate. Labour resented both having to rely on Liberal votes in the House of Commons and the proposal put forward by the Liberals for PR. The PLP rejected a majority recommendation from the Cabinet to support PR. So incensed were Labour backbenchers that it was decided 'by a large majority' to leave the Bill to a free vote but to give it no facilities if it passed the second reading. The argument ran that since the Liberal Party failed to bring in PR when they thought it would be helpful to the Labour Party, why should the Labour Party help the Liberals when they think it will be helpful to them.[41]

Herbert Morrison, Labour MP for Hackney, seconded the rejection of the Bill. Morrison considered that under PR it would be impossible for candidates to make themselves known and impossible for candidates when elected to keep in touch with their constituents afterwards, thus emphasizing the constituency link. Under PR the tendency would be for 'special groups representing minority opinion on special questions to make immoral bargains in the House of Commons, and that in fact the whole philosophy behind PR was the elevations of the minority and the subjection of the majority to specialist opinions of cranks and freaks'. Any theory of government based on the coming together of antagonistic opinions was wrong and contrary to the interests of democracy and of the country. In a swipe at the Liberal Party, Morrison affirmed PR was the natural philosophy of decaying parties and it was not natural to strong men and women who wanted the country to be governed wisely and firmly. FPTP did maintain secure representative government and the present political situation was temporary and would return to that of two parties.

Henderson, the home secretary, deemed that while the government would have been willing to consider AV, it could not do the same for PR. Firstly, no party had made reference to the issue in their manifestos; secondly, the division which existed in all parties; and thirdly, the treatment PR had received in previous parliaments and its rejection. Referring to the 'ultimatum' delivered by the Liberal Party, Henderson encouraged Labour opponents to turn their threats into action and attempt to remove them from office.[42]

The actions of the Liberals potentially reinforced the growing scepticism towards PR in the Labour Party since the 1916–17 Speaker's Conference. Joining with the Conservatives to reject the measure by 238 votes to 144, only 28 Labour MPs voted in favour and 90 against, in total a majority of 94 against. Of those who voted in the Cabinet, four supported PR and two voted against. James Maxton epitomized Labour's attitude in an address to a May Day 1924 rally in Glasgow. The Liberals, he said, had tried to drive them into a particular lobby, but they had decided to tell Asquith, Lloyd George and the rest to go to hell. He added that the Liberals threatened to hold weekend meetings throughout the country. 'God help Asquith and Lloyd George if they tried to address a meeting at Bridgeton Cross on a Saturday night.'[43]

By rejecting PR, Labour had put at risk the parliamentary support of the Liberals, not to the disappointment of some Liberals. As the *Times* reported, the 'Patient Oxen' were uneasy[44] and could no longer endorse policies which transgressed 'liberal principles'. Accordingly, the days of the first Labour government were numbered and during the August and September of 1924, the government came under increasing pressure. Two treaties with the Soviet Union and the Campbell Case – the charge of 'incitement to mutiny' against a British Communist newspaper editor and the Labour government's decision to suspend prosecution – led to a perception that Labour was sympathetic to communists, providing ammunition for Labour's opponents. On 31 September the Conservatives registered a motion of censure, and the Liberals followed with an amendment calling only for a select committee inquiry. MacDonald and the Cabinet treated both issue as a matter of confidence on the government. On 8 October, the Conservatives abandoned their censure motion and voted for the Liberal amendment. Duly, the government was brought down by 264 votes to 198, ending the Labour Party's first government.

As MacDonald had first stated in the House of Commons, the Labour Party was 'not afraid of what fate we may meet in the process'. The fact that the Labour government had been removed from office on a Liberal motion reinforced the perception that the Liberals were opportunistic and unsympathetic to the Labour Party, thus legitimizing MacDonald's policy of keeping them at arm's length. The relationship between the two parties had disintegrated during the 1920s. The Labour Party felt a socialist majority was on the horizon. At the 1926 Labour Party Conference, George Lansbury thought that 'the majority of the decisions under the present system had worked for the other people; but if they were wise, they could now make it work for themselves.'[45] Therefore, reliance upon the Liberals for parliamentary support would be a thing of the past. Moreover, electorally in 1924 it appeared Labour was on course to displace the Liberals as the main opposition to the Conservatives, gaining 1 million more votes than in 1923 and the lead over the Liberals widening to 2.5 million in 1924. Indeed, between 1925 and 1929 Labour won eleven seats from the Conservatives in by-elections, plus a further two seats from the Liberals. Labour was learning and experiencing how to win under FPTP in the 1920s and the objective of a return to a 'two-party' system was coming to fulfilment, with the Liberals in the process being reduced to a rump of MPs.

In addition, there was a general satisfaction with FPTP amongst Labour-supporting intellectuals. Here we can see the influence of Fabianism. Traditionally, the Fabians considered society should be engineered by administrators from the top-down – preferably Fabians or Labour people – who could govern on behalf of the working class. Reform of society could be achieved by having like-minded individuals in positions of power – permeating the establishment – implementing reform through the parliamentary route, thus committing the Labour Party to equality and efficiency through a centralized state. Thus, what was required was extending the British state, underpinned by the belief that the British state was fundamentally neutral. Ensuring that the right class of people, or at least, representative of the right class, were in position was critical, namely controlling a majority in the House of Commons committed to socialism. Sidney Webb, a leading Fabian, argued:

> For the Labour Party, it must be plain. Socialism is rooted in political democracy; which necessarily compels us to recognise that every step towards our goal is dependent on gaining the assent and support of at least a numerical majority of the whole people.[46]

Strong, decisive and responsible government would result, entailing a rejection of a written constitution and PR, as both would undermine the Westminster Model, the sovereignty of parliament and importantly reduce the opportunity of a parliamentary majority. Marxism was rejected because evolutionary socialism was inevitable – the 'wave of the future' – rather than violent revolution, and through 'gradualism', 'moderation' and a 'step-by-step' approach, socialism could be introduced. Webb based organic reform on four principles: that it is democratic, acceptable to the majority of people; gradual, thus causing no dislocation; regarded as moral by the mass of the people; and constitutional and peaceful.[47] The British State, duly reformed, would become, in the words of George Bernard Shaw, 'A first-rate practical instrument of democratic government'.[48] Underpinning this approach was the continuity and durability of British political institutions and appealing to different stands of thought from British history. Direct democracy and participation were impractical.

> The utmost function that can be allotted to a mass meeting in the machinery
> of democracy is the ratification or rejection of a policy already prepared for
> it, and the publication of decisions to those concerned.[49]

A Fabian Tract published in 1924, written by Herman Finer, deemed 'What Government are we going to make?' was the ultimate electoral question.[50] Finer argued that the workings of Parliament force 'men to leave their small caves and enter into larger combinations for the support of a common programme', meaning the exactness of representation is 'neither real nor ultimate political moment'.[51] The single-member constituency encouraged MPs to fulfil their duty in return for recompense. Additionally, MPs are representatives not delegates, 'subject to a possessive relationship with his constituents' with whom he can consult and in turn who the constituents can blame or praise. Consequently, the single-member system is 'highly representative' whilst also giving 'a predictable sphere of independence for the Member'. Given that a parliament cannot foresee everything that is going to happen, the close connection of MPs and electors guarantees 'popular consultation' along with the importance of by-elections in gauging political opinion.[52]

Furthermore, a Cabinet must rest upon a party organization and to 'be effectively responsible to the country must rest upon the support of a single party'. The electorate then 'is best able to know who is to praise or blame' at a general election.[53] Secondly, the need for political bargaining with 'ministrable' groups – a reference to small parties who could expect to become government ministers – is avoided during coalition negotiations. Finer also considered that AV did not offer a majority in the 'English political sense of the word i.e. a majority of positive supporters'. Moreover, and in accordance with the objectives of MacDonald and the Labour Party, 'it is likely that within 15 years the Liberal Party will be electorally defunct … It would be the height of political unwisdom to introduce a new and vicious element into the constitution to counteract a temporary ill.'[54]

1929–31 – the second Labour government

The 1929 general election produced a hung parliament. Labour returned 287 MPs, despite polling over 300,000 fewer votes than the Conservatives who had finished second with 260 MPs. The Liberals finished third on an improved fifty-nine MPs. It was the best electoral result for Labour in both votes and seats. Stanley Baldwin, the sitting Conservative prime minister, resigned immediately and advised the king to send for MacDonald, as anything else might have seemed 'unsporting'. Baldwin was determined, wrote the historian A. J. P. Taylor, that Lloyd George should not get the credit for turning the Conservatives out – or still worse, for keeping them in[55] – negating any possibility of the Liberals putting Labour into office. Baldwin's actions further marginalized the influence of the Liberal Party, suggesting the Conservatives were at ease with British politics revolving around the Conservatives and the Labour Party. On 5 June 1929 MacDonald became prime minister for the second time.

The Liberal Party understood that only through political bargaining and coalition building would they be able to influence government policy, a consequence of now being the third party in British politics. Parliamentary mathematics necessitated Labour would be able to form only a minority government, reliant on the support of Lloyd George and his truncated Liberal Party. Notably, it contained a significant minority of MPs inclined towards the Conservative Party rather than Labour. There was no guarantee that Lloyd George could hold his party together and force it to vote with Labour. However, Lloyd George could turn out the Labour Party by aligning his party with the Conservatives. MacDonald's distrust of Lloyd George, a feeling shared in Labour and across the House, had not mellowed even in light of the precarious parliamentary arithmetic. A diary entry in 1929 claimed the Liberal leader was 'like Samson shorn of his locks and bent on destruction … one of those men who are never happy unless they are the leading figures or are pulling down others.'[56]

The Liberals sought to gain electoral reform, particularly a form of PR, from any bargaining, preventing terminal electoral decline. The Labour Party knew that conceding demands on electoral reform had the potential to perpetuate the Liberal Party and give them a significant foothold in British politics indefinitely. A former Liberal, Pethick-Lawrence, commented on Labour's favourable electoral position. He urged MacDonald to avoid any deal with Lloyd George, especially on the electoral system:

> PR would be the devil. It would destroy our constitution and substitute the folly of continental politics. The alternative vote would postpone an absolute Labour majority – perhaps for a generation … There is a great feeling in the

party against electoral change. It might be induced to support it but it would be against its conviction, and this would be very bad for the morale of the party.[57]

In his government's first king's speech, MacDonald wondered whether Parliament could consider itself more a 'Council of State', focusing on the nation as a whole. His speech is often interpreted as the first overtures at a 'National Government'. He had, of course, ruled out coalition in 1924. His statement included a direct reference to electoral reform. Yet, in the ensuing debate, MacDonald's position on the matter appeared noncommittal as to which alternative was preferable, and importantly added what he considered to be the objective of an election:

> One view of Government is the static view where we are in exact replica, on a very small scale, of the millions of electors … But the other view is that the real, final purpose of an election is to elect a Government – and I use the word rather apart from merely electing a House of Commons.[58]

Fair records how MacDonald, after consultation with the Cabinet and leaders of other parties, proceeded to set up a Speaker's conference led by Viscount Ullswater, who had presided over the conference on electoral reform in 1917–18 and on devolution in 1919–20. Preparations for the Conference consumed four months, much to the annoyance of Lloyd George, before the deliberations began on 4 December 1929.[59] Ullswater records: 'It was arranged that the conference should itself determine the subjects which it would consider, in the light of the suggestions made by the parties, and the order in which they would be taken.' Ullswater also noted in his report that the chances of a successful conference were hindered by the lack of framework and parameters, leading him to speculate 'whether it reflects the attitude of the Prime Minister to the whole subject of the enquiry'.[60] MacDonald's decision not to provide strict terms of reference suggests he intentionally desired the Conference to get bogged down in wrangling, thus scuppering the chances of the Conference.

The make-up of the Conference reflected the House of Commons with seven Labour members, seven Conservatives, four Liberals and four representatives from the House of Lords, including the chair. The Conference decided to look into electoral funding, using motor vehicles to transport voters and relaying election speeches to other locations by radio. Importantly, they agreed to examine plural voting. MacDonald explained to Ullswater that it was necessary to enquire into the workings of the electoral system and whether reform would 'sacrifice other requirements of an efficient democratic machinery?'[61]

In spite of its minority position, the Labour Party was conscious of the need to give the impression of credibility and respectability, tying it to the British State and showing the electorate it was capable of governing. In December 1929, the government faced difficulties in passing a 'Coal Bill' and without the support of Liberal MPs it would be defeated. Lloyd George sought to use the Coal Bill to prise electoral reform out of the government. Morrison told the Liberals they had a choice: vote for the Coal Bill and be a progressive party or bring down the Labour government. Moreover, the political outlook for the Liberals was bleak as the country was steadily getting back to the two-party system.[62] MacDonald and Lloyd George met at the beginning of February 1930, in an attempt to bridge the gap between the two men. MacDonald reflected that the 'bargain proposed really amounts to this: we get two years of office from the Liberals and give them in return a permanent corner on our political stage'.[63]

The successes gained by the Labour Party throughout the 1920s at waging electoral war on the Liberals were, through electoral reform, at risk of being undone. After all, the Labour Party was the biggest party in the House of Commons for the first time. Legislating for an alternative electoral system ran the risk of undermining MacDonald's aim of returning to a two-party system. In a memorandum, MacDonald outlined his scepticism towards any deal with the Liberals, preferring an arrangement which did not hamper the freedom of the Party.[64] An agreement which lacked detail, whilst giving both parties freedom, would have offered very few guarantees for a full parliament. Interestingly, MacDonald listed seven difficulties the Labour Party would face if it were to go further than a loose agreement, ranging from the spirit of the Party, strengthening Lloyd George's position and the long-term costs a deal would impose on the Party.[65] Compromising the independence of the Party, responsibility and accountability led MacDonald to express reservations at the prospect of a pact with the Liberals.

A report appeared in March 1930 claiming MacDonald was complaining that Lloyd George was intriguing with Labour people behind his back. Liberal obstruction continued, and it became increasingly clear to the Labour government that only electoral reform would overcome the Liberal impasse. On 18 March 1930, the Labour leadership agreed to introduce an electoral reform Bill, conceding AV, and the Liberals duly abstained. However, MacDonald's scepticism towards electoral reform, its impact upon the independence and electoral capability of the Labour Party, along with the distrust of the Liberals surfaced quickly.

> From the birth of the Party until now we have held rigidly to the position that we were standing on our own legs and that has been inculcated as a cardinal principle from John O'Groats to Land's End. It has become part of the very nature of the Party … the scheme proposed by the Liberals would secure for them the very maximum possible representation, and for us the minimum.[66]

Additionally, it was apparent that any such electoral innovation would induce an end to the two-party system in which his party had only recently become a vested member, with any Labour government reliant on the Liberals.

Labour representatives in the ongoing Speaker's Conference, which had reconvened on 8 May 1930 after the recess, were deliberately obstructive, seeking to change electoral practices and finances – destroying the plural vote and the perceived financial advantage of the Conservatives – rather than the electoral system per se. Indeed, the idea of adopting an electoral system which boosted the Liberals at the expense of the Conservatives seemed unattractive. The Tory members thought it best to 'let sleeping dogs lie' and sought to wreck any proposals. However, they voted with the Liberals that if any change were to be made, it should be the adoption of PR, perhaps fearing a combination of anti-conservative forces in constituencies. John Campbell, the political biographer, wrote that Labour representatives would hear nothing but AV, which the Tories vetoed, and duly the conference broke up in July without agreement.[67]

PR was unacceptable to the Labour members of the Conference. Lord Arnold, Paymaster-General in MacDonald's government, claimed that parliament had no mandate to introduce PR and that it was only a means of representing minorities. According to the Conservative Samuel Hoare, 'Socialist after Socialist (damned) PR with bell, book and candle'.[68] Labour members of the Conference were willing to concede AV, conditionally on adopting other reforms such as expenditure and University representation.

There is disagreement in the literature regarding where Labour committee members were receiving instruction. Butler, Fair and Skidelsky suggest the NEC proposed committee members to 'offer a modicum of alternative vote on the condition that their list of reforms in the election law also be accepted', a view supported by Snowden in his memoirs. Marquand concludes otherwise, believing Labour members were told to oppose AV.[69]

James Maxton, a leading Clydesider, during the second reading of the Representation of the People (No. 2) Bill, declared himself as not at all enthusiastic about this measure, as it showed the power of Lloyd George over the government rather than the more important matter of the implementation of socialism. Furthermore, emphasizing the social and economic factors above issues of political reform, Maxton desired attention be paid to the 'immediate and urgent problems confronting the country, the first being that of the social condition of the people and the problem of poverty, and secondly, the general problem of economic reconstruction'. These issues should take precedence. 'Our Parliamentary machine runs along very clumsily, and places upon every one of us a terrible restraint. The question', he continued, 'of how we are going to operate when we get here is one that ought to be decided as a question of more importance than how we are to adjust the machinery which sent us here'.[70] Consequently, what mattered for Maxton was not the method of election but what happened once one was in the House of Commons. Voting on the second reading divided along strict party lines, 290 votes to 230.

In March 1931, the clause allowing for AV carried by 277 votes to 253. Despite the whips, 11 Labour and 2 Liberal MPs voted against it and 27 Labour members were absent unpaired. Beckett, the Labour MP for Camberwell was critical of the Labour Government supporting AV, reminding the House of MacDonald's previous statements that the 'hopeful future he said the Labour Party would have under the present system was to be sacrificed to prolong inordinately the dismal present'. J. M. Kenworthy, MP, who sat on the Bill's committee stage, spoke out against AV. Firstly, it was a sell-out to the Liberal Party which were a 'dying party', secondly, it would perpetuate the three-party system, and thirdly, 'make the winning of a majority by the Labour Party almost impossible'.[71] Regardless of Labour Party opposition, the Bill was finally passed in the Commons by 278 to 228 votes on 2 June 1931.

Continuing reliance on Liberal votes in the House of Commons during 1930 and into 1931 raised the prospect of closer ties between Labour and the Liberals, to ensure the government's survival for the whole parliament. By May 1931, the regular meetings between the Cabinet and Liberal leaders led to speculation there would soon be Liberals in government, something Skidelsky believes MacDonald seriously considered.[72] Owen writes that Lloyd George, in a memorandum to his secretary in July 1931, recorded a conversation with MacDonald, in which MacDonald had said that the Labour Party wanted an alliance. Moreover, he hoped that Lloyd George would join the government as foreign secretary or chancellor of the exchequer. This is disputed in the academic literature. Thorpe states the document cited by Owen has never been found since and, in turn, references a paper in which Lloyd George tells Lansbury that if he joined Labour it would antagonize millions of Liberal supporters. For Thorpe, 'the case for arguing that a Lib-Lab coalition was about to be formed in July 1931, therefore, is virtually non-existent'.[73] What did exist, however, was a situation whereby it was clear to all that the Liberals were keeping the Labour Party in government, without being bound to the government through Cabinet positions, ministerial roles and therefore collective responsibility.

The Bill progressed into the House of Lords where it was subject to wrecking amendments, with the peers focusing on the lack of a mandate for reform and seeking to restrict its implementation to the 174 seats in boroughs with more than 200,000 people. Thus, the passage of the Bill was delayed to the extent that the government would not have an opportunity to reconsider it until parliament reconvened in the autumn. The Parliament Act was one option available to the government to introduce AV, as neither Labour nor the Liberals were optimistic about their electoral chances during deep economic problems. However, the financial crisis of 1931 led to a split in the Cabinet over cutting unemployment payments, thus causing the collapse of the Second Labour government. MacDonald would go on to form a 'National government' with the Conservatives and the Simonite Liberals, resulting in a Labour prime minister leading a government dominated by Conservative MPs.

MacDonald's act would go down in Labour folklore as the 'Great Betrayal' impacting on the Party's attitude towards coalition at Westminster, and what this means for the working class whom the Labour Party represents. Miliband affirmed that whatever the Labour leaders had not learnt from 1931 'they had learnt that never again must any Labour leader propose any kind of collaboration with Labour's opponents'. As such, 'there was the fear of anything resembling alliance with non-Labour and anti-Labour elements',[74] thus ruling out a coalition with the parties of capital. Roger Eatwell and Tony Wright write that Labour had learnt that never again should it form a minority government. This lesson made sense, 'in so far as a socialist party could hardly hope to implement socialist measures when dependent on non-socialist support'.[75]

Here, we can see something of Labour's working class ethos. Henry Drucker wrote: 'Nothing better exemplified that ethos than the determination built up after the 1931 debacle never to form a government again without a parliamentary majority'.[76] MacDonald's actions convinced the Labour movement to avoid such arrangements, for it is the Labour Party which is the guardian of workers. Later, the Lab–Lib Pact of 1977–8 differed, borne out of political necessity, ensuring the government's survival rather than believing in the merits of power-sharing and coalition government. Drucker considered that the Lab–Lib Pact may further weaken the old working-class ethos. Yet, as we will see, its legacy still shapes attitudes towards electoral reform and coalition government.

Summary

A debate has existed about the electoral system within the Labour Party since its inception. Whilst the Labour Party has flirted with electoral reform on several occasions, the Party has been committed to introducing PR for the House of Commons during 1910–11 and 1918–26. AV was a device hoped to ensure the survival of the second minority Labour government for a full term and, whilst close to becoming law, was supported with little enthusiasm. A range of factors shaped the Labour Party's attitude towards electoral reform in the period analysed: the best method to increase parliamentary representation, the relationship with the Liberal Party and the influence of the Party leadership. Interest in reform duly subsided as Labour's position in the two-party system strengthened.

As the Party grew as an electoral and political force throughout the 1920s, experiencing minority government in 1924 and 1929–31, it moved away from PR. Many in the Labour Party considered the Liberal Party a 'decaying corpse', in terminal decline and soon electorally defunct, meaning British politics would once again revolve around two parties: Labour and the Conservatives. Therefore, the adoption of an electoral system which perpetuated the three-party system was highly disagreeable to many within the Labour Party, for it would continue the situation through the 1920s in which the Labour Party had to rely on the Liberals. The experience of government had taught the Labour Party two vital lessons: firstly, minority government reliant on the support of other political parties was restrictive and therefore was to be avoided; and secondly, with a parliamentary majority, the workings of the British State would enable the Labour Party to enact its brand of democratic socialism.

MacDonald displayed a split attitude towards electoral reform but the evidence indicates a preference for FPTP and a reluctance towards reform. Importantly, it was his underlying belief that British Politics should revolve around a Conservative Party and a Labour Party that has had a great bearing on the governing ideology of the Party. The Labour Party should be independent, capable of fighting and winning elections across Great Britain and forming single-party governments, emphasizing to the country that it was capable of governing. Consequently, it was vital to marginalize the Liberal Party and neuter its capability as an electoral force.

2

Labour and the electoral system in historical perspective, 1931–87

This chapter charts the Labour Party's interest, or lack thereof, in electoral reform and proportional representation, beginning with the years following the fall of the second minority Labour government. The chapter will then move on to the post–Second World War era and the height of the 'two-party' system. Finally, the chapter will outline the growing interest in electoral reform in the 1970s, the impact of Callaghan's minority government and the Lib–Lab Pact and the election of Margaret Thatcher's Conservative government. As such, the chapter will take us up to the growth in pressure for voting and wider constitutional reforms discussed in the following chapter on the Plant Report.

1931–45

Jennifer Hart refers to this period as the 'Barren Years'.[1] The National Government had seen no need to pursue the Labour Government's Electoral Reform Bill, particularly in light of its vast parliamentary majority. The Labour Party, bar a few voices, had little interest in changing the voting system despite suffering the heaviest loss of seats to befall a major party from 288 MPs to 52 MPs.

From without the Party, Harold Laski, the influential academic, made the case for FPTP. Interestingly, his political journey covered pluralism, Fabian socialism and Marxism.[2] From his early concern that the 'belief in state sovereignty placed the state above the moral law and the conscience of individuals', he attempted to reconcile a Marxist analysis of British capitalism with the possibility of achieving socialism by constitutional means.[3] He reflected:

Mr MacDonald's victory is so disproportionate to the votes cast for him in the country, that the claims of proportional representation have been urged with added vigour since the election ... [such] a change in the system of election would assume the proportions of a serious disaster. For it would perpetuate the dangers which would attend upon minority Government not only maintaining in being the three-party system, but quite probably encouraging further fission. Thereby, it would weaken the executive power at a time when only strength and coherency can make for honest and straightforward government ... Our system has, of course, its limitations; but worked with goodwill and common sense, these do not seem likely to destroy the purpose at which it aims.[4]

By default, those who had chosen in the Labour Party not to serve in the National Government were the only credible opposition. Indeed, in light of the 'Great Betrayal' it was probably considered this was a reasonable result. The Labour MP J. R. Leslie described himself as among the 'lone scouts' in the Labour Party for PR.[5] Elsewhere, Cecil H. Wilson, Labour MP for Sheffield, Attercliffe, and an advocate of PR, was bemused at the leading figures in the Labour Party, such as Dalton and Morrison, who wished to maintain the present system.[6] Morrison, as shown, was staunchly in favour of FPTP, a position he unwaveringly held both pre– and post–Second World War.

In 1935 the Labour Party still fared badly – 40 per cent of the votes won them less than one-quarter of the seats – but the Party remained loyal to the system which seemed to offer them the best chance of gaining a clear parliamentary majority. Crossman, who would in the Wilson governments of 1964–70 be a leading figure in promoting a range of constitutional reforms, noted in his 1939 *How Britain Is Governed* that the electoral system in Britain created a 'temporary dictatorship'[7] between elections. However, this was beneficial for government, as a system that encouraged more than two parties tended to lead to weaker governments:

Proportional representation in parliamentary elections would be a national disaster. It would of course make the strength of the parties in the House reflect more accurately the division of opinion in the country; but in so doing it would ensure the survival of the third party and encourage the formation of a fourth and fifth.[8]

Moreover, weakening of government would be disastrous for the Labour Party and the working classes, as change and reform would be impossible. In 1963, Crossman reiterated his objection to PR, arguing wherever it has been tried 'it has fulfilled his (Bagehot's) prediction that it would undermine the independence of the MP and increase the powers of the party managers who control the electoral lists'.[9] Crossman's biographer writes he never considered electoral reform again, 'but his lack of action on the issue suggests that he remained very sceptical about the benefits of electoral reform generally, and proportional representation specifically'.[10]

The Cabinet, which by May 1943 included Labour ministers, had managed to ignore 114 MPs from all parties who had supported G. W. Rickard's motion calling for a conference on electoral reform. Nevertheless, the wartime coalition was forced to include methods of elections in the terms of reference of the 1944 Speaker's Conference, a result of a two-day Commons debate in February 1944. On 8 February 1944 Sir Winston Churchill formally invited Colonel D. Clifton Brown to Chair the Conference. Nine Labour MPs along with James Maxton (Independent Labour Party) and Denis N. Pritt (Labour Independent) constituted the Labour membership. Pritt dismissed AV as it did not go far enough, whereas STV had the great benefit of resolving the redistribution problem and the 'extreme misrepresentation' of the present system would be replaced by 'actual opinion.'[11]

The main issues for Morrison, the Labour Home Secretary, 'were the principles of redistribution and the fusion of the local government and parliamentary franchise; he did not think there would be much interest in proportional representation'.[12] What occurred was a repeat of the previous Conference. Labour and the Conservatives were hostile towards any reform, with STV being rejected by twenty-five votes to four and AV by twenty votes to five.[13] Some Labour members felt that only by a combination of the Liberal and Labour votes, which would be made possible by the AV, would the Conservatives ever be defeated. This relied on the assumption that Liberal voters were more inclined to put the Labour candidate as the second preference rather than Conservative, an issue which has raised considerable intrigue. Two Labour members of the Speaker's Conference, having failed to convince their colleagues, abstained from voting on this issue,[14] and the adoption of AV at any election in a single-member non-University constituency was rejected. Once again, the Labour Party had come down on the side of FPTP and confirmed its opposition to AV.

Post–Second World War: 1945–74

The wartime coalition broke up on 23 May 1945 and the general election was held in July. The result was a Labour landslide victory with a Commons majority of 146 seats, a net gain of 209 seats of which 79 were constituencies which had never previously returned a Labour MP. Breaking into territory which had never previously been captured and winning 394 seats, the Conservatives had gone down to their biggest defeat since 1906. The Labour Party polled 48.2 per cent of the vote and a national swing was 12 per cent. Notably, the Labour Party did not need to seek alliances and negotiate with the Liberals, as they had done previously, and the long-term objective of replacing the Liberals as the main opposition to the Conservatives had been achieved. Clement Attlee became Labour prime minister, the first leader of the Labour Party with the ability to utilize a parliamentary majority. For the first time in the Labour Party's history, the workings of FPTP had handed the party such a victory that it could enact its manifesto commitments of 'Let us Face the Future Together'.

Indeed, significant importance was attached to the doctrine of the 'manifesto and the mandate'. Morrison told the Labour Party conference in 1945: 'Only by a Labour majority – a coherent Labour majority – can our programme be put through. I make no promise about what will happen to that programme if we do not get a clear and coherent and united majority.'[15] The intellectual climate within the Labour Party towards the British state was one of acceptance, believing that having captured a parliamentary majority, they could control the machinery of government. Dalton, when opening the second reading debate on the Bank of England Bill, stated: 'I hold in my hand a document entitled "Let us Face the Future, a Declaration of Labour Policy for the Consideration of the Nation". The nation considered it and having done so elected this House of Commons. We have an unchallengeable popular mandate to carry out all that is contained in this document.'[16]

Such was the confidence in the reforming capabilities of a Labour majority in Parliament, that talk of coalition and a deal with the Liberals was unnecessary. Butler notes that many of the policies enacted by the Labour government solidified the Liberals in opposition to it. Talk of coalition came from the Conservatives, led by Winston Churchill. He had never heard of a 'Liberal-Socialist', and therefore held out hope for an anti-Socialist agreement between the Conservatives and the Liberals. The 'Woolton–Teviot' agreement of May 1947 made possible 'Conservative Liberal' mergers, and in the 1950 General Election fifty-three candidates stood under miscellaneous headings such as 'National Liberal and Conservative', 'Conservative and National Liberal', 'Conservative and Liberal' or 'Liberal and Conservative'.[17] Such varied headings would continue on into the 1960s.

In 1950 Attlee referred to a rejection made in 1944 in refusing the Liberal leader Clement Davies's calls for a new inquiry into electoral matters.[18] Five years previously, the Labour Party had won its first landslide victory and during the Parliament had not lost a by-election to the Conservatives. Furthermore, in the 1950 General Election, Labour polled 13,267,466 votes, at that time the highest poll ever won. However, boundary changes by the then Home Secretary, Chuter Ede, harmed the Labour Party, with the changes favouring suburban and middle-class constituencies.[19] The result was a majority of five, thus making for a more insecure and weakened government. The cause of Labour's downfall was England, for both Scotland and Wales increased their representation. Industrial working-class constituencies returned Labour MPs with extravagant majorities, whereas suburban England reverted to the Conservative Party.

For eighteen months the Labour government battled on through Cabinet resignations and divisions until Attlee, under no constitutional obligation, called an election for 25 October 1951. Whereas in 1929 Labour had won more seats on fewer votes than the Conservatives, the system 22 years later had worked to the disadvantage of Labour. On a 48.8 per cent of the vote, a total poll of 13,948,883 – an increase of 2.7 per cent on 1950 – Labour suffered a net loss of 19 seats and won only 295. Cook claims the cause of Labour's defeat was the Liberal Party, who fielded a mere 109 candidates, forcing erstwhile Liberal voters into the hands of the Conservatives. Accordingly, Labour faced the Conservatives in 495 straight fights in 1951 compared to 109 in 1950.[20] Ironically, the reduced electoral capability of the Liberal Party – the abiding wish of the Labour Party – had hurt Labour's electoral chances.

Returning to the opposition benches did not dampen Labour's enthusiasm for FPTP. Morrison wrote of the benefits of the two-party system and rejected PR in a Labour Educational Series booklet. The Labour Party had always been independent and the British two-party system 'leads to greater coherence and responsibility in government and opposition and the work of parliament'. Recognizing Labour and the Conservatives were made up of individuals who, whilst subscribing to fundamental principles, differed on certain matters, believed the electors had to make a 'broad choice as to which of the two great political parties more generally represents their point of view'. PR would result in 'a series of minority groups to Parliament would make it very difficult to form majority governments … If there is no majority for any Party in Parliament, it means that coalitions have to be formed and bargains have to be struck, with the result that governments are unstable and firm, consistent policies are difficult to carry out.' Both parties are against PR 'based on substantial constitutional considerations of public policy'.[21]

Morrison offered a traditional defence of the Westminster model and the working of British parliamentary democracy. He considered the 'British Parliament is one of the most efficient and up to date instruments for its purpose'. Specifically, on the workings of the electoral system and its impact on the British political system Morrison considered a backbench MP was a representative not a delegate, 'acting in the general public interest'. An MP also must uphold the government, realizing that the alternatives are 'either a Government formed by the opposition or a general election in which he will be involved'. FPTP was a 'safeguard against the development of minor or splinter parties' which was one of the reasons why the British people opposed PR, as PR would result in 'no chance of forming a Government and no chance of getting their policies adopted except as a result of bargaining with other parties'. This view was recognized as beneficial by the British people due to their practical nature, 'that when they vote they are voting for a Government, and that their votes are wasted if they are spent upon a party which has no chance of forming a Government at any foreseeable date'.

Additionally, a two-party system leads to an effective government and an effective Opposition. After all, agreement over policy occurs within parties. For Morrison, a democratic country with many views faces a choice. It can organize points of view into separate parties 'for the reconciliation between them to take place as a result of bargaining at the general election and in Parliament itself'. However, the preferred method is reconciling different views 'within the framework of the parties, each of which within itself contains the elements from which a Government can be formed'.[22] In 1953 Herbert Morrison looked back at the Attlee administration and praised its record on parliamentary reform. Reducing the delaying power of the House of Lords, the abolition of University Seats, the final remnants of plural voting and increasing MPs salaries by two-thirds had all played their part in transforming the House of Commons from a 'talking shop' to a 'workshop'.[23]

In his textbook, *Government and Parliament*, published in 1954, Morrison declared the importance of the mandate given by the British people, writing that the opposition has a moral duty and justification to sustained opposition should the government try and introduce controversial legislation for which there is no mandate. So attached had Morrison become to the workings of the British constitution that 'if the Opposition is to be given no moral case for obstruction, the Government must "play the game" and respect the principles of parliamentary democracy, otherwise representative government will be endangered'. Furthermore, 'the British people rightly attach importance to a party being sufficiently coherent and united to give the country a Government not only of sound policy but of adequate strength and unity of purpose'. Indeed, Morrison goes on to write, perhaps influenced by the 1950–1 Labour government, 'let the electorate remember that whilst there are objections to excessively large parliamentary majorities, there are even greater objections to a majority so small that the legitimate freedom of the MP is gravely limited'.[24]

Laski, who had defended FPTP in the 1930s, was influenced by the success of the Attlee government, affirming that the purpose of a general election was the creation of strong government. Laski rejected claims that Parliament should represent a microcosm of society and in England and America 'you have no law prohibiting the existence of social groups and you get a two-party system'. He turned his attention to the European continent, where 'you get a proliferation of groups that in turn leads to an unstable ministerial system; and where there is ministerial instability, you get, I suggest, the development of revolution'. This made Laski hostile to PR, for it multiplies groups. He suggested the 'business of a legislative assembly is not to mirror the variegated opinion of a democracy but to make possible the existence of an executive with some degree of permanence.[25]

He reiterated this point in *Reflections on the Constitution* that as a strong believer in a 'stable executive with sufficient authority to drive important and substantial programmes through the House of Commons in the life-time of the Parliament of five years, I remain completely unconvinced by advocates of proportional representation, in any of its numerous forms, or of kindred expedients like the alternative vote'. Such was Laski's faith in FPTP he did not think it important that

> from time to time, a minority of the electoral votes may give a party a majority of seats so that it is able to form a government. For it would be a very stupid party, obviously courting defeat, which failed to remember that it must not outrage the Opposition, that it must show a real respect for a minority of importance, and that it must pay careful attention to the currents and cross-currents of opinion outside the House of Commons. Consequently, constitutional reforms that pose a threat to the clarity and consistency of government, especially a socialist government, should be rejected, where compromise naturally inhibits the implementation of controversial or radical policies.

Moreover, Minority government, he argued 'is invariably uneasy government, and usually cowardly government.'[26]

Unsurprisingly, losing despite receiving more votes than the Conservatives in 1951 provoked little comment in the Party as did Labour's under-representation in 1955. Three successive election defeats in 1951, 1955 and 1959 did not make Labour more favourably disposed towards reform. In the 1959 General Election, six Liberal MPs and an independent Conservative were the only non-Labour or non-Conservative MPs returned to the House of Commons. The Scottish and Welsh Nationalists remained peripheral. Few worried about the electoral system, leading Birch to comment that in the 1960s the electoral system was 'no longer a bone of contention.'[27]

Labour returned to office in 1964 with a slim majority of four. Harold Wilson had no contingency plan for such a small majority, intending to govern as though he had a larger majority and enact the government's legislative programme accordingly. Two backbench Labour MPs, Woodrow Wyatt and Desmond Donnelly, suggested a Lab–Lib understanding. Yet Jo Grimond, the Liberal leader, rejected this. One of the features of the consultations with the Liberals in 1964 was electoral reform. During the summer of 1965, Wilson had allegedly looked seriously at changing FPTP in exchange for parliamentary support, 'albeit without in any way committing himself'.[28] Yet, Wilson's biographer Philip Ziegler adopts a different view, affirming 'Wilson was forthright in his denunciation of anything smacking of a coalition, even if it were merely to involve accepting Liberals in a few of the less important jobs'. However, Wilson was forced to look seriously at the matter in August 1965. Gerald Kaufman took soundings amongst backbenchers; broadly, three were against a Lib–Lab pact for every two in favour of it, one uncommitted, and Wilson could dismiss the possibility. Even if they had wanted to seek a deal with the Liberals, the Parliamentary Labour Party 'would never let them get away with it'.[29]

Unlike in the 1940s, no attempt was made to exclude methods of election from the terms of reference for the Speaker's Conference on Electoral Law, which addressed such things as registration of voters, the voting age, absent voting, election expenses, television and sound broadcasting, election petitions, and relief. When the Conference came to discuss STV, all Labour members denounced it. George Strauss considered FPTP had two major benefits: direct representation and effective government. For Strauss, the effectiveness of parliamentary democracy most importantly depended on a 'close association of Members of Parliament with their constituents'.[30] A government with a majority was essential, as it took responsibility for its actions without any excuses.[31]

John Mendelson, Labour MP for Pensitone, believed that pressure from academic circles and the Electoral Reform Society was simply to increase third-party representation for the Liberal Party 'and saw no reason why the baby should not ever be mentioned by name'.[32] Mendelson dismissed PR supporters who argued they were the 'superior custodians of purity of democratic representation; because accuracy of representation ... is only one half of the problem of government', the other being 'effective government'. In sum, 'all discussion about accuracy of representation are academic'.[33] Mendelson deemed that once the first proposition – specifically that third-party representation hindered the chances of forming a single-party government – had been accepted, the second inevitable proposition was the 'casting about for possible arrangements on a political programme which no single party wants'.[34] The seriousness of this was based on two factors. Firstly, 'the essential basis of a democratic system of Government must be the ability of the electorate to place responsibility where it clearly belongs'. After all, 'it is the job of government that the electorate have to judge'. Secondly, Coalition government makes it 'difficult to judge where responsibility really belongs' leading to more political cynicism.[35]

James Idwal Jones, a Labour MP from Wales, understood that a general election 'is to choose a government, a government according to a political policy' and the 'task of a minority ... is to seek a majority'.[36] Jones thought this should be done by the hard work of the third party, not by changing the rules and the altruism of a major party. Jones refuted that safe seats were necessarily negative, stating 'security of tenure for Members means security of tenure for governments as well', although qualified the statement arguing 'the best thing for a government at times is to be put on the opposition benches'.[37] Samuel Charles Silkin 'always unhesitatingly' came down on the side of 'effectiveness'. He continued: 'No democratic system can survive unless it is effective and that one has to subordinate even justice to that principle.'[38] When the vote took place during Conference on STV, nineteen to one voted against; the one dissentient being the Liberal MP, Eric Lubbock, the grandson of the founder of the Proportional Representation Society.

Leading Labour figures rebuffed Lubbock when he subsequently tried to raise STV in the Commons. The purpose of the electoral system for James Callaghan, the then Home Secretary, was to elect a government, not to be fair to the Liberal party.[39] He sympathized on behalf of the Liberal Party, but it was 'one of the inexorable facts of life that third parties come up against when a general election arises'. In effect, this was to rule out coalition government. Another minister, Merlyn Rees, when arguing against a change, referred to Laski's (mocking) assertion that there were 949 different methods of proportional representation. Rees was confident that 'our democracy works', one reason for which was 'the clear majority which is given to the government of the day'.[40]

It was clear in the post–Second World War era that the electoral battle lay between the Conservatives and Labour, with the Liberals few in number and only on the margins of British politics. The importance of the Labour victory in 1945 would live long in the Party's collective memory, enacting social reforms to the benefit of the working class through the traditional practices and workings of the British State. On the matter of constitutional reform, it is as Miles Taylor states, that legislative efficiency was the ultimate consideration.[41] Legislative efficiency – free from the parliamentary wrangling with smaller parties – would be aided by a socialist majority in the House of Commons. The best way to deliver a majority was through FPTP, and when it did come to reform the Labour Party was more concerned with electoral practices – the law relating to broadcasting during elections and the lowering the age of voting from twenty to eighteen which had been recommended by the Conference – than with voting methods. Wilson dissolved parliament in 1966 and won a 96-seat majority in the general election. Whatever troubles and failures the Wilson government faced, and the ensuing defeat in 1970, they remained convinced of the merits of FPTP.

The post–Second World War Labour revisionists, notably finding expression in Crosland's *The Future of Socialism*, had little interest in the political and administrative machinery through which redistribution and public expenditure would be achieved. Labour politicians, including Crosland, were concerned about the political implications of an increasingly affluent working class.[42] The belief in the neutrality of the state meant that its power could be harnessed for social purposes, and under successive Labour governments a socialist Britain could be realized. Little attention was paid to the possibility that the structure by which Labour hoped to achieve reform was permeated with values opposed to theirs, and therefore attempts to enact their values might be defeated. Instead, Labour politicians could utilize the existing structure of the British State to change society following their values, and as such, the policies would be implemented through the existing parliamentary machinery, including the Cabinet and Whitehall. All that was required was a parliamentary majority, and this would withstand attempts at 'obstruction by the City, by industrialists, by the capitalist-controlled mass media and by international financiers'.[43] In Harold Wilson's phrase, the state could be driven anywhere depending on who was in the driving seat.

> What matters is the driver. If the man behind the machine is a Labour man, the machine will move towards Labour. Not only Parliament, but the vast machinery of the State which it controls … are politically neutral, loyal to their political masters.[44]

Such an approach did draw criticism from the pluralists, who deemed that the Westminster model concentrated power at the centre. Mackintosh accused the parliamentary reformers in the 1960s of naiveté and foolishness for thinking reform was possible without diminishing the power of the executive.[45] Mackintosh was critical of the workings of Parliament in an era when the Labour Party was satisfied with the constitutional setup. He considered that the executive had become too powerful and this needed to be checked by a stronger parliament. Moreover, 'the old, straightforward parliamentary system of democracy has been added to and been confused by other concepts of legitimacy and other methods of obtaining and demonstrating support'.[46] A parliamentary majority no longer conferred 'moral authority' on to laws. This was rejected by a Peter Shore, a Cabinet minister and contemporary of Mackintosh. In the annual Nye Bevan lecture in 1976, Shore rebutted the 'elective dictatorship' thesis articulated by Lord Hailsham and defended parliamentary sovereignty. For Shore, it was parliamentary sovereignty that had allowed for the peaceful evolution of British society.[47]

The Right critiqued Labour's state-centric approach in *Adversary Politics and Electoral Reform*. Indeed, in the 1970s it was the Conservative Party who were more inclined to electoral reform forming the 'Conservative Action for Electoral Reform' in 1975, fearing that the Labour Party would continue to form governments on reducing vote shares, thus introducing socialism without popular backing. Anthony Wigram believed that through PR they had the power to extinguish the possibility of an extreme left-wing government indefinitely.[48] With four out of the last five general elections delivering Labour governments (albeit only 1966 with a landslide victory) Conservative statecraft and their ability to win elections was questioned. This was against a declining number of Scottish Conservative MPs from thirty-one in 1959 to sixteen in 1974, and the group enjoyed the support of such backbenchers as Nicholas Scott, Anthony Kershaw and Douglas Hurd.

1974–83

In February 1974, Edward Heath called an election on the issue of who governs Britain – the trade unions or the government at Westminster? The reply from the British electorate was inconclusive. The Conservative polled 100,000 more votes but the Labour Party won 4 more seats returning 301 seats to the House of Commons. As the sitting prime minister, Heath had the constitutional right to seek to form a government; he spent three days attempting to guarantee the support of the Liberal Party offering a Speaker's Conference on Electoral Reform. When this was rejected, Wilson's Labour Party formed a minority government, intentionally avoiding the support of the Liberal Party. During the parliamentary vote to pass the queen's speech, Callaghan deemed 'it would be frivolous to think you could defeat the Government on their programme without serious consequences arising'. Moreover, the behaviour of the opposition parties was irresponsible and seemed to be 'little more than a simple desire to bring down a Labour Government no matter what its policies, so that the Conservative and Liberal parties may climb into office on the back of a spurious national coalition'. For Callaghan, belief in coalition government was misguided: 'A coalition is like a mule. It has no pride of ancestry and no hope of posterity.'[49]

For the first time since 1929, FPTP had failed to produce a clear winner. As such, some started to doubt the electoral system's legitimacy. Two months into the Labour government, during a Cabinet meeting on 4 April 1974, Roy Jenkins brought up the question of Edward Heath's Speaker's Conference, which had ended with Parliament's dissolution in February 1974. Barbara Castle notes in her diaries how the conversation transpired. Jenkins claimed the Conference had 'unfinished business left over from the last Parliament and he was thinking of reconstituting it. But before he did he wanted to discuss how we should handle the matter of the single transferable vote', an electoral system not favoured by the Labour Party since pre–First World War. Jenkins continued:

> If we did not include it in the terms of reference we should look as though we were the only party not interested in electoral reform. As the Liberals were very likely to propose its examination, it would be better for us to take the initiative. He suggested therefore that we should get the Speaker's Conference to examine it in a 'low pressure way'.

The response to Jenkins's suggestion was critical. 'Bob Mellish looked alarmed at this, while Mike (Michael Foot) came in emphatically: "Once we get into this it will grow and grow," he protested. "Why hasten the conference at all? I have always believed the Tories would come down for the alternative vote because it is in their interests." '

Bob Mellish approved Foot's criticism and added that he was darn sure the Speaker was in no hurry to have the conference reconstituted. Willie Ross (the secretary of state for Scotland), in his lugubrious way, pointed out that all this was linked with the Kilbrandon Report, which had itself recommended a form of proportional representation as the only way of eliminating the perpetual Labour majorities in Scotland and Wales which devolution would produce. Castle continues:

> If we were not careful we could see the end of any possibility of a Labour Government. Harold reminded us that nothing could stop the Speaker's Conference from producing an interim report – particularly if we put on it some of the Labour maverick types like George Strauss as we had done before. It was obviously best to let this sleeping dog lie as long as possible. So we sent Roy away with a flea in his coalition ear.[50]

In the days running up to the October 1974 general election Harold Wilson affirmed that whilst he remained leader of the Labour Party he would not enter a coalition with any party, and proceeded to damn the tactics of the Liberal Party. It was the dream of 'manipulating voices' that the result of a general election would be the Liberals holding the balance of power, meaning 'permanent majority for the Conservatives by the creation of a new Liberal Party out of the ashes of the Labour Party. They are wasting their time. This party is not for burning.'[51] The electorate gave the Labour Party a majority of three in a different political climate across Great Britain. Whereas in 1964 the only non-Labour or non-Conservative and Unionist MPs were nine Liberals, by 1974 thirty-nine MPs were neither Labour nor Conservative. Importantly, eleven of whom were from the Scottish Nationalist Party (SNP) who would play a pivotal role through the course of the Parliament. The fracturing of the two-party system in the 1974–9 parliament was not necessarily harmful to the Labour government, as the Conservative opposition was reliant on agreement amongst a disparate group of political parties.

Wilson affirmed at the 1975 Party Conference that Labour was 'the natural party of government',[52] implying a satisfaction with the electoral mechanism which was delivering Labour governments, having only lost one election since

1964. The Labour Party was fulfilling its objective of governing in the same manner as its Conservative opponent. However, this did not prevent Roy Jenkins on Tuesday, 18 November, raising the issue of proportional representation and the Speaker's Conference in the Cabinet. Castle claims it was 'pleasant to have Roy Jenkins slapped down'. Jenkins gave his excuse that the Conference ought to be reconvened to discuss certain outstanding items of electoral procedure and that it would be very difficult not to refer electoral reform to it at the same time. What was worrying was that, with Harold's connivance, he had already sounded out the Opposition on this possibility. Ted Short, who ought to know better, supported him. There was, he said, 'great pressure for it', though 'we must watch it very carefully'. However, Castle declares the rest of the Cabinet turned on them. Denis (Healey) who

> with good pragmatic vigour, denounced the idea as 'absolute madness'. Even people like Roy Mason, Fred Peart, Malcolm and Willie Ross were against. Only the hard core of Jenkinites coalitionists (Harold Lever, Shirley Williams and Reg Prentice) were in agreement. So Harold had to sum up that the idea was turned down. But those rightists will go on beavering away, with Harold and Jim as their instruments, until they have finally destroyed the Labour Party's independence and power to govern single-handedly.[53]

Ron Hayward, former general secretary of the Labour Party, speaking in 1976, warned PR would mean 'coalition government at Westminster, on the lines of our European partners, and it is goodbye then to any dreams or aspirations for a Democratic Socialist Britain'.[54] On the other hand, Mackintosh outlined the benefits of the Lab–Lib Pact in the *Scotsman*: a 'counter-weight to the Left and puts Labour in touch with five million voters who, in 1974, rejected both the traditional main parties'; politicians having to consider the impact of policies on people not the manifesto or party; and lastly the government's survival rests on its relationship with the Commons. The objective of a realignment would be to 'produce a major left-of-centre party which would be tied neither to Marxist dogma nor the trade unions'. Debates over the mixed economy would cease and those who wished for state ownership 'would have to make their case to the electorate'. Lastly, a realigned party could 'shed the desperate constitutional orthodoxy of the left and accept the development of democratic controls over government, from Parliament downwards'.[55]

The Labour Party lost its parliamentary majority in April 1976 and as the government could not deliver on the guillotine on the committee stage of the Devolution Bill, the attitudes of nationalists hardened against Labour. The Conservatives saw their opportunity to strike and put down a motion of censure for 23 March. Callaghan needed to appease the minority parties and established a Speaker's Conference to examine representation in Northern Ireland to buy Unionist support and Proportional Representation for European Elections and Devolution for David Steel's Liberals. Callaghan and Steel were wary of the need to avoid a general election, fearing heavy losses. On 23 March 1977 the 'Lab–Lib' Pact was born, with the Labour government and the Liberals announcing the formation of a Joint Consultative Committee, designed to examine policy and the practicalities of such an arrangement.

This period reveals the weight of feelings and tension within the Labour Party in the debates over PR for Europe and the proposed devolved assemblies in Scotland and Wales. Callaghan told Steel, 'As he would understand, proportional representation was an animal of a very different colour, for the party was against it and so was I.'[56] Consequently, forcing the Labour Party to walk through the lobbies in favour of a Regional List for the European Parliament would split the Cabinet and the Party. Accordingly, Callaghan suspended collective responsibility, agreeing to 'commend' the Bill, thus ensuring a 'free vote'. By the Second Reading, collective responsibility was suspended and the Bill passed by 381 votes to 98. However, 74 Labour MPs opposed the Bill and 90 abstained including Cabinet ministers; Foot, Benn, Orme, Shore and Silkin, all of which was overlooked by Callaghan.[57]

In December 1977, during the Second Reading of the Bill, Pugh emphasizes that Labour opponents of the scheme 'interpreted the question purely as a device by the Liberals to edge the country nearer to a general PR system; Fred Willey tried to damn the idea by referring the House to the effort of the 1929–31 Labour government to do a deal with the Liberals over PR.'[58] Kirkup charts the course of events. Willey tabled an amendment calling for a vote to strike out the government's preference for Regional List and replace it with FPTP, already in place as a schedule to the Bill, passing 321 votes to 224. Eighty-five abstentions yielded a majority of 98. The PR clause was defeated by 319 to 222 votes, with the Labour Party dividing 147 for PR (including 60 ministers) to 122 against and 46 Labour MPs abstained. Twenty-five government ministers either voted against PR or abstained.[59] Clearly, a substantial section within the Labour Party were against the Regional List System, particularly when the Commons majority of 183 against PR for the devolved assemblies is considered.

The Lab–Lib Pact ended in June 1978, placing the Labour Party in a precarious parliamentary position. Callaghan considered calling an election for the autumn but held back only for the 'Winter of Discontent' to harm the electoral chances of a Labour victory. Margaret Thatcher brought forward a 'vote of no confidence' for 28 March 1979, on which the government fell by 311 votes to 310. The Scottish Nationalists sided with the Conservatives, seven MPs from Ulster, and an Independent. The Liberals, who were partaking in the Lab–Lib Pact nine months prior, supported the Conservative motion. As Callaghan stated immediately after the Commons vote, echoing MacDonald's view in 1924, 'We shall take our case to the country.' In the ensuing general election, the Conservative Party won a working majority.

Prior to the Conservative Party election victory in 1979, and considering the governing difficulties of the 1970s, Roy Jenkins had voiced his concerns about the two major parties moving away from the centre ground. Only a 'new' kind of politics could resolve these problems. Jenkins gave a speech titled 'Home Thoughts from Abroad' in which he criticized the 'constricting rigidity – almost the tyranny – of the present party system' and believed that 'the case for proportional representation (to be) overwhelming'. Instead of coalition government being feared, it should be embraced, as it was 'essential for democratic leadership'. Furthermore, 'the test is whether those within the coalition are closer to each other, and to the mood of the nation they seek to govern, than they are to those outside their ranks'. As we will see, he repeated this argument in his report on the voting system in 1998. In his closing remarks, Jenkins, advocated for 'a strengthening of the radical centre',[60] suggesting that the formation of the Social Democratic Party (SDP), of which he would go on to be a founding member, was already in his thoughts.

Not all looked so favourably upon constitutional reform and embracing electoral reform. In his autobiography, Healey reflected on the Lab–Lib Pact and the whittling down of the Labour majority through by-election defeats and defections. Released in 1990, the same year the Plant Commission was set up, potentially as a repost to the growing demands for electoral reform within the Labour Party, he dismissed PR, coalition government and defended FPTP and single-party government. It is worth quoting Healey in full.

> Labour cannot escape from its problems through alliances with the Centre parties, or through proportional representation. The non-Labour majority is probably as large as the non-Conservative majority; there is no guarantee that members of the Centre parties would vote Labour if their own candidates stood down – or vice-versa. Proportional Representation could not be introduced in Britain without years of wrangling over its precise form; previous attempts to change the British constitution, over devolution or the House of Lords, are not an encouraging precedent. The experience of PR in other countries shows that it has many defects. It tends to give excessive influence to tiny political parties ... and rarely produces a government which can act decisively in a crisis.
>
> In any case, if the Labour Party cannot defeat the Conservatives on its own, it is unlikely to do so in an alliance with the Centre or Nationalist parties; it is even less likely to form an effective government with them if it did. The Centre parties are deeply divided both on their values, their policies and their leadership; and each Nationalist party has only one aim, which none of the other parties share.[61]

The Labour Party after the defeat in 1979 could not have foreseen the eighteen years in opposition that awaited and the internal trauma caused by Militant and the breakaway SDP. Militant and the problem of entryism prompted interest in internal Labour Party democracy, and as Roy Hattersley commented, attempted to use the Labour Party as a vehicle for their ideas which were alien to Labour's tradition. Paradoxically, for Hattersley, both the Trotskyites and the SDP gave the same reason for their actions: 'Democratic socialism seemed out of fashion'.[62] As for the SDP, the 'the gang of four' – Roy Jenkins, Shirley Williams, William Rogers and David Owen – who sought to 'break the mould of British politics' committed, to many in the Labour Party, an act of treason akin to Ramsay MacDonald in 1931.

As the 'mould' was to be broken through PR, the SDP were guilty by association and responsible for returning the issue to the political agenda. Tom Ellis, a Labour MP before becoming a founder member of the SDP, developed a wide-ranging case in favour of reform. This included linking the failings of the parliamentary system to economic decline, the perverse idea of the mandate and the advantages of participatory democracy. He was rebuffed by Rosaleen Hughes and Phillip Whitehead in an equally wide-ranging defence, dismissing the fanatics of proportionality as irrelevant.[63] For Shore, the SDP's obsession with PR and restructuring British politics was little more than self-interest and revealed a poverty of thinking over the real problems facing the country.[64] Anderson and Mann state that at that time 'proportional representation was too closely associated in most Labour minds with the hated SDP defectors and their Liberal allies to make any headway in the party'.[65]

In 1983, the Labour Party manifesto was dubbed the 'longest suicide note in history' and was rejected by the British electorate, with Margaret Thatcher winning the first of her landslide victories. Labour achieved only marginally more votes than the SDP/Liberal Alliance, but considerably more seats; 8.4 million votes won 209 seats compared to Alliance who polled just below 7.8 million votes but won only 23 seats. Bogdanor calculates that the Labour Party received thirty more seats than it would have achieved under PR. Curtice and Steed made two calculations, estimating on a national PR system Labour would have won twenty-nine fewer seats, and a local PR system estimating the Labour would have returned twenty-two fewer seats.[66] Having become one of the two major parties in British politics, the Labour Party's position in the system was secure under FPTP even in the face of an electorally dominant Conservative Party and a resurgent third party.

When the issue was raised from within the Party, it was mostly dismissed: Jack Straw considered PR to be about 'giving parties who get the least number of votes the most power. It's very clever.'[67] Peter Hain penned *Proportional Misrepresentation* in 1986 rejecting PR as it suffered from many flaws, although favoured AV for the House of Commons. Without, figures on the Left criticized Labour's acceptance of FPTP and parliamentary approach. Hilary Wainwright, a leading figure in the New Left, deemed the New Left more critical in every way of Britain's parliamentary institutions. Westminster is not the hallmark of democracy that it is for the Labourist left due to the New Left experiences of campaigning in close cooperation with other organizations on the left. As such, the New Left is less protective of the Labour Party's monopoly of working class politics, part of Labour's opposition to PR. Working in alliances with other organizations on the left has led to the belief that the consequences of PR are not considered a threat. Moreover, PR would allow a party of the left 'to establish an electoral competitor to the Labour Party'. The present situation of electoral competition emanating from the centre and right results in 'the all-powerful pressure within the party is to silence the left in the mad rush for the centre'.[68]

Arthur Scargill, the then president of the National Union of Miners (NUM), saw PR not as a device for compromise and coalition but as the exact opposite: 'a means of *polarizing* political views around alternative programmes and class approaches, of clarifying the fundamental contradictions within capitalism and exposing the class nature of this society, thus involving more and more people in the struggle to transform it'.[69] Consequently, PR would allow ideological and political purity – winning power 'for my class and its allies'[70] – unlike the collusion of the Labour Party with capitalism under the present system. Socialism will lack support and legitimacy unless a majority can be garnered in favour and therefore what is required is an 'electoral system which gives an appropriate number of parliamentary seats in direct relation to the number of votes cast'.[71] Echoing the sentiment of Wainwright, Scargill writes: 'No change in electoral process will on its own alter the nature of a society.' However, PR does 'help provide the basis for carrying that tradition forward within the structures already familiar to the British people. Furthermore, it demands levels of political campaigning and education sadly neglected in recent decades by the leadership of the Labour Party and key organisations in the Labour movement'.[72] The inherent fairness of PR will be a 'vote for clarity, for participation, for mobilising the British people to build a society worth living in. A vote for proportional representation is a vote for democracy, and a vote for socialism'.[73]

Summary

MacDonald's attitude towards elections and governing were shared by subsequent Labour Party leaders and prominent figures, becoming the dominant view. Attlee's 1945 reforming government fulfilled Labour's promise in the 1920s, utilizing a parliamentary majority to enact social reform. Indeed, from the 1930s through to the mid-1970s, there was a lack of voices willing to make a case for electoral reform; a minority pursuit within the Labour Party and wider society. Labour's position in the two-party system was secure and they were now the only opposition to the Conservative Party. With governments being returned on well over 45 per cent of the vote, few worried about any theoretical injustice to the Liberals, the third party.

The 1970s witnessed the decline of the combined vote share and seats for both Conservative and Labour parties, with the rise of the Liberal Party and the SNP. For Joyce Gould, the February 1974 general election shifted the focus in both the Labour and Conservative parties on to the legitimacy of FPTP. It was a 'watershed moment' highlighting 'the unfairness of FPTP in terms of votes and seats became clearly apparent for the first time since World War Two'.[74] Yet, many in the Labour Party cared little about the perceived unfairness of the electoral system when PR was discussed for the proposed devolved assemblies and European elections. It was viewed then as the thin end of the wedge, leading people to question the legitimacy of the Westminster electoral system and eventually prompting a move away from FPTP.

The core tenets of the British constitution were accepted by the Labour Party, choosing to prioritize economic issues rather than constitutional reform. Whatever electoral and political difficulties the Labour Party faced, few within the Party believed it could escape them through PR and coalition. On the occasion when a deal had to be made, it was out of necessity rather than a conviction in the merits of parliamentary deals. In the period analysed a variety of system were put forward by dissenting voices, yet it was the perceived benefits FPTP that held sway within the Labour Party. The arguments for electoral reform and the introduction of PR could easily be dismissed as special pleading on their part, out of kilter with the desires of the nation who were choosing between two competing policy platforms.

Coalition and the policy compromise involved, an event judged to be more likely under PR was inferior to single-party government, as moderate Labour MPs and Cabinet ministers such as Healey deemed. The argument from the left during the Lib–Lab Pact was unhappiness at the thought that thirteen Liberal MPs had more influence over the government than the eighty Labour MPs in the Tribune Group; a belief that the tail could wag the dog and a further watering down of the commitment to socialism. In addition, political events have shaped Labour attitude including MacDonald's 'great betrayal' and the breakaway SDP in 1981, whose acts constituted betrayal of the Labour Party and the working class they sought to represent. The SDP were guilty by association in their support of electoral reform and Labour politicians considered that those who joined were traitors or cowards, and whose actions hindered the Labour Party's ambition of returning to office.

The Party considered that other reasons resulted in the defeat in 1979 and the electoral meltdown in 1983, not the fault of the electoral system. Instead, it was a failure of policy – 'the longest suicide note in history' – leadership, presentation and organization in the face of the electoral populism of Thatcherism. The Labour Party was deemed to be unelectable, and given the internal Party strife with entryism and the hard left, PR was low on the agenda. After the second Thatcher landslide in 1987, an election in which the Labour Party considered it ran a successful campaign in terms of presentation and organization, four percentage points gained had translated into only twenty more seats, a disappointing return. Consequently – and for reasons outlined in the following chapter – interest in constitutional reform and, importantly, electoral reform and PR grew.

3

The slow rise and quick fall of the Plant Report

The *Plant Report: A Working Party on Electoral Reform* was an internal Labour Party enquiry that met from 1990 to 1993. The enquiry looked at potential electoral systems for the European Parliament, regional and devolved assemblies, a reformed second chamber and subsequently developed a remit for local government. The chapter's main focus will be the House of Commons and will begin by outlining the circumstances in which the Plant Report was written, the reasons for the growing pressure for reform and why the Labour leadership felt compelled to hold the enquiry. The chapter will then move on to the 1991 *Democracy, Representation and Elections* document, referred to in this chapter as the 'Interim Report', outlining the remit of the Working Party, theoretical issues and the nature and implications of different voting systems. In 1992, a short summary was released, referred to as the 'Second Interim Report', informing the progress the committee had made and the issues looked at to date. The third and final report was published in 1993. It stated the arguments for and against reform of the electoral system and, through a series of votes on the committee, recommended electoral systems for the House of Commons, the Second Chamber and the European Parliament. The chapter will establish how proportional representation became a defining issue for the Labour Party in the late 1980s and early 1990s, how conclusions were reached on the Plant Report and how the leadership sought to influence and ultimately contain PR.

The growth in pressure for voting reform

Prior to 1979, the Conservative Party had broadly supported the social and economic settlement introduced by the Attlee governments. However, the election of the Conservative government under Margaret Thatcher in 1979 embarked upon a series of economic, political and social reforms that ran contrary to the ideology of the Labour Party: privatization of nationalized industries, restriction of trade union practices, restructuring the welfare state, all of which suggested the 'post-war consensus' had ceased. The Thatcher government was committed to the New Right ideology: shrinking the size of the state, cutting spending and liberalizing the economy. Whilst pledging to 'set the people free', the power of local government was limited, the Greater London Assembly was closed down and the government utilized Royal Prerogatives and Privileges in order to pursue its agenda. Such significant social and economic changes, it was argued by electoral reformers, should have been supported by the majority of the electorate. On a minority of the popular vote deep societal and economic changes were driven through parliament, disregarding the views of the opposition inside and outside Parliament. Moreover, such an argument was used with increasing regularity by the opposition parties in parts of Britain where the Conservatives were in electoral retreat, specifically in Scotland.

The introduction of New Right economics and social policies – individualism, consumerism and personal responsibility – undermined the planks of social democracy, shifting the debate away from collectivism. Hirst and Khilnani considered that 'in the name of greater economic efficiency and respect for individual rights Conservative governments since 1979 have accumulated unprecedented powers for the central government'. This has been achieved by two means: the doctrine of parliamentary sovereignty and the freedom of an unwritten constitution.[1] Thus, new governing foundations were required, for whether government was too weak or too strong, both lacked political endorsement. From within Labour, Robin Cook, who would later become a Cabinet minister, declared:

> The appalling insight supplied by the Thatcher experience is that there are no real checks and balances in the British Constitution. The doctrine of the sovereignty of Parliament means that the tyranny of parliamentary majority is absolute. Yes, the first-past-the-post system has given us strong government and I for one have had strong government up to the back teeth.[2]

As Labour struggled against the dominant statecraft of the Conservative Party during the 1980s and 1990s, its position encouraged thoughts of coalition and electoral pacts, gaining favour with journalists, politicians and academics.

Authors including Paul Hirst, Will Hutton, Michael Keating and David Jones, and David Marquand critiqued the British constitution, advocating reform of the electoral system and promoting a pluralistic approach. The celebrated British constitution of 'good government' consisting of a stable, two-party politics, delivering what 'people wanted', requiring the occasional modification began to come under a wide-ranging critique. As for the Labour Party, its electoral and political troubles raised issues for its acceptance of the norms of the British constitution. Jones and Keating wrote that 'the strategy's acceptability was dependent upon success measured in terms of winning control of Parliament and upon the state's ability to deliver the economic goods. By the 1980s neither expectation appeared well-founded.'[3]

Marquand's *The Progressive Dilemma* sought to analyse the reasons why Labour had struggled electorally and politically during the twentieth century. It had not fulfilled its promise due to the narrowness of its electoral coalition which was based on the Labour interest and ethos. This fuelled a link between the working class and voting Labour – 'the world of Labour' – but was limited in its appeal, defensive and inward-looking. Marquand summarized the problems this posed for progressive intellectuals. Firstly, how to transcend Labourism without betraying the Labour interest? Secondly, how to bridge the gulf between the old Labour fortresses and the anti-Conservative but non-Labour hinterland? Thirdly, how to construct a broad-based and enduring social coalition capable not just of giving it a temporary majority in the House of Commons, but of sustaining a reforming government thereafter?

Marquand argued in favour of a 'radical' anti-Thatcherite coalition which could also attract conservative interests and tendencies. The Labour Party had been unable to construct the type of coalition that the Liberals had formed pre–First World War, leading Marquand to write: 'Seventy years of British history suggest that neither the Labour Party nor the SLD can do this all by itself.' On the matter of PR, it was an 'indispensable first step towards a citizen democracy' and electorally for the Labour Party, allow it to gain seats in the south of England. To succeed, the electoral pact would have to be based on a political policy, a shared policy agenda. 'People are increasingly prepared to listen to each other' and 'party frontiers are simply too restrictive for creative political and intellectual debate.'[4] The shame of British politics had been a disunited left, allowing the Conservative Party to dominate electoral politics in the twentieth century.

Hirst echoed Marquand's preference for PR and coalition, writing that it would change our political system. Moreover, Labour had accepted Conservative myths about FPTP and the idea that they could repeat 1945, which was an 'exception'. Coalition was preferable as it was based on a 'collaborative political culture', in which governments had to work through 'large sections of the public through informed consent and dialogue' – not simply manifesto or conference decisions – and this was the only method to tackle the social and economic problems facing Britain.[5]

Pressure groups formed campaigning for constitutional reform notably the Labour Campaign for Electoral Reform (LCER) and Charter 88, a reawakening of interest in civil liberties and in new forms of government. Charter 88 was critiquing not only the actions of the Conservative government but the perceived constitutional conservatism of the Labour Party. It followed *Samizdat*, a non-party newsletter committed to bringing together all anti-conservative forces publishing under the auspices of the Constitutional Reform Centre, for a new legal settlement. Such was the weight of intellectual opinion that Lord Norton, a constitutional expert, noted how the intellectual climate in this period meant 'few (appeared) willing to challenge publicly and in print the views expressed' despite the case for a new constitutional settlement being 'in substance flawed … Dangerous, then, and pretentious'.[6]

Roy Hattersley, former deputy leader of the Labour Party was one figure who was prepared to challenge the pluralist reasoning and he mockingly dismissed Charter 88 as 'the Charter of despair'.[7] Hattersley's objection was threefold. Firstly, British exceptionalism and the sovereignty of Parliament, entailing majority government, allowing a Labour government to enact redistributive policies; secondly, the impracticality of the liberal rights agenda, the power afforded to the judiciary and a belief that democracy is best fulfilled through 'good government'; and thirdly, individual rights have no meaning unless they can be actualized.[8] Neil Kinnock succinctly dismissed Charter 88 as 'whiners, whinges and wankers',[9] emphasizing both Labour's belief in the traditions, norms and practices of the British constitution and the scepticism in which constitutional reformers were held.

The Labour Party having been sceptical of wide-ranging constitutional reform in the post–Second World War era, had become convinced of the need to alter Britain's constitutional settlement. Had Labour won in 1992, several new institutions and other changes would have been introduced – a Scottish Parliament, Welsh Assembly, signing up to PR for the European Parliament, an elected House of Lords by some system other than FPTP – all of which required the Labour Party to have a view on constitutional issues and PR. Had Labour pledged to introduce these institutions with no clear view, basis and agreement would have provided the Conservatives with an 'open goal' to attack Labour, arguing constitutional upheaval would result from a Labour government who had not considered the implications of its policy.

Elsewhere, the Scottish Constitutional Convention and the Executive of the Labour Party of Scotland were heavily engaged in drumming up support for a Scottish Parliament, perhaps realizing that promoting a Scottish Parliament as a 'one-party state' was going to be a hard sell. As with the Labour Party south of the border, the need to keep the Liberal Democrats on board kept the option of electoral reform alive. It was decided at the Dunoon Conference in March 1990 that it could not accept FPTP elections for the Scottish Parliament. As the Labour Party was the dominant party in Scottish politics regarding votes and seats, Kinnock announced that 'no one can claim that our party is examining the detail of methods of electing the Scottish Assembly from any position of weakness or supplication. We are doing it from a position of strength and in the interests of democracy.'[10] Advocating an electoral system other than FPTP for a Scottish Parliament was presented as an indication of the seriousness of the Labour Party's commitment to a more pluralist and consensus-based politics. Consequently, the pressure for reform from different parts of Britain forced the Labour Party to look more closely at new ideas.

Hattersley led the arguments against reform over the Plant process. He maintains that in this period 'PR was very fashionable and there's nothing more damning I can say than the word "fashionable".'[11] PR was one of many 'fanciful ideas', an outpouring in Hattersley's mind of 'radical chic' that would disappear once poll ratings improved. However, such ideas did find favour. Mary Georghiou commenting in the electoral reform edition of *Samizdat* argued that democracy should be Labour's elusive 'big idea' as people wanted to change the way the government is elected. If the party were to adopt electoral reform it would be seen as a symbolic indication that the voters could trust Labour with power and Labour trusted voters.[12]

Dame Margaret Beckett shared Hattersley's sentiment, stating that there was 'plenty of talk about how the electoral system cheated the British people and what people wanted was fair votes – that this demand was increasing'. With this feeling in the air, the Labour Party felt compelled to look into the matter. For Beckett, the analysis was fallacious, as it was only a small but vocal minority demanding reform, not representative of the majority who were not interested.[13] Alan Duncan from the GMB Union and Alun Michael, the MP for Cardiff South and Penarth concurred. At the 1989 Labour Party Conference the former affirmed: 'There are some in this party who would have us believe that electoral reform is a burning issue, high on the political agenda. It is not' as the debate 'has no interest or concern amongst the people we represent'. The latter was 'not surprised *The Guardian* leader writer is urging us to go on this detour' though in truth it was 'an irrelevant trip down a blind alley'.[14]

Although the evidence from the period suggests that support for electoral reform among the electorate is somewhat weaker than was acknowledged by its proponents,[15] polling emerged of the electoral benefits for the Labour Party if it committed to electoral reform. The extra votes and seats would increase the likelihood of forming a government. The influence of academic commentators like Patrick Dunleavy on the Labour Party is understandable, given the political climate and the electoral appeal of Thatcherism. Dunleavy stated: 'There would be about a three per cent net gain of Labour support which is in excess of 1.25 million votes nationwide. If you looked at the change from the 1987 figure, you would be looking around 80 seats.'[16] A poll for MORI conducted on behalf of the Electoral Reform Society suggested a fifth of centre party voters would switch their votes to the Labour Party if it committed itself to PR, a 3 per cent swing among the population at large. Backing PR would increase Labour support particularly among middle-class men living in the south-east, with 'fairness' and 'increased democracy' the main reasons given for supporting PR.[17] The opportunity to win over a considerable number of voters could not be passed up for a party seeking to return to office and would not have escaped the attention of Labour MPs.

The need to look for different ways of attracting support stemmed from the question of whether Labour could win again under FPTP. Three successive general election defeats, seemingly unable to make electoral advances against the popular appeal of Thatcherism, had dented the belief that the electoral pendulum would swing to Labour. According to Lord Rosser, a member of the Plant Report, there was a feeling that FPTP 'wasn't very friendly to the Labour Party. The prospect of returning to office were not necessarily that great.'[18] Others shared the pessimism of Labour's electoral situation. Linton and Wintour, commenting in the *Guardian*, argued, 'three successive election victories and dismay on the Left at the prospect at its impotence at preventing a fourth and even fifth Thatcher win.'[19] Whether accurate or not, the prospect of Conservative hegemony ratcheted up the pressure on the Labour Party to consider other election methods if it was ever to have the opportunity to govern.

The Labour Party, even if it performed well at the next general election, still faced the possibility of a hung parliament with no party able to form a majority. Therefore, if a coalition were necessary, in all likelihood with the Liberal Democrats, the Labour Party would have to table an offer on electoral reform, the starting point for negotiating with the Liberal Democrats. Consequently, having a concrete proposal would show the Liberal Democrats that the Labour Party were serious about electoral reform, power-sharing and reforming the British constitution. The Liberal–SDP Alliance had performed well in terms of vote share in both 1983 and 1987 yet had been hindered by the workings of FPTP, receiving fewer seats than its national vote share warranted on a proportional basis. Observing two opposition parties to the Conservatives fuelled the 'progressive-left' thesis, overlapping in some policy areas, with a combined vote totalling more than the Conservatives. This led some to conclude that there was a progressive majority in Britain.

As the talk of a 'progressive left' grew, John Evans MP for St Helens North, a leading ally of Neil Kinnock, argued in late 1988 for an electoral pact in sixty key marginal constituencies in an attempt to defeat the sitting Conservative MP. Evans had in mind thirty in which the Labour candidate would stand down and thirty seats where the centre candidate would stand down. It was time, to quote Evans, 'to think the unthinkable'[20] and break with Labour's historic fear of pacts and coalitions. Charles Clarke, Kinnock's chief of staff from 1983 to 1992, accepted that Labour had to be more open to new ideas, potential strategic alliances, working with others and recognizing strands such as feminism and human rights. 'Neil's leadership was very much about being open to different forms of approach.'[21]

The Labour Party's adherence to a more equitable and fair society led some to question how a party committed to an equal society could support an electoral system with a clear disparity between votes cast and seats won. Where was the equality and fairness in supporting an electoral system that acted so unfairly towards the SDP–Liberal Alliance or to the millions of Labour voters in the south of England who repeatedly end up with Conservative MPs? Moreover, the issue of equality and fairness spread further than votes translating into seats. Baroness Gould states: 'The reform issue was part of a wider movement outside of electoral politics. Equality and Fairness along with women's representation were part of the deep societal changes happening in the 1980s'[22] emphasizing the pluralistic changes Britain was experiencing.

The LCER – an internal Labour Party grouping – grew dramatically by 1993, gathering a following of over two thousand members and the sponsorship of over sixty Labour MPs. Despite Labour riding high in the polls by 1993 the group became the largest campaigning group within the Labour Party.[23] Dale Campbell-Savours, the Labour MP for Workington, announced in the *Times* that of 125 Labour MPs he interviewed over the past nine months, 108 were in favour of some change in the electoral system. A party spokesman dismissed the survey as 'a series of informal discussions over a period'.[24] To further counter the Campbell-Savours poll, a Market Access International survey consulted thirty-five MPs, of whom twenty-five said they did not support electoral reform.[25]

Despite the arguments for reform and the increasing popularity of PR amongst Labour MPs, the Labour leadership and the wider Labour movement were not yet ready to reverse their opposition to electoral reform. The Party leadership was under pressure by a succession of conference resolutions concerning electoral reform, although a strong retort met these at the 1987 and 1989 Conferences by those who still favoured FPTP.[26] At the 1987 Labour Party Conference in Brighton a representative from Mole Valley moved Composite 27 in favour of setting up a Working Party on Electoral Reform. Whilst the Composite was seconded by Chorley and did receive support from representatives from Watford, it was contested by Kevin Stephens (Gloucester CLP) arguing the electorate have 'seen what the economic doctrine of the Liberals and the Tories mean to them – it means redundancies. They need protection and they need jobs along with a National Minimum Wage and only a Labour government can deliver that.' Peter Hain (Putney CLP) offered a traditional defence of the British system of representative government asking: 'Is it really a priority to tinker around with the electoral system when we confront much more important issues of democracy?' Siobhan McDonagh (Mitcham and Morden CLP) argued the Labour Party lost because 'not enough people wanted to vote Labour' and Labour will win 'fighting on the issues that people find important'.

The most vocal critic of electoral reform and PR was Hattersley who claimed supporting this composite would be 'interpreted as, and in fact is, support for proportional representation' and would be 'absolute folly'. Much to the enjoyment of the floor, Hattersley bashed the SDP, asserting they are 'united by only two principles: the first is a hatred of David Owen and the second is support for PR.' Furthermore, he went on to deliver a classical defence of FPTP; damaging our traditional system of democracy and eroding the rights of people to vote for the policies which they support – the manifesto and the mandate – and the unaccountable backroom deals and blunting of radical policies through 'soggy compromise' associated with PR. Hattersley closed his speech by affirming

> the belief that we can win on our own, the certainty that we will win on our own, on our own policies, our own programme and our own philosophy. The only way forward for this party is to fight on its own policies and to win on its own policies. That is why we must defeat this resolution.[27]

It became apparent that the issue of electoral reform would not disappear. 'Democracy and the Individual' headed by Hattersley was one of Labour's policy review groups. According to Hughes and Wintour, Hattersley realized he could sideline the most important issue in his remit – PR – by tying it to regional representation and reform of the House of Lords, an idea he first floated on 20 September 1988. It attempted to 'snare proportional representation in the lobster pot of constitutional reform'.[28] No member of the group supported PR. Besides, 'a scheme different from that by which Members of Parliament are elected' was possible as no minister would be drawn from the second chamber.[29] This provided the opportunity for the final six paragraphs of its report to condemn proportional representation, citing reasons such as the confusion of coalition government, disproportionate influence over policy by smaller parties, the questioning of the 'resolve of the Labour Party win outright' and PR would decrease democracy, through the watering down of manifesto commitments.[30] Elsewhere, Hattersley wrote:

> Critics of our present system underestimate the importance of the twin doctrines of the manifesto and the mandate – parties publishing their programme before the election and promising that, given the chance, they will do their best to put it into practice after polling day. With proportional representation that process – offering the electorate the chance to reject or endorse specific policies – is rendered impossible.[31]

Evidently, governments face unexpected events and it is not possible for a manifesto to foresee all actions, and therefore contain the relevant policies. Yet, the actions of the government are not rendered illegitimate and nor is the authority of the government brought into question, due to the 'implied manifesto'. The longstanding ideology and values of the party permits the electorate to have a reasonable expectation of policies.[32] Hattersley believed that in times of recession, the electorate would broadly predict and understand the policies of a Labour or Conservative government. He affirmed:

> The government can't promise all it's going to do, it can't do all it promises. With FPTP you sort of know which side the Party is going to be on when the crunch comes even if events arise that government had not anticipated. That is possible under FPTP but not under PR and coalition.[33]

Whilst electoral reform was not a key issue at the 1988 Labour Party Conference, one year later the issue had returned, with a motion – Composite 29 – calling for 'an urgent study on electoral reform in its widest sense', in practice, a Working Party on electoral reform. Once again it was rejected, for it would have been a diversion from winning the next general election. Hattersley damned PR and its consequences for Westminster, claiming 'proportional representation would diminish, not increase genuine democracy in the country' as it is in 'the House of Commons that governments must build their majorities and introduce their legislation and for the House of Commons, PR would in consequence be a reduction, not an extension of democracy'. Furthermore, he attacked the smaller parties, believing at the end of a week in which Labour had honed its policies the party was going to contemplate 'bargaining that away in a smoke-filled room with Mr Paddy Ashdown,

Dr David Owen or anybody else to bargain away our manifesto. It would be an act of historic folly.'[34] The resolution was duly defeated 4,592,000 to 1,443,000 a majority of 3,149,000, a substantial majority of 3:1. However, the losing side drew comfort from the result, emphasizing 1,443,000 votes had been cast in the cause of electoral reform, affirming the issue was here to stay. Tony Benn notes in his diary that the Conference National Executive Committee (NEC) discussed PR, 'which was supported by Robin Cook, Ken Livingstone, John Evans and Clare Short. Hattersley, Kinnock, Bryan Gould, Beckett and I spoke against it. In the end there was a vote, with 23 to 4 against even having an NEC inquiry into it.'[35]

The culmination of the policy review was *Meet the Challenge, Make the Change* published in 1989.[36] The document described FPTP as 'the most honest, the most efficient and the most effective form of government'. Moreover, the document warned of the dangers to be associated with PR. 'Talk of proportional representation or any alternative voting system would cause the electorate to question our resolve, our commitment, and our self-confidence.' Bryan Gould writing in *A Future for Socialism* considered PR generally suffered on a number of counts against a socialist criterion of diffusing power: the loss of direct representation through multi-member constituencies, the elector's uncertainty of the ultimate destination and purpose of his or her vote because of transferable votes, and a significant increase in the power of Party officials to determine who should be elected as a result of national or regional Party lists.[37]

The Labour leadership was divided. Hattersley considered even the most minimal softening of the position on PR a sign of weakness on behalf of the Labour Party and a whim that would evaporate once poll ratings rose. Kinnock was more flexible in viewing the issue as not yet fully discussed in Britain: 'Those people who are entirely defensive about the possibility of change are much more dynamic and forward looking than some politicians give them credit for.'[38] He thought debate was essential if widespread support was to be built. In addition, an open-minded approach had the potential to foster more votes for the Labour Party, attracting support from those leaning towards the centre parties. Lord Whitty, the then general secretary of the Labour Party, considered Kinnock and those around him were 'quite positive' towards electoral reform and although 'Neil would never say he was completely convinced, he would say he was more favourably inclined than any leader before or since'.[39] Beckett agrees with Whitty, yet implies that Kinnock was 'got at' by those around him, who had 'convinced themselves that this was the only way Labour could win, who were very strong advocates, persuading Neil that this was a valuable modernisation reform'.[40] Exactly who 'got at' Kinnock, Beckett was not prepared to say.

For the 'modernisers' within the Party, electoral reform was useful in distinguishing the present Party from its past and would result in a Labour government being pulled away from socialism towards the centre. Electoral reform would 'reassure' voters who perhaps did not yet trust the Labour Party that a Labour government could marginalize its more extreme elements. Philip Gould, a key strategist for the Labour Party, states: 'The drive towards proportional representation came from a belief that it was the only certain way to make Labour safe. If you have PR, Labour can never govern alone. It was always to be neutered, a consensus not an extreme government'.[41] Butler and Kavanagh reflected that 'Mr Kinnock's flirtation with PR and his subsequent emphasis on a broad-based co-operative approach to government was designed to soften Labour's image and allay fears about a Labour government.' Patricia Hewitt and Clive Hollick thought PR might provide reassurance that the Party sought consensus and would not give in to the unions or the left wing.[42]

The Labour Party produced a policy document titled *Looking to the Future* in May 1990, asserting 'Labour (was) opposed to changing the electoral system for the House of Commons'. It reiterated how the House of Commons is the primary institution and, as such, a fundamentally different institution to all others. However, throughout 1990 the pressure for reform continued to grow, with Party leaders showing an increased willingness to consider PR for the European Parliament, a reformed second chamber, a Scottish Parliament and regional assemblies for England and Wales. A Working Party was to be set up by Labour Party Conference, as had been agreed by the NEC, without considering PR for the House of Commons. Gavin Laird, general secretary of the powerful Amalgamated Engineering Union, questioned the logic stating it was 'not credible then to say we are not going to look at the system, examine the system, for the House of Commons'.[43] Labour leaders believed that including the Commons in the Working Party's remit would allow the Tories to claim Labour had abandoned hope of winning under the FPTP.[44]

The opposition to the consideration of PR for the House of Commons – the position of the leadership – was defeated at the 1990 Labour Conference. By 2,766,000 to 2,557,000 the Conference approved a study on proportional representation, rebuking Hattersley, who once again had promoted FPTP. Linton and Southcott write that it was the moment that 'Labour moved from outright opposition to an agnostic position on electoral reform'[45] signifying a considerable change of attitude towards the electoral system, not seen since the 1920s. It is noteworthy that the decision to include the House of Commons in the Working Party's analysis may have been even closer, had the builders union, UCATT, which opposed electoral reform, not lost its 160,000 strong voting card, eventually forcing it to abstain. Laird argued that Labour would get an 'even bigger' majority at the next election if it committed itself to PR in advance of the poll, and raised questions of credibility if the Labour Party were to consider PR for other institutions but not the House of Commons. By contrast, Ron Todd, the transport union leader, remained neutral on the issue, proposing only that it be debated.[46]

Pressure for reform of the electoral system came from a variety of sources and for a variety of reasons. Whereas the Labour Party had shown very little interest in electoral reform and PR during a prolonged period of opposition between 1951 and 1964, the situation in the 1980s was fundamentally different. The Conservative government had embarked on a socioeconomic course committed to the free market and undermining the planks of social democracy. Conservative statecraft was perceived to be hegemonic, and the third party – now the Liberal Democrats – along with the nationalist parties had fractured British politics, promoting the 'progressive left' thesis. This raised the possibility of a hung parliament and the need for a coalition, encouraging thoughts that a commitment to electoral reform was an avenue back into government. Indeed, for some, electoral reform was a prerequisite for realigning the British left. Constitutional reform had found favour, especially in intellectual and academic circles, and increased popularity with a certain section of the electorate.

However, the restructuring of the British economy, the malleability of the British constitution, and considerable talk of 'trust', 'modernisation' and 'centrism' were only part of the rationale behind the increasing interest in electoral reform and PR in the late 1980s and early 1990s. The fate of the Party at the ballot box encouraged a reappraisal of attitudes and objections to PR, electoral reform and coalition. Successive heavy defeats resulted in the Party engaging with ideas such as PR, emphasized by the votes at Labour Party Conference, the increased membership of LCER, a more prominent role for electoral reformers such as Robin Cook and Marjorie Mowlam – individuals willing to make the political, moral, social and economic case for reform – and the increased sympathetic tone adopted by Kinnock. Primarily, PR was a response to the electoral despair and the method that would broaden Labour's electoral appeal and put it into a position where it would enter government, as a single party or in a coalition with the centre. Consequently, PR was part of a wider strategy for power.

The Plant Report

Kinnock indicated, 'What we are initiating is a formalised debate about electoral systems, not deciding in favour of PR – far from it.'[47] Nonetheless, the enquiry, *Democracy, Representation and Elections* was the first serious study into the matter in the Labour Party since MacDonald, Anderson and Roberts investigated proportional representation prior to the First World War. The Working Party was made up of different parts of the Labour Party; MPs Bryan Gould, Alistair Darling, Margaret Beckett, Hilary Armstrong, Geoff Hoon, John Evans; peers Reg Underhill, Patricia Hollis and from 1992 Raymond Plant; Members of the European Parliament (MEPs) Geoff Hoon and Gary Titley; academics Raymond Plant and Ben Pimlott; trade union representatives Richard Rosser, Judith Church, Tom Burlison and members from the nations Murray Elder from Scotland, Ken Hopkins from Wales and Jack McConnell as Scottish general secretary of the Party. Thus, the committee contained a broad span of views and attitudes towards the electoral system due to the variety of Labour backgrounds of the membership. The objective, according to Plant was to encourage a debate about the nature of representation and democracy.

All constituency parties were invited to present evidence, the PLP allowed MPs to respond as individuals, Labour peers were canvassed and set up a Working Party to respond, along with a visit to the European Parliament to discuss with Labour MEPs and other socialist delegations elected by proportional representation.[48] Dr Tim Lamport, secretary of the Working Party deemed that it was different from a normal Labour Party policy committee as it had more autonomy. Moreover, it reported to the NEC, who set it up, determined who was on it and did not report to the Home Policy Committee.[49] This increased freedom, particularly from the Home Policy Committee, who would have had an explicit interest in the matter, allowed the committee to carry out its work free from direct interference from the leadership. However, with the Working Party involving individuals such as Beckett, a sceptical leadership could be assured that the committee would avoid advocating anything too radical.

Plant's original stance on electoral reform is contested. Beckett believes 'Plant changed his mind. When Plant was appointed and one of the reasons Plant was appointed, I suspect, was because he was a FPTP man.'[50] Rosser disagrees along with Clarke and Lamport. Rosser always got the impression Plant was a 'genuine agnostic on the issue. Therefore, he was not starting with a particular stance or position and looked at the issue openly' a view shared by Lamport.[51] Clarke claims:

> Plant was not particularly committed to any direction. He was certainly open-minded, to put it mildly. He was not an advocate and not one of these liberal types who thought it was the most important thing in politics. He was certainly ready to give it a thorough investigation. On the other hand, in the event he looked at it properly and thought it was not a starter, he would have been ready to say it was not a starter.[52]

Regardless of opinions on where Plant started, there is agreement Plant changed his mind as the Working Party progressed. Whether he started out as a FPTP supporter or an agnostic his finishing position was pro-reform, not only in coming out in favour of a different electoral system but by joining the LCER. Rosser considers that Plant 'became convinced of the need for change'.[53] Beckett shared Rosser's view that Plant changed his mind but was less sympathetic, returning to the idea that those around Kinnock swayed Plant's judgement.[54]

Hattersley chose Plant to be chair, not wanting 'some fashionable PR advocate to do it absent-minded because it was the new idea of the day, "we've got to change", "modernisation"'. Plant was a 'man you could trust, believe in his integrity' and perhaps most importantly given the attitude in the Party at the time, appeared to be 'opposed to PR'. The argument for Plant's chairmanship was based on the belief that Plant was a FPTP man and he would not have been appointed 'had I not thought him to be FPTP'. Hattersley is unequivocal and was in no doubt: 'Some months before he told me he was FPTP and he was appointed for that reason,' reaffirmed on the day of the first meeting.[55]

When asked about his attitude towards electoral reform before chairing the Working Party, Plant stated: 'I suppose I went into it, insofar as I thought about it at all, that I was in favour of FPTP.' When Hattersley asked for Plant's view on the electoral system, Plant replied he had no views on the matter, the answer he wanted to hear, illustrating for Plant what Hattersley thought about PR. However, Plant changed his mind due to the Working Party's evidence and the result of going to Germany. 'FPTP no longer really mapped the range of interests in the country accurately and you needed – not necessarily a more proportional – but more pluralistic kind of system.'[56] Hattersley allegedly described Plant as a 'political innocent',[57] suggesting that Plant's lack of political experience was also part of why he was chosen, which Plant took as a compliment.

Hattersley's decision to appoint his friend Plant as chair meant that someone who supposedly had very little prior interest in electoral systems and electoral reform – a 'political innocent' – was leading Labour's first serious enquiry into electoral reform since prior to the First World War. An academic from a background in political philosophy was chairing a group of individuals who were in the main politicians, resulting in the committee containing a range of opinions, some passionately held, with significant hostility to reform from elements of the leadership who did not wish to be seen as coming down in favour of reform. Yet, this neutrality would be vital in avoiding the perception of bias and allowed the Labour Party to argue it was starting with a blank sheet of paper, and as Charles Clarke affirms, the conclusions needed to carry weight.[58] Plant's appointment also sidestepped a potentially damaging split in the Labour Party. Hattersley considered that there was a majority in favour of FPTP at the time so we 'avoided a row by having someone who was regarded as agnostic'.[59]

The Interim Reports

In 1991, the *Report of the Working Party on Electoral Systems* was released, stating two important caveats. Firstly, 'the appropriateness of an electoral system is going to be governed to a large extent by our view about the nature of representation and by what we think that elections are actually for' drawing a distinction between a 'legislative' body and a 'deliberative' body.[60] Plant expanded on the argument made by FPTP supporters that small or single-issue parties threaten the capability and existence of a parliamentary majority committed to socialism.

> Those in favour of the first past the post or majoritarian systems tend to take the view that the House of Commons is the arena in which competing political philosophies or ideologies are locked in a constant combat and effectiveness depends to a large extent on parliament being able to continue to provide this kind of forum.[61]

He also considered the view of electoral reformers.

> Advocates of proportionality, on the other hand tend to stress the idea of Parliament as a deliberative assembly in which the range of opinions reflected in proportional membership are negotiated and to some extent blunted by the almost inevitable coalition building that goes on.[62]

The traditional socialist response to those who advocate Parliament reflecting society at large – a microcosmic view – has been twofold. Initially, 'such a view of the function of electoral systems is highly individualistic. It is concerned only with fairness to individual preferences and does not consider any other sorts of social values at all.' A socialist, for instance, would concern themselves with the solidarity of a community voting for the socialist candidate. Even if the Labour candidate failed to win, the electors have shown unity in opposition to the parties of capital. Secondly, supporting an 'electoral system purely on the grounds of a rather formal understanding of fairness, it might under a PR system introduced for such reasons, find it impossible to form a government which would be committed to securing greater social and economic justice or fairness'.[63] He continued:

> In the view of the defender of FPTP it is more important to have the capacity to fight for a substantially fairer society than to superimpose some abstract and procedural idea of fairness and justice on a much less than fair society.[64]

As such, the electoral system might be 'fair' in relation to a preset criteria if the percentage of votes cast matches the number of seats won. Yet, the society under PR might be very unequal and unjust, the opposite of which the Labour Party strives to create. Therefore, voting is not an end in itself but considered a means to an end, which is a more egalitarian society.

Describing parliaments and assemblies as either 'legislative' or 'deliberative' did draw criticism, for failing to acknowledge that a legislative body has a deliberative function and a deliberative body has a legislative function; legislation must be debated and requires a parliamentary majority for it to be passed into law, emphasizing that an institution such as the House of Commons has a dual function. Furthermore, in the British political system with the executive emerging from the legislature, the executive must have the consent of a majority of the legislature. The Second Interim Report offered a response admitting that the House of Commons is both a 'legislative and deliberative chamber' and institutions are 'not necessarily static'. However, this was qualified by reiterating a distinction, at least in terms of emphasis between the House of Commons and that of other institutions envisaged by Labour's constitutional reform agenda. The committee maintained 'that this distinction has a central although not necessarily a determining role to play in selecting an electoral system'.[65]

The second caveat mentioned by Plant centred on the idea that 'no voting system can simultaneously satisfy a set of obvious conditions for social choice in a democratic society'.[66] This is a result of the idea of 'fairness' and to whom we are seeking to be fair – electors, political parties, minorities, women and geographical regions – and the 'hierarchy of fairness' in which one puts them, are shaped by values. As Plant notes: 'The important point is that the claim to fairness does not stand on its own, it is, rather, fairness given a particular assumption about the nature of representation.'[67] He elaborated in *Parliamentary Affairs*: 'Electoral mechanisms cannot be assessed in a wholly neutral way, as it were giving them points against a set of neutral criteria.'[68] Indeed there are cases where by seeking to be 'fair' to one group you may hinder another, and returns to Plant's original assertion that what you consider to be fair is dependent upon what you consider elections to be for. Moreover, different forms of PR contain different assumptions about some of the central features of representation, the role of parties and the nature of accountability.[69]

Importantly, given the Labour Party's commitment to devolved assemblies, it was agreed that different electoral systems can be used for different institutions, as the role and function of the institution varies depending on its powers and remit, a key factor in light of the Labour Party's constitutional reform agenda. For instance, when the electoral system for the Scottish Parliament was discussed, it was recommended that FPTP was maintained to ensure constituency accountability but supplemented by additional seats to ensure a greater degree of proportionality. This decision was reached by acknowledging that a Scottish Parliament could not be seen as a 'one-party state' which would have undermined calls for greater pluralism; the Scottish Constitutional Convention had coalesced around the need for an alternative system; and the Scottish Parliament was to be fundamentally different from Westminster.[70]

As both caveats suggest, there is no perfect electoral system and therefore a case can be made for using more than one system in different government areas. 'The nature of representation in an institution', wrote Plant, 'has to be linked to the function of that institution rather than determined on abstract and contested ideas like "fairness". What we should be looking for is fairness in relation to function.'[71] Therefore, the argument is entwined due to different electoral systems fostering different views of the nature of representation, and the type of representation might be more suitable for one institution than another.

For the House of Commons, the Plant committee recognized the legislative function of the House of Commons and considered there was a 'powerful case' for leaving untouched the central elements of the representative and electoral system. This included clear accountability through a constituency base, thus ruling out multi-member constituencies as in STV as well as national or regional List System. Having just emerged from years of in-fighting the idea, to quote Plant, 'of setting up an electoral system that actually encouraged people to stand against one another wasn't going to be something they were going to embrace very fondly'.[72]

Furthermore, the committee questioned the role of top-up MPs under the Additional Member System (AMS)/Mixed Member System (MMS). Lord Whitty, a supporter of AMS, considered that the Labour Party could not back an electoral system that did not maintain a constituency link, believing 'MPs do really identify with their constituents, either in a negative sense that they're causing trouble, or in terms of the next election – the accountability.

The trouble with a too broad electoral system is you lose that accountability.'[73] Rosser, also a supporter of AMS, attempted to dispel the argument that electors would question who the top-up MPs represent. 'Most people would feel they still have a constituency representative, namely the person who won the constituency.'[74]

Plant considered the constituency link to be key, ensuring a direct link between constituents and legislators which would be weakened in a multi-member constituency. 'In relation to predominantly legislative bodies we do believe that the constituency basis of representation is very important in terms of securing the accountability of an elected person to a clearly identifiable group of people.'[75] Maintaining the direct constituency link was criticized from some quarters prompting a response in the *Second Interim Report*. The report argued that the direct constituency link keeps the MP in touch with grassroots feeling about policy and its implementation, rather than becoming preoccupied with Westminster politics. Furthermore, given the Labour Party's historic commitment to community it would be paradoxical for the party to commit to diminishing the role of communities in electoral terms.[76] Bryan Gould, considering himself 'something of a romantic' on the history of British parliamentary democracy 'liked the thought that each MP was sent to Westminster primarily to serve his or her constituency rather than a particular party'. When challenged in the House of Commons by a Liberal MP on the grounds he had only received 37 per cent of the vote and could therefore not claim to represent his constituents, Gould replied rhetorically, 'Who would you replace me with – someone who got only 19%?'[77]

Elsewhere, Plant thought it undesirable that there has been a decline in FPTP ability to closely equate share of the vote and share of seats. While the system does not aim at proportionality, 'there has to be some rational and predictable relation between votes and seats if there is to be a defence of First Past the Post as a legitimate system even on its own assumptions'.[78] Therefore, if the chief virtue of FPTP – single-party government – could be achieved on a percentage vote share in the low thirties then this would bring into question the legitimacy of the system, particularly if the winning party in terms of seats continually polled fewer votes across Great Britain.

The interim reports were the building blocks for the committee to move on to the final report where it would go on to make firm recommendations, and therefore the two interim reports did not clarify the Labour Party's policy on PR for Westminster. They were more concerned with electoral theory – unsurprising, given Plant's academic background in political philosophy – with the interim report making clear there is no such thing as a perfect electoral system and the assertion of fairness does not stand on its own but to the criteria by which one is judging fairness. Importantly, given Labour's constitutional reform agenda, different institutions can use different electoral systems. Indeed, Plant acknowledged that the House of Commons was still going to be the primary legislature even within the devolved settlement, resulting in a 'powerful case for leaving the central elements of the representative and electoral system ... of vital importance to the legislative function of the place'. The report concluded that it would still be advantageous to maintain an electoral system that produces majorities and therefore the power to elect a government which will initiate legislation. Importantly, the power of making and unmaking government should be in the hands of electors, not politicians in 'smoke-filled rooms' who cobble together coalitions after the election.[79] Consequently, the interim report does hint that the options available to reformers were limited to AV, SV or a variation of AMS, rather than STV or regional or national list systems.

The 1992 general election, Labour and proportional representation

The polls in the lead up to the 1992 general election placed the Labour Party ahead of the Conservatives, on course to be at least the largest party. However, the lead in the polls evaporated in the final few days and the election held on 9 April 1992 gave the Conservative Party under John Major their fourth successive general election victory achieving just short of 14.1 million, the highest poll in a British general election. However, rather than the commanding lead in popular vote translating into a third successive landslide for the Conservatives, FPTP had only given the Conservatives 336 MPs, a slim majority of 21. The Labour Party had won 271 MPs on 11.5 million votes, an improved showing on 1987.

During the final few days of election campaign the issue of PR emerged. The 1992 *Labour Party Manifesto*, 'It's Time to Get Britain Working Again', stated that the Working Party would continue with an extended membership and enhanced authority. Contingent on a Labour Party victory, Kinnock elaborated on the function of the Working Party suggesting it could be converted into a formal government inquiry reporting to the prime minister, possibly even a Royal Commission, and its membership would be widened to include members from outside the Labour Party, including business, trade unions, churches and members of other political parties. Consequently, the Labour Party had gone further than it had before in endorsing PR, and the Liberal Democrats were invited to join the Plant Committee. According to one academic commentator, the Labour government would respond by determining its own policy on the matter, which would then be laid before the electorate at the next general election.[80]

Charter 88, under the guidance of Anthony Barnett, arranged 'Democracy Day' on 2 April 1992, the moment in which the Labour Party would announce its support for PR. It was, according to Beckett, 'a sign of lack of confidence' feeding the view 'which was untrue, that we did not stand for anything and we would say anything to try and get elected, desperate to get the Liberal vote, saying something we probably did not mean.'[81] It also ensured the newspaper headlines would focus on hung parliaments, coalition, the Liberal Democrats and the nationalists, away from the more salient economic issues. Clarke considers that the issue of PR and the shadow budget were the two big issues that had not been fully thought through by the party, 'manifesting uncertainty about what we were going to do' resulting in the Labour Party looking 'untrustworthy' and as such was a 'weakness'. Accordingly, 'the electorate were not clear whether we would do something or would not do something, and this was exposed in the last few days before polling.'[82]

Kinnock faced difficulties on the *Granada 500* programme on 6 April, failing to provide a direct answer to the question of whether he was in favour of PR, responding, 'Yes, sure – well, quite no, it is not quite so simple', saying that he was waiting for the Working Party to report. Kinnock's position was understandable for in public he had attempted to remain neutral on the issue, to avoid being drawn on either side of the argument. An open declaration of support could be interpreted as a loss of faith in Labour's ability to win.[83] In an attempt to balance the views of defenders of FPTP and reformers, along with his own preference which was becoming increasingly sympathetic to PR, Kinnock had to do so without providing the Conservative Party the opportunity to attack him for appearing to fudge the issue, a lack of principle and a lack of confidence in the Labour Party's ability to win. Kinnock's view was that in any event an electoral mandate would be required to make such an 'irreversible and significant' change to the future of our political democracy.[84]

Butler and Kavanagh conducted a post-election survey amongst Labour candidates, with many quick to condemn PR, believing it showed weakness, distracted from the National Health Service (NHS) and taxation or they were opposed to PR.[85] Clarke is of the view that in 1992 Labour could not win unless the Party 'reassured electors that it was safe to come back to Labour, for all sorts of reasons; winter of discontent and other points in between', with the issue of PR as noted hampering Labour's chances of success.[86] However, Hattersley disagrees, believing it had no effect. 'If you wanted PR passionately you would have voted Liberal' as it was a 'niche issue'.[87] Hattersley reflected:

> Unfortunately, we actually lost support by what appeared to be a sudden conversion to constitutional reform. The proposals set out during two press conferences (exactly a week before polling day) had been official party policy for years. But the unexpected enthusiasm with which the plans were advocated appeared to be the product of sudden panic.[88]

Post-election research demonstrates how different election systems would have affected the 1992 general election result. A different majoritarian system would have resulted in the Labour Party standing still or decreasing, and therefore would have provided little or no electoral benefit, refuting the argument that a different electoral system would have been beneficial in 1992. Indeed, the only party that stood to benefit in 1992 was the Liberal Democrats, with a swelled number of MPs, increasing the likelihood of coalition. Under a proportional system the Labour Party would have had fewer seats and been reliant on the parliamentary support of the Liberal Democrats. Moreover, the Conservatives would still have been the biggest party.[89]

Evans offered an analysis of tactical voting in the 1992 general election. Contrary to the 'progressive-left' thesis, the Conservative Party would have been the main beneficiary of tactical voting in 1992. Indeed, a *Sunday Telegraph* Gallup poll, published only four days before polling day, showed that if minor parties were to hold the balance of power, 45 per cent of Liberal

Democrat supporters favoured keeping the Tories in power compared to 41 per cent who preferred the Liberal Democrats leverage being used in favour of the Labour Party.[90] Whatever electoral benefits had been advocated by reformers prior to the election – whether backing PR or electoral pacts – were not borne out in the post-election study. The Conservatives could in 1992 equally have argued that there is a split on the Right of British politics, that a vote for the Liberal Democrats was a vote against the Labour Party. Rather than the overtures towards the Liberal Democrats resulting in a broadening of Labour's electoral appeal, it encouraged wavering Liberal Democrats and those instinctively anti-Labour into the arms of the Conservatives, therefore having the opposite effect.

Kinnock stood down as leader of the Labour Party, replaced by John Smith, with Margaret Beckett becoming his deputy. Smith's proposals for constitutional reform included incorporating the European Convention on Human Rights into British law, devolution for Scotland and Wales, House of Lords reform, a freedom of information bill and regional government. He had attacked the 'relentless centralisation of power' under the Conservatives that had rendered Westminster 'dictatorial and remote'.[91] However, electoral reform at Westminster entailed different issues compared to the electoral systems for the proposed devolved assembles. For Smith, it was 'more complicated' than other aspects of constitutional change, and he did not want to prejudge the debate within the Party.[92]

According to Smith's biographer, Andy McSmith, in 1991 Smith discussed with Ashdown in a taxi the possibility of PR. Smith's version of the conversation was that 'we did not talk specifics'.[93] However, according to Ashdown's office, the gist of it was that Smith was ready to concede PR for the Commons, the Scottish Parliament and regional assemblies, in return for Liberal Democrat support for a minority Labour government, should there be a hung parliament. The *Ashdown Diaries* record a conversation between Smith and Ashdown during a gathering of the Bilderberg Group in Spain in May 1989, in which the shadow chancellor rejected the idea of electoral pacts, believing that Labour would win outright. Consequently, the Party's leadership was, concerning the reform of the Westminster system, at best sceptical, as Smith, from the Right of the Party, was unenthusiastic, and Beckett originally from the Left of the Party was outright hostile. The prevalent view was one more general election would see Labour back in office. While Whitty deemed that the problems facing Labour had not changed, 'in one of the meetings, in late 1992, John sent Margaret to tell the committee that the leadership will not support, if you go for electoral reform. It poured cold water on the work they had been doing for the last eighteen months.'[94]

The final report, 1993 – 'Report of the Labour Party Working Party on Electoral Systems'

Having met on twenty-eight occasions, taken advice from both those inside and outside the Labour Party, interested individuals and groups and academics, visited Europe to gain an understanding of the German AMS, the final report appeared in April 1993. Whereas the interim report was interested in assessing the criteria by which electoral systems can be judged, the final report sought to make recommendations for the House of Commons, as well as the Second Chamber and the European Parliament. The arguments put forward in chapter one – 'The Case for Reform' – and chapter three – 'The Case for First Past the Post' – are of interest given they set out the arguments in favour of and against reforming the Westminster electoral system, which is set against the background of the Labour Party's wider commitment and enquiries into constitutional reform.

'The Case for Reform' acknowledges Labour's constitutional reform package is, in part, a recognition of the growing pluralism in British society, whether it be individualism, particular groups or the distinctive identities found across the UK. For Plant, FPTP failed to recognize the growing pluralism in British life in terms of party representation, as there are regions of Britain where substantial support for a political party does not return MPs. In order to be consistent with Labour's wider constitutional reform agenda, an electoral system should be adopted that reflects and provides opportunities for new voices to be heard. If one party dominates in a particular part of Britain, it could lead to alienation and frustrations, excluding the representation of others, particularly with the growing north-south political divide.

Secondly, the issue of having more women in Parliament was considered, as in the interim report; and the same conclusion was reached that the electoral system has little impact on the number of women MPs as it was a matter of social context. Changing social attitudes towards minority and ethnic groups along with positive discrimination in the form of all-women shortlists, was the preferred method. Thirdly, the suitability of FPTP must be questioned in relation to devolution and its inability to be sympathetic to local and regional issues, with the potential for devolved assemblies to claim more legitimacy as they are elected under an alternative electoral system, based on increased proportionality. For those who favoured electoral reform it was necessary for the Commons and central government to have enhanced legitimacy, even if they have a diminished sphere of power within Labour's proposed programme of constitutional reform. Plant claimed: 'This can only be achieved by a change in the electoral system which makes central government more sensitive to local and regional issues and interests, as represented and expressed in the House of Commons.'[95]

Whilst Maurice Duverger maintained 'the simple majority single-ballot system favours the two-party system,'[96] 'The Case for Reform' considered that due to a decline in 'Cube Law', FPTP is likely to lead to more hung parliaments. Consequently, part of its rationale, namely single-party government, would cease. In a multinational state like the UK, with strong regional identities and a separate ethnic-based politics in Northern Ireland, the two-party system comes under pressure from the forces of pluralism. It is also claimed that the geographical concentration of the vote leads to areas of the country becoming 'no go' areas for political parties.

Consequently, the claim a government receives a 'national mandate' from the electorate is problematic when the winning party's support is concentrated in particular regions of Great Britain. The recent experience of the policies pursued by the Thatcher government and the landslide victories in 1983 and 1987 would have been fresh in the mind. Not since 1935 and the National Government has the government received over 50 per cent of the vote, thus implicating the notion of the 'mandate' and the legitimacy this provides. For Plant, a government that seeks to implement fundamental changes should be widely supported 'if they are to be seen as legitimate and not undone by some incoming government with a different ideological perspective'.[97]

When interviewed, Plant considered the idea of the mandate to be 'laughable'. A party having to do something because it's in the election manifesto even though the policy is 'outmoded' is awkward.

Only a minority of the voters who have read the manifesto to start with and more importantly a minority of voters have voted for the manifesto under whatever favourable electoral considerations. You have always got to go outside the box of Labour interests and Labour values to enable the Party to galvanise enough support to form a government. More importantly, is how you can write a manifesto that has sufficient flexibility if you like, to make it possible for people outside of the Labour movement to vote for you.[98]

The ability of FPTP to deliver pure ideological values – a vision and introduction of democratic socialism – is questioned. Firstly, according to Plant, FPTP cannot be defended on the grounds that it is in the electoral interests of the Labour Party. At best, deemed Plant, FPTP's ability to produce democratic socialist values had been 'extremely intermittent'.[99] Secondly, and based on Downs 'majority principle',[100] FPTP encourages parties to move towards the centre, as this is where both the beliefs of the median voter reside and the bulk of the electorate. Thus, 'the critic of PR cannot claim that First Past the Post provides an unalloyed opportunity for parties to preserve ideological purity'[101] as internal compromise on policy in political parties must take place in an attempt to win as many votes as possible.

Consequently, the Plant Report suggests that coalition government may be preferable to single-party government, carrying out a 'very substantial part of a programme' rather than being left powerless in opposition.[102] The reasoning was based on the work of Max Weber who put forward a distinction between the ethic of conviction and the ethic of responsibility, the latter being a willingness to compromise in order to gain a particular electoral benefit. Coalition was justified on the following basis:

> Adherents of the ethic of responsibility who are concerned to achieve something, if not everything, of what we stand for are in a more defensible position, mainly because we have to be concerned about the needs of those who depend on a strong Labour input into government, rather than maintaining a high level of ideological purity at the cost of political impotence.[103]

The ability of FPTP to continue to deliver strong government is brought into doubt by the fragmentation of the party system, with smaller parties winning and holding on to seats. Moreover, strong government is not necessarily a desirable criterion, as 'strength has to be linked to effectiveness to produce a reasonable criterion of judgement'.[104] Indeed, Plant deemed that an effective government is one which has 'policies to meet the needs of the country and the political will and capacity to implement them', something that is more likely to come about through a different electoral system as 'it will embody a wider degree of consent and legitimacy. Under a reformed system, a government will have a greater incentive to seek wide consent and thus greater legitimacy for its policies with Parliament.' The ensuing change to the British political tradition that would follow a change to the electoral system would correct 'some of the most intractable British problems, impeding the possibility of our development into a modern democratic society and of a successful economy'.[105] Plant wondered whether supporters of FPTP within the Labour Party would not seek power because it entailed political negotiation with other parties, considering that party leaders would take on board the views of MPs, peers, party officials and the electoral. He continued:

> Labour would be the biggest party in any coalition and as such would have the democratic legitimacy to enact the bulk share of its manifesto whilst making minimal concessions to the junior coalition partner. A changed electoral system would provide incentives to see greater legitimacy and consent within parliament changing the behaviour of parties making more likely a climate for greater collaboration within British politics.[106]

Lamport recalls spending a whole afternoon going through 'The Case for First Past the Post' with Beckett, agreeing with her on what it could say.[107] The Labour Party should commit to pluralism. However, rather than seeing pluralism within the House of Commons, defenders of FPTP who see pluralism as valuable to the Labour Party suggest pluralism between institutions is more worthy – inter over intra institutional pluralism – with decentralization and devolution of power a key part of the Labour's commitment to constitutional reform. The basis of this argument lies in the House of Commons producing the executive while all other institutions, although important, do not carry the same legislative function. Different electoral systems for the devolved institutions, rather than undermining the legitimacy of the House of Commons, is perfectly compatible with FPTP for the House of Commons, for checks and balances would be provided by the devolved institutions.

The diagnosis offered in the 'Case for Reform' that the vote share of the two main parties is decreasing and hung parliaments are likely to occur more often is rejected: it is 'entirely speculative' and is 'not a good basis on which to embark a fundamental reform of the electoral system'. Even if it were accepted to be correct, the 'development of policies with a strong national and regional appeal and by improved organisation'[108] was required for electoral victory. The pursuit of power relies on creating converts not the 'artificial device of changing the electoral system'.[109] Pressure for reform had arisen from a prolonged period in opposition, but the possibility of single-party government was not going to be traded away 'for an electoral system which seeks to incorporate regional differentiation at the cost of permanent coalition' and having to rely on support from other parties.[110]

'The Case for First Past the Post' makes a traditional defence of the 'mandate and the manifesto', something that is argued to be crucial to democratic accountability. Political parties are by their nature coalitions of left and right, and therefore policies have already been discussed and compromised between diverse interests. Under a different system, manifesto commitments would be traded away post-election. Therefore, 'the electorate has no way of expressing a view about the policies which emerge from such negotiations' and is in fact undemocratic, for the electorate can exert no influence at that stage. FPTP 'enables the electorate to have a clear choice of government'. The question asked when the electorate go to the polls is '"which government do you want?" ... making government accountable to the electorate in a way that no other system can'.[111] The electorate in 1992 were not 'cheated' through the electoral system failing to give expression to the anti-Tory majority. Instead, the electorate through their actions of voting for political parties other than Labour acquiesced to the return of a Conservative government. Only by retaining 'a sense of integrity in relation to their own values and retaining a sense of honesty, fair dealing in relation to the electorate and a proper sense of accountability'[112] will the Labour Party win an election. Although there is concern about a strong executive elected on a national vote share in the low forties, 'under PR, smaller parties could exercise pivotal power with a much lower percentage vote'.[113]

Recommendation, reaction and impact

For a legislative body it was considered the electoral system should ensure as far as possible 'direct accountability to the electorate'. Therefore, the Working Party was 'not prepared to endorse an electoral system for the Commons in which individual representatives do not face the electorate directly and in which direct accountability to the electorate is diminished'.[114] Consequently, both regional and national list systems were rejected along with STV for both are based on multi-member constituencies. This left AV, SV and MMS, devised by Rooker, with 500 seats won under FPTP and the remaining 150 top-up seats won by candidates who had stood in a constituency. The system shared similarities with the system recommended by the Hansard Society in 1976. Here, three quarters of the House of Commons to be elected in single-member constituencies under FPTP and one quarter regionally according to a more proportional system, with those elected on the top-up having to stand for direct election.[115]

None of the interviewees who sat on the committee were prepared to say who supported which system, claiming they could not remember given the length of intervening time. Whilst entirely plausible it could cynically be described as a 'vow of silence', unwilling to divulge the way the committee divided, and as the votes were not recorded it makes it difficult to know how each individual voted. Two reports appeared in the press firstly in the *Financial Times* and secondly in the *Times*. Combining the two articles suggests the Working Party voted ten votes to six in favour of reforming the electoral system, deciding eleven votes to four that any new system had to be based on MPs representing individual constituencies rather than being elected in strict proportion to the number of votes a party wins nationally. In deciding which electoral system to recommend, the committee agreed by nine votes to seven SV.[116] The numbers put forward coincide with Plant's comments that MMS was 'rejected by a majority on the Working Party' whilst there was also a 'majority on the Working Party which favoured moving away from First Past the Post'. The position was best summarized as a 'clear majority in favour of a single-member constituency majoritarian system'.[117]

Yet the decision that was reached came as somewhat of a shock to Plant and Lamport. Plant wrote it appeared to him to be a 'small majority in favour of an additional member system but between these straw polls and the final meeting of the Working Party at which final recommendations were made some change came about in the intimated voting intentions of certain members of the Working Party'.[118] The shift, according to Plant, was a result of Smith 'getting at' members of the Committee – 'certainly the MPs' – having everyone in separately telling them which way they should be voting.[119] Lamport shares Plant's view, recollecting some on the Working Party 'changed their position', wanting 'to be seen as going the way the leadership wanted it to go', leading him to be surprised because 'one or two didn't take the same position they had indicated previously'. He continued:

> Either they were leaned on or felt this is the side the bread is buttered and I'm going to do what the leadership want me to do ... I think there was less support for the proportional system than there probably had been, people didn't want to be seen to be going for that.[120]

Indeed, Plant found himself voting in favour of an electoral system he didn't support, to ensure the Working Party would recommend reform. 'I did not want the Supplementary Vote', stated Plant, however, 'I did in fact vote for it or else otherwise the majority would have gone for FPTP which I didn't want. To keep the issue alive it seemed to me best to vote for the Supplementary Vote.' According to Plant, Rooker, when he realized MMS was going to be rejected, voted for FPTP as opting for SV was worse than retaining FPTP.[121] Mark Stuart, John Smith's biographer, claims Rooker had unsuccessfully argued for a top-up of about 100–150 members to make SV more proportional.[122]

Regardless of the role Smith played in encouraging the committee to reject PR and come out in favour of FPTP, some members took it upon themselves to make the workings of the committee as difficult as possible. Prior to the Working Party voting on which system to recommend, according the *Financial Times*, Beckett attempted to deliver a 'Minority Report', containing only a menu of options and not making any firm recommendations to the NEC, a position that was rejected by Plant. Beckett wanted to 'try and make it absolutely plain that we didn't all go along with this aim of changing the electoral system and to put the argument across for FPTP, which otherwise were not going to be put'.[123] The *Times* reports that Beckett was so angered after the Working Party had opted for SV, she walked out the meeting and continued to demand a minority report.[124] Bryan Gould saw himself in a 'spoiling role', not wanting to 'provoke an outright split', contenting himself with 'trying to ensure it arrived at no meaningful conclusion'.[125] Baroness Armstrong, who at the time was Smith's Parliamentary Private Secretary (PPS), replaced Jo Richardson when she fell ill, chosen in effect to 'spy' on the Working Party. 'John felt that he could not get a hold of what was going on in there. And he didn't want a surprise. So he put me on so I could tell him what, politically, the issues were coming out.'[126]

'In a sense', wrote Lamport when reflecting on the Plant Report, 'SV was perhaps the lowest common denominator or "least worst" option. Some may have backed it on the basis that, if there were to be change, this represented the minimum'.[127] Lamport later reflected that some understood that they could not get away with supporting FPTP, even though that's what they wanted. Consequently, 'SV was the minimum change they could get away with'.[128] Armstrong considered it was 'alright at the time but it was a fudge'.[129] Whitty thought it was an attempt to keep everyone happy but rejected it was a 'fudge' as the Working Party had 'gone through the system of exhaustive ballot, so it was never the majority view of the committee. It was the one that people had the least objections towards, which is one of the problems.'[130] The recommendation of a not very proportional system was a fudge, Plant deemed in the *New Statesman & Society*, along with the committee's decision to emphasize the function of voting systems rather than their fairness. 'The political dynamics of the working party made it rather difficult to have entirely sharp priorities without risking the whole thing.'[131]

Advocacy of change was always likely to meet resistance. In January 1993, Beckett is supposed to have told colleagues on the Working Party at a two-day meeting, 'if you lot carry on like this there's going to be a fucking great row in the party.'[132] David Hill, Labour's communication director, informed the final meeting of the Working Party on 31 March 1993 that he had 'come to put a lid on all of this'.[133] The response of Smith and Beckett to the recommendations was, perhaps given their known positions, unsurprising. Smith and Plant had already had an argument at the 1992 Conference over whether the Working Party should be allowed to make recommendations on the House of Commons rather than arriving at conclusions of BBC-like impartiality.[134] Plant considered that the Working Party must deliver a firm recommendation to the NEC as not making a fixed recommendation after two and half years of work would have made a mockery of the Working Party and undone all the work hitherto completed. Smith and Beckett considered it to be a diversion from vital modernizations required to make the Labour Party electable, particularly One Member One Vote (OMOV). A commitment to changing the electoral system was an unnecessary diversion from winning the next general election.

On 19 May 1993 Smith released a press statement thanking the Working Party for all its efforts but going no further and stating his own position and that of the Labour Party. 'Most electors', Smith affirmed, 'vote for a party with the intention that with their support it should form a government. That is not a relevant consideration to, for example, the European Parliament which does not have the obligation to produce and sustain a Government.'[135] MMS was rejected due to the dilution of the constituency link and having two classes of MP. Secondly, 'it would make a coalition government the most likely outcome of an election' and the electorate according to Smith were entitled to vote for a 'set of distinctive policies and for a government which will carry them through'.[136] The course of action given its 'constitutional significance' was, for Smith, pledging a referendum to be held during the first parliament of the next Labour government.[137]

When Plant floated the referendum at a meeting of the Working Party he found little support.[138] Yet Smith's decision to refer whether to reform the Westminster electoral system to the British electorate kept both reformers and traditionalists happy, for it did not fully close the door on reform nor come down in favour of reform. The referendum was also a device that prevented the Labour Party from splitting in the run up to the next general election, and although it meant the issue did not go away, it was sidelined. In effect, pledging to hold a referendum was a party management device.

According to Beckett, Smith believed in removing things that caused divisions and problems, as voters do not like divided parties. 'He was no great enthusiast for this type of constitutional reform, thinking one of the ways to curtail the issue was to say, "well you think the British people demand this, but no one has ever asked the British people. Why don't we ask the British people?"'[139] However, Beckett may have been understating her role in convincing Smith to commit to a referendum. In an interview in 1994 with *the Times*, Beckett affirmed she had persuaded Smith to make the offer.

A referendum was the right answer, affirmed Beckett, as 'the British people are being sold a pup' based on a 'snare and delusion ... that if they had PR it would be easier to influence and change the decision of government. I think it would be more difficult ... Speaking as a practical politician, there is only one way to put to bed this constant clamour'.[140]

The Plant Report received a variety of praise and criticism from both within and outside the Labour Party. At a meeting of the PLP, MPs passed judgement. Tony Wright argued 'to retreat now from the point we have reached – that first-past-the-post is no longer good enough – would be an act of electoral suicide'. Others such as Derek Fatchett, chairman of Labour's FPTP group warned of 'coalition by stealth', whereas Gerald Kaufman deemed the Party 'was spending too much time on irrelevancies such as this', questioning 'Who is going to volunteer to be replaced in a Labour Cabinet to make way for coalition partners?' John Spellar and Bruce Grocott condemned PR, the former stating 'it is not our job to prop up the Liberals', while the latter desired the Labour Party to 'kill the debate stone dead'.[141]

Outside of Labour, David Butler called it a 'revolutionary document' as it sought to move the Labour Party away from constitutional conservatism. However, he considered SV a 'silly answer' which 'has probably set back the cause of electoral reform'.[142] Others of the left and right variously described it as a 'half-baked compromise' and 'the worst option'.[143] Georghiou deemed it would encourage tactical voting[144] and Wainwright thought SV could actually produce more disproportionate results than First-Past-the-Post[145] as can happen under redistributive majoritarian systems due to the distorting effects of the second and, under AV, lower preferences.

Those who were willing to partake in the research offered a range of views on its impact on the Labour Party. Beckett considered that it did have 'quite a big impact on Labour MPs because they were also going through the same arguments. Nothing excites MPs quite like a change which might affect their own circumstances'.[146] Rosser deemed that the impact of the report was not as much as reformers might have hoped.

> Within the Labour Party outside the commission, there were still very polarised views. The majority of the Parliamentary Labour Party and probably the membership outside, still wanted FPTP. It is not a Report that has led to radical change across the democratic system in this country.[147]

The most damning account of the response to Plant Report from within the Labour Party came from Whitty, claiming most Labour MPs 'couldn't understand why we were bothering'. While he thought his 'short-sighted' and debated the merits of reform with colleagues, 'it was never going to receive an easy ride in the PLP, as they prefer the majoritarian system'. Moreover, 'given that the Leader and the Deputy Leader were adamantly opposed to electoral reform, it wasn't going to get anywhere anyway. The bulk of MPs were against it, and by and large the Unions were against it so it was regarded as an intellectual exercise.' Had the Leader had the will and political capital to follow through with electoral reform for the House of Commons 'there would have been tensions and they would not have been able to get away with it.' It had also become apparent by the time the final report had been released that John Major's Conservative government were deeply unpopular and there was a feeling in the Labour Party of ' "well what's all this about? We're going to win." '[148]

Summary

The issue of electoral reform and PR became important within the Labour Party in the late 1980s. The dominance of Conservative statecraft had prompted people to look at the economic, moral and political case for constitutional reform, coinciding with sections of the Labour Party losing confidence in FPTP, searching for other avenues to return to office, one being proportional representation. Reformers argued FPTP was the vehicle that delivered aggressive free-market policies, with negative social effects. Electoral reform and PR became fashionable as a device, it was believed, that could taper the excesses of Thatcherism and put the Labour Party back in touch with centre voters, thus offering a route back into power.

External factors, mainly those of electoral failure, created the internal pressure within Labour, leading to pressure groups such as the LCER, conference votes and a more prominent role for those sympathetic to reform. Appearing to be unable to escape the demands for an enquiry, the leadership acquiesced, agreeing to hold an enquiry but omitting the House of Commons, yet were subsequently defeated at the 1990 Labour Party Conference when the widest possible remit to the enquiry was awarded. Hattersley duly appointed his friend, the academic Raymond Plant – someone Hattersley could trust and thought would deliver the answer he wanted to hear – to chair a Working Party looking at a wide range of constitutional issues. For three years the Working Party, consisting of individuals from all parts of the Labour movement and with a wide range of views, met and debated the vices and virtues of the arguments for reform and different electoral systems, taking evidence from academics, interest groups, trade unions and Labour politicians, ultimately producing three reports.

The first report was theoretical – unsurprising given Plant's academic interests – outlining the issues of electoral reform and proportional representation, the second was an update on the committee's work, and the third and final report stated the case for reform, the case for retaining FPTP and made specific recommendations. Consequently, the Working Party moved from predominantly theoretical arguments of democracy and representation to issues of party politics, specifically relating to the Labour Party. Key ideas are outlined across all three reports: there is no such thing as a perfect electoral system, with opinions based on what individuals consider to be the purpose of elections, and 'fairness' does not stand on its own and must be 'fairness' in relation to a preset criteria. Importantly, given Labour's commitment to altering Britain's constitutional settlement, institutions entail different purposes and therefore a different electoral system can be adopted. The constituency link was key, maintaining a direct link between legislator and elector, and therefore electoral systems involving multi-member constituencies were ruled out as the dilution of the constituency link was contrary to Labour's historic emphasis on community. Moreover, a system such as STV contained the prospect of Labour Party candidates from different wings of the Party competing against one another.

The final report sought to reconcile a range of views, made more difficult by the leadership's actions, particularly once the leadership had been assumed by Smith and Beckett. Both sought different ways to disrupt the Working Party. Furthermore, with Bryan Gould openly admitting that he sought to prevent the committee from arriving at any meaningful conclusions and Baroness Armstrong openly divulging she was sent on the committee to report back to John Smith, the report was unlikely to receive an easy ride from both those on and those outside the committee. The steadfastness of the FPTP cohort led Bryan Gould to affirm: 'The pro-PR people were not strong or committed enough to overcome the determination of the FPTP people to let the exercise just run into the sand.'[149]

When it came to the recommendation for the House of Commons the leadership was successful, discouraging the committee from coming out in favour of the more proportional and pluralist MMS. Instead their actions made SV the only viable system for reformers; otherwise the Working Party could have come out in favour of the status quo. SV was therefore the 'least worst' option, significantly less proportional, maintaining many of the features of FPTP. Plant became convinced of the need for reform, originally starting out as pro-FPTP, but ultimately considering the Labour Party had little to fear from coalition, as Labour would be the biggest party, and would be able to implement considerable parts of its manifesto, a bold and controversial statement in light of Labour's aversion to coalition.

Far from the 1992 general election emphasizing the need for electoral reform, it, if anything, had the opposite effect. When the issue of PR emerged in the final days of polling, the Labour Party looked unprincipled, unable to say whether it supported the present system or favoured reform, putting off potential voters. This uncertainty was duly apportioned blame for contributing to Labour losing the election. When John Smith replaced Neil Kinnock – who was becoming increasingly sympathetic to reform – as leader and Beckett became his deputy, the two top positions in the Labour Party were held by individuals hostile to this type of constitutional reform. The Working Party was closed down in autumn 1993, not allowing time for the committee to look at local government. With the next Labour government committed to holding a referendum on the electoral system, and the increasing unpopularity of the Conservative government, the Labour Party continued with its internal party and policy reforms, focusing on the next general election.

4

Realigning the left and the Jenkins Commission

This chapter charts Labour's interest in electoral reform between 1994, with Blair winning the leadership, and the end of Labour first term in office in 2001. Bartle writes that the 'period from July 1994 to June 2001 witnessed one of the most fascinating experiments in British politics for a century', as Blair and Ashdown 'followed a sustained strategy of co-operation although there was no immediate need for it'.[1] A key event was the Independent Commission on the Voting System, commonly known as the Jenkins Commission. Consequently, the chapter establishes and explores the personal view of Blair and other leading figures who rose to prominence under 'New Labour'; the relationship between Labour and the Liberal Democrats and the desire, or lack thereof, for coalition; the general election result and its impact on the introduction of electoral reform at Westminster and a coalition with the Liberal Democrats; and the arguments put forward by the Jenkins Commission and the reaction to its recommendations within the Labour government and Parliamentary Labour Party.

The Plant process and subsequent referendum commitment by Smith, had to some degree, contained the matter, although it was far from settled. Yet, the more pertinent question remained, namely whether the Labour Party would be able to win a parliamentary majority at the next general election and form a government or whether they would have to rely on the parliamentary votes of Liberal Democrats. With the death of Smith in 1994, a leadership contest was fought between Margaret Beckett, John Prescott and Tony Blair, with the last of these emerging victorious, ensuring the modernization process would continue. All three had committed to upholding Smith's referendum pledge on reforming the Westminster electoral system during the leadership contest,[2] likely wishing not to be seen to be going against a policy pledge made by the well-regarded Smith and accepting the Party management benefits the referendum commitment entailed. Given the candidates' views, it was far from an endorsement of PR. Indeed, despite a concerted attempt to drop the pledge at the 1995 Labour Party Conference, the New Labour leadership retained the commitment, with known PR sceptics such as Jack Straw speaking in its defence. As we will see, ensuring good relations with the Liberal Democrats was just as important as the emotive reason of Smith's pledge.

Blair, proportional representation and the Liberal Democrats

Blair's views carried significant weight due to his position and could direct Labour Party policy. Privately, he was concerned about the response of the written press if there was an attempt to move towards a proportional scheme, a theme he would return to throughout his time as leader.[3] Publicly, Blair would be noncommittal, remaining 'unpersuaded' of the case for PR. Indeed, Blair's earlier writing on the matter were sceptical. Writing in the *New Statesman* after Thatcher's second landslide victory in 1987, in which Labour's vote had increased for the first time since October 1974, he stated that PR was not the answer to the electoral problems facing the Labour Party. It would instead lull the Party and electoral reformers into a false sense of security about Labour's electoral prospects, rather than tackling the big and necessary issue of modernizing the Labour Party in order to win.

> Labour's new enthusiasts for PR put their case not primarily on grounds of constitutional principle, but as a strategy for power. The implications of their case are fundamental: that Labour cannot ever again win a majority of seats in parliament; and that what cannot be achieved through the front door of majority government can be bundled in by the back door of coalition and electoral pacts … The real question for the Labour Party is why it is not achieving sufficient electoral support. It must face this question irrespective of whether we retain the present electoral system or change it, whether we stand for election alone or in a pact. The campaign for PR is just the latest excuse for avoiding decisive choices about the party's future.[4]

After a fourth successive general election defeat in 1992, Blair would affirm the need for continued modernization. 'The issue for Labour today', he told journalists, 'is not change or no change but what type of change. Nobody should be under any illusion that the route back to power can be achieved without fundamental reform of ideas and organisation.'[5] For Mandelson and Liddle, this was an attempt to ensure there was no rolling back of the reforms enacted by Kinnock 'but also at others – including, they thought, Kinnock himself – who might now advocate an immediate commitment to reform of the electoral system'.[6] Whatever view Blair and Brown held about PR, 'they argued that you do not win elections by changing the rules'. What mattered was building upon Kinnock's achievements, turning the Labour Party into a 'broad-based party of the left and centre, rather than watch it turn into a minority left-wing party that would have to rely on electoral reform to unseat the Tories'.[7]

Consequently, the Labour Party could not escape its policy and organizational problems through electoral reform and PR. If the Party did avoid the difficult decisions it would not be in a position to win an election. Blair returned to the issue in the *New Statesman* in 1996. On this occasion, his reasoning went further than PR resulting in reluctance to modernize. When asked whether he was against PR, Blair said, 'Yes. I have never been convinced that small parties do not then get disproportionate power.' Emphasizing social and economic factors as greater priorities for the electorate than constitutional reform, Blair considered, 'Whether you change the voting system or not the hard decisions still remain and people want to know where you are on the economy and jobs, health and education', all areas 'Labour has to get right'. He continued:

> My worry is more about what I used to call the unilateralist and PR option for the Labour Party. You carry on with policies the electorate won't support, change the voting system and hope you can somehow gain power by joining forces with other political parties. It doesn't work.[8]

In September 1996 Blair wrote a special piece for the *Economist* on the constitution. Commenting on the House of Commons, Blair deemed 'effective democracy was dependent on, above all, quality'. While Blair adopted the popular electoral reform phrase of 'elective dictatorship', he remained unpersuaded on the merits of PR and stressed that the purpose of the House of Commons is to form and uphold a government.

> It is not, as some claim, a simple question of moving from an 'unfair' to a 'fair' voting system. An electoral system must meet two democratic tests: it

needs to reflect opinion, but it must also aggregate opinion without giving disproportionate influence to splinter groups. Aggregation is particularly important for a parliament whose job is to create and sustain a single, mainstream government.[9]

Whether Blair was convinced on an intellectual level about the merits of pluralism and electoral reform, or whether his interest was tactical, is open to debate. By January 1997, Blair's position had supposedly shifted and his opposition to reform had softened. In a meeting with Ashdown, Blair is quoted as saying: 'I have told you privately I am in favour of a change to the voting system provided we retain the single-member system' implying AV or SV. However, he could not say so publicly until a commission had reported its findings, and it was a way of opening up a relationship with the Liberal Democrats.[10] The question remained whether Labour could ever win again and despite the strong showing in the polls. According to Whitty and Lipsey, Blair remained sceptical of Labour's electoral chances, remembering what had happened in 1992 when the poll lead evaporated in the election campaign's final few days.[11] As such, overtures were made towards leading figures in the Liberal Democrats, as early as October 1994 in which Blair and Ashdown discussed options for cooperation in the next parliament, ranging from independence, broad cooperation and full partnership.[12]

In 1994, in an interview with the *Observer*, Blair had made pluralist overtures towards the Liberal Democrats. Labour did not solely occupy the centre-left, but also the Liberal Democrats. Indeed, the Liberal Democrats had an important role in constructing a centre-left political philosophy.[13] At the 1995 Labour Party Conference Blair listed his political heroes to include Lloyd George, Keynes and Beveridge. Publicly, Blair was making inclusive statements designed to bring the Liberal Democrats into his 'big tent', both electorally in terms of voters and on a personal level, as Blair found many Liberal Democrats from their social-democrat wing much more collegial than many Labour colleagues. Importantly, Blair's conference speech suggested the Labour Party did not have a monopoly on good ideas, and the Liberal Democrats had valid policies. John Edmonds, then leader of the GMB Union, thought this an 'incredible' and 'extraordinary' speech, not for its brilliance but for 'a leader of the Labour Party openly regretting the foundation of his Party, because it splits the left. He believed deeply that we need to reunite the progressive forces that are always in the majority in this country.'[14]

The Liberal Democrats abandoned 'equidistance' in May 1995, aligning themselves politically with Labour. Blair considered this to be necessary, wanting an agreed approach on the constitution because it would help politically, both in opposition and government, negating the possibility of the Liberal Democrats opposing as a matter of course should Labour only achieve a small majority.[15] Foley writes that cooperation with the Liberal Democrats entailed further benefits for the Labour Party. Firstly, acting as a 'mutual defence alliance against Conservative attempts to divide and rule the centre left', protecting 'the coherence and integrity of Labour's own constitutional agenda from ambush with the Liberal Democrats'. Secondly, this would prevent constitutional reform from becoming defined by the Liberal Democrats. Thirdly, the Liberal Democrats would turn their attack almost exclusively at the Conservatives.[16]

In the summer of 1996, Blair and Ashdown asked Robin Cook and Robert Maclennan 'to explore the possibility of co-operation between the Labour and Liberal Democrat parties in relation to constitutional reform'. Cook invited Plant to contribute to Cook-Maclennan, and for Plant it gave expression to what he had outlined in his Report, namely broadening Labour's appeal by attempting to put into the public arena the idea that people could vote Labour knowing that the Liberal Democrats still supported part of Labour's manifesto.[17] Both parties were committed to constitutional change, sharing a common view of the need to reform our democratic institutions and to renew the relationship between politics and the people. Following progress in the initial discussion, the two parties agreed in October 1996 to establish a Joint Consultative Committee (JCC), exploring the extent to which there was common ground on a legislative programme for constitutional reform. On the matter of PR, on which the entire constitutional reform agenda could well have foundered, the JCC resolved it in time for the general election: a single-question referendum between FPTP and an alternative held within the first term of a new Parliament.[18]

The JCC extended its remit to cover Europe, welfare, health and education. However, in both parties some felt they had been 'bounced' into an arrangement they did not want to be in, and the leadership only conducted the 'project' with little influence given to the backbenchers. Rawnsley dismisses the importance of the JCC as a 'presentation token of his [Blair] often voiced desire to embrace a more inclusive, more pluralistic style of politics'.[19] By the beginning of 2001, Charles Kennedy had replaced Ashdown as leader, revealing the JCC and 'the project' were in a 'coma', waiting to be revived if people wish.[20] In September 2001, the Liberal Democrats withdrew from the JCC, having only met twice in the last two years.

Blair, in the April of 1997, asked Alistair Campbell, his press secretary, 'How would you feel if I gave Paddy a place in the Cabinet and started merger talks?', something Blair allegedly had mentioned previously, the rationale being 'we could put the Tories out of business for a generation'.[21] In the days after the 1997 general election, according to Ashdown, Blair mentioned 'a merger' of the two parties, an idea that left Ashdown cold, preferring positions for Liberal Democrats on Cabinet committees.[22] Derek Draper wrote an account of Blair's first 100 days in office, also mentioning the potential for a merger.[23] Blair continued to state his desire to reshape British politics around two progressive parties and, in August 1998, sent a fax to Ashdown believing it could be achieved 'without electoral reform'. Whilst Blair did acknowledge this was an important issue for Liberal Democrats, the Jenkins Commission 'will provide the means, but not the end in this process. Our task will be to convince our parties, and the country, of what we are trying to do'. The best option was either FPTP or AV with top-up, although 'it will be very difficult to get through parliament in the face of such a heavy programme of legislation on schools, hospitals and other measures of constitutional change'. Additionally, the boundary changes legislation would not be passed in time to take effect for the next general election. Consequently, the best time for the referendum would be at the same time as the next election.[24]

A month later, Blair would send another fax to Ashdown further explaining his position on electoral reform, repeating many of the same points made in the earlier fax, whilst also suggesting compromises to appease the Liberal Democrats. Furthermore, it was 'clear that if it were to be pushed, we would be fighting a referendum with a Labour Party badly divided (possibly with a majority anti) … the real danger then would be *losing* the referendum'.[25] Ashdown pressed Blair to go for a coalition in November 1998, after Jenkins had published his report, creating a window of enthusiasm for the Liberal

Democrats towards the Labour Party. However, no coalition materialized then or over thirteen years of government, and the JCC was as close as the Labour Party and Liberal Democrats came to forming a coalition at Westminster. It is worth exploring why this happened.

During Labour's first term in office, those individuals who were willing to pursue 'the project' left government; Peter Mandelson, supposedly an advocate of Lab–Lib relations, left the government over the 'home loan affair' and Ashdown stood down as Leader of the Liberal Democrats in 1999. Charles Clarke confessed that when he was chair of the Labour Party in 2001 there were late night meetings with the Liberal Democrats at County Hall going through various policy issues. Yet, Lab–Lib Democrat relations between 1997 and 2001 were 'very much a minority pursuit around Number 10 and a few of his [Blair's] very close people. Nobody thought this was really where you want to go, partly for the reason that the "why do you need it?" factor was so deep.'[26] The lack of voices at the top of each party willing to make a case for cooperation naturally meant the merits of the argument were not made or heard in significant numbers, as Cabinet ministers focused on their department and the concerns of practical politics.

Mandelson records in *The Third Man* that the general election 'killed (or) at least was sure to delay' the formation of a coalition, as not only had Labour won a landslide, but also the Liberal Democrats were up from twenty seats to forty-six seats. Furthermore, 'for many in the Labour Party, especially those who still seethed over the SDP split, the idea of offering the rebels' successors a place in government was unpalatable, to say the least.'[27] Blair's account, *A Journey*, gives no mention of electoral reform or PR, yet he admits from the outset he wanted the Liberal Democrats 'in the big tent' as 'their leadership was sound' and 'some outstanding people in their ranks' politically aligned with New Labour. Yet, the project failed as the Liberal Democrats lacked the 'necessary fibre to govern', capable of 'breath-taking opportunism', and although agreement was found on issues 'that didn't touch voters immediate lives they opposed the necessary public sector reforms 'which most directly touched people's lives'.[28] McFadden concurred with Blair's analysis, stating: 'Whilst PR was an area of common interest, it was not a strong enough subject matter in itself and there was a lack of common purpose in other areas that New Labour felt were important: public services, pensions and other domestic issues.' Blair's faith in the Liberal Democrats withered, as they opposed reforms to higher education, schools and hospitals.[29]

Philip Cowley and Mark Stuart analysed Liberal Democrat voting in the House of Commons from 1992 to 2003. Although voting in the House of Commons is binary, Liberal Democrat voting behaviour changed, shifting 'from being almost undisguisable from Labour in their behaviour to their becoming a *bona fide* party of opposition'.[30] The Liberal Democrats tendency to vote with the Conservatives grew from 27 per cent in the first session of the 1997 Parliament, to 40 per cent in the second session, 44 per cent in the third, 47 per cent in the fourth, then reaching 54 per cent in the first session of Labour's second term. During the 2002–3 session, Liberal Democrat MPs voted against Labour in 251 of the 352 Commons whipped votes in which they participated, meaning they opposed the government in 75 per cent of the votes.[31] The move away from Labour during the parliament would have done little to convince Labour politicians that the Liberal Democrats would be reliable in a coalition, particularly as the 'objective was to get them, a couple of years down the track when we were established, as being more supportive'.[32]

The Jenkins Commission, 1998

By the time of the general election in May 1997 the Labour Party had concluded that electoral reform at Westminster was conditional on an electoral commission and a referendum.[33] Despite constitutional reform coming sixteenth out of sixteenth in the concerns of voters during the 1997 election campaign,[34] the Labour Party had committed to a raft of constitutional reforms: devolution in Scotland and an assembly in Wales; a continuation of the peace-process with a power-sharing executive in Northern Ireland; an elected second chamber replacing the House of Lords; regional assemblies in England; locally elected mayors across England's towns and cities; and a Freedom of Information Act. The closed regional list (d'Hondt) system was adopted for the European Parliament – although it faced considerable opposition in the House of Lords – bringing Great Britain in line with the rest of the European Union, with Northern Ireland using STV. Notably, 'one MP attributed Straw's introduction of a closed list system for European elections to a cynical desire to discredit PR, commending him on "playing a blinder",[35] thus negating PR becoming the thin end of the wedge for FPTP elections to Westminster. Indeed, all the elected devolved bodies introduced by the Labour government were committed to using something other than FPTP.

To fulfil the manifesto commitment and to ensure 'the project' remained on course, the Labour government announced a commission with a remit to recommend an alternative electoral system to be put before the British electorate in a referendum. Holding the enquiry into reforming FPTP conveniently deferred a pronouncement on the matter, pushing the date back before a decision had to be made. The prominent 'centrist' Roy Jenkins was chosen as chair in the summer of 1997,[36] an individual who had a chequered history with the Labour Party. The former Labour chancellor of the exchequer, president of the European Commission, member of the 'Gang of Four' who founded the SDP and president of the Liberal Democrats had sought to 'break the mould' of British politics, the means to the end being PR.

As such, not all in the Labour Party viewed Jenkins as benevolently as Blair. Many considered him now charged with the task of concocting an electoral system that had the potential to reduce Labour representation and ensure that the Labour Party would never govern as a single party again. The choice of Jenkins as chair was, for Edmonds, a gesture not just to the right of the Labour Party, but mainly, a gesture of reaching out beyond Labour, leaving 'tribal' Labour such as himself, questioning where it was leading. Moreover, Jenkins was a 'political move in a way that Plant was not. Plant was party management, Jenkins was completely different.'[37] Tribal Labour 'questioning where it was all going' is exemplified by the anecdote of Blair informing Prescott of his decision to appoint Jenkins as chair: 'It was a very good thing he [Prescott] was sitting down, because he exploded.'[38]

A five-strong Commission was announced in December 1997. Joining Jenkins was Lord Alexander of Weedon, a Conservative peer with a career in law and banking; Baroness Gould of Potternewton, a former national organizer for the Labour Party and member of the Plant Report; the civil servant Sir John Chilcot, former permanent secretary at the Northern Ireland Office; and David Lipsey, a special advisor to Tony Crosland and political editor of the *Economist*. The *Economist* considered four of the Commission to be declared reformers. Jenkins had long promoted electoral reform, whilst suggesting he would accept something less than STV, the favoured system of the Liberal Democrats. In his book, *The Voice of the People*, Lord Alexander announced his 'tentative personal preference' for STV. Lipsey had argued for AV, and Baroness Gould had sat on the Plant Commission and backed the majority vote for SV.[39] Chilcot had not publicly declared his personal view, although in his role as permanent secretary at the Northern Ireland Office he would have witnessed the workings of STV first-hand.

For Gould, she and Lipsey were chosen by Blair and Straw as they understood we would consider the electoral consequences for the Labour Party of any proposed system. Indeed, this explains their lack of enthusiasm for proportionality, mindful of Labour sensitivities. Gould affirmed: 'David and I were very clear that we could only come up with something that didn't do any damage to the Labour Party.'[40] During the Commission, Lipsey wrote to Jenkins urging him to understand the importance of gaining Labour support, which was taken 'but not undiluted'. To do this, they could not push too hard.

> My reason for wanting to avoid introducing a system that would damage Labour too much in relation to first-past-the-post is essentially political. I want electoral reform. I think we can only get it if it has the backing of Tony Blair, his Cabinet and the majority of the Parliamentary Labour Party. And making all allowance for the virtues of magnanimity, that means we cannot ask them to swallow too much.[41]

Straw, the then Home Secretary, gave the remit for the enquiry in a written parliamentary answer. The Jenkins Commission was given one year and the freedom to recommend an alternative to FPTP. Four requirements were outlined: (1) broad proportionality; (2) the need for stable government; (3) an extension of voter choice; and (4) the maintenance of a link between MPs and geographical constituencies. The members – perhaps bar Jenkins – had not been consulted on the terms of reference. It was noted that the four requirements were 'not entirely compatible' and that none of the requirements were 'absolute'; otherwise its task would have been impossible due to the irreconcilable terms of reference. As such, they adopted a semi-flexible attitude towards the terms of reference to reconcile the criteria.[42]

Dunleavy and Margetts suggest the brief included two 'Labour' criteria – keeping the link to constituencies and stable government – and two 'Liberal

Democrat' criteria – proportionality and extending voter choice. However, proportionality was modified to broad proportionality by Labour.[43] For Lipsey, the nature of the criteria suggested that it had been drawn up by a Cabinet committee on which both pro-and anti-reformers sat.[44] Whether the Labour leadership intended to create a situation for the Commission which ruled little out, whilst also not ruling anything in, is a possibility. Mclean considered the terms of reference an attempt by Blair to 'find something which satisfies reformers just enough to count as barely acceptable to them, while comforting conservatives that it is the minimum you could offer'.[45]

Interestingly and importantly, Jenkins added three further criteria: the system should be 'intellectually acceptable', should represent 'a significant change' from the existing system and should have a 'reasonable chance of coming about politically'.[46] The additional criteria added by Jenkins suggest the original criteria as outlined by Straw were going to play only a minimal role in influencing the outcome. Indeed, Lipsey went further, stating:

> The terms of reference we were given were brilliant and completely contradictory and enabled us to do whatever we wanted to do because of the contradictions within them. They were brilliantly drafted to be completely impossible to fulfil. If we had tried to take the terms of reference seriously we would have had to 'square the circle'. In a sense what we ended up doing was providing a system which offered an appropriate balance of the contradictory requirements within the terms of reference.[47]

The overriding concern of the Commission was putting forward an electoral system that had the potential to be introduced, not the intellectual puzzle of solving them. Lipsey continued: 'The driving force was to find a change that was big enough to be worthwhile which nevertheless had some chance of success.'[48] As such, little time was spent defending FPTP, as it was believed that that case would be made in the referendum campaign. Instead, the Commission outlined what they saw as the failings of FPTP, including distorting representation, poor-quality legislation, perverse results, restricting choice, safe seats and the inability of the system to deliver single-party government.[49]

The Commission travelled to Germany, New Zealand and Australia on fact-finding missions, held open meetings for voters in the UK and took soundings from experts and interested parties. The public influenced the Commission's decision by showing antipathy towards strengthening the Party's influence in placing candidates on the top-up lists. Consequently, top-up members were to be chosen locally for 'smallish' areas. Importantly, and implying that the Commission was keen on receiving the backing of the three major political parties, their views were taken into account.[50] Labour's ruling National Executive Committee (NEC) submitted a document to the Commission on 6 July 1998, asking to 'bear in mind the need for a system which sustains, open, stable and accountable Government'.[51] The constituency link was and should continue to be the 'bedrock of the parliamentary system ... ensuring MPs are clearly representative of and answerable to a clearly defined group of electors',[52] making the retention of the constituency link vital in any alternative electoral system. A stable government was considered 'a government which is generally able to last its full electoral term and which is also able to carry though its manifesto pledges', deemed a vital consideration as in the UK it was expected the House of Commons would sustain a government with a clear mandate and also a strong opposition.[53] Over the past fifty years Britain had enjoyed a stable and representative government, aided by 'the preponderance of single-party majority administrations'. Crucial in a democracy was the 'power to throw out an unpopular government' and the submission deemed it should be maintained in any alternative to FPTP.[54]

The submission judged there to be a trade-off between stable government and proportionality, with pure proportionality most likely to lead to coalition. Coalitions are 'not by definition unstable' claimed the submission, but the process of forming a government can be 'consuming and divisive, and small parties can gain a pivotal position where they wield power which is disproportionate to their degree of electoral support'.[55] Additionally, the document declared: 'We do not believe the electoral system should result in perpetual coalition' nor 'was a government illegitimate if it received less than fifty per cent of the vote'.[56] Concerning broad proportionality, the submission desired the Commission to look into proportionality of representation and power, for the two were deemed not to be the same. 'It would be a mistake to place so much stress on pure proportionality of representation that small parties are given disproportionate power compared to the level of support in the country'.[57]

Regarding voter choice, the document reasoned on two aspects: the choice of the individual voter and whether the overall result in terms of the government supported by the House of Commons can be said to reflect the broad choice of the electorate as a whole. 'Systems capable of producing clear winners help to ensure that governments are held to account between elections ... Systems which inevitably lead to coalition can undermine the direct accountability which other systems produce', an 'excuse for non-delivery of manifesto promises'. Post-election deals result in voters not knowing until 'after they have voted the precise programme to which the resulting government will be committed'.[58] The document highlighted the strength of opposition towards PR and a satisfaction with FPTP emphasizing many of its perceived benefits. According to the *Guardian*, the only vote against the NEC document was by Dennis Skinner, the then Labour MP for Bolsover, who opposed PR.[59]

Having taken on board the submissions, the Commission turned its attention to alternative electoral systems. SV, the Second Ballot and 'Weighted Vote' were considered unsuitable. AV fulfilled three of the four terms of reference: AV maintained the constituency link, increased voter choice through preferential voting and it was unlikely to lead to unstable government. However, it would fail to address the electoral deserts for major parties in parts of Great Britain, and AV can produce more disproportional results than FPTP. For the remit to be met there had to be some modification to the maintenance of the constituency link.[60] This led to the exploration of the suitability of STV, believing it 'maximises voter choice, giving the elector power to express preference not only between parties but between different candidates of the same party' achieving a 'significantly greater degree of proportionality'. Furthermore, 'it avoids the problem of having two classes of member, as is the case with the Additional Member System'.[61] However, as with Plant, STV was unfeasible, even as part of a hybrid scheme. Constituencies under STV would contain *c*.350,000 electors entailing a 'very long ballot paper and a degree of choice which might be deemed oppressive rather than liberating'.[62] Additionally, it was deemed unlikely that electors would know significant differences between candidates from the same party and there was little evidence to suggest STV encourages participation. Furthermore, it would be challenging to reconcile using STV as part of a hybrid system, explaining to electors why voters are using a different method for the same institution in different parts of the country.[63]

Lipsey records that Jenkins had in mind a 'fanciful anti-Labour' scheme with different systems in town and country: AV in the country, multi-member constituencies in the cities. According to Jenkins, this was an adaptation of Britain's electoral system in the nineteenth century. For Lipsey and Gould, who were determined not to let Labour be negatively affected by any change, it was not lost on them that AV would squeeze Labour in rural areas and the Tories would benefit at the expense of Labour in the cities. The bias against Labour meant it was duly dropped.[64] Consequently, a hybrid system was recommended – AV+, a variation of AMS – based on 80–85 per cent of MPs representing parliamentary constituencies elected under AV, and the remaining 15–20 per cent elected from county top-up areas – chosen as it was deemed a limited modification, less unfair to minority parties and avoiding electoral deserts for the two major parties.[65]

It was also argued to be the system that came closest to fulfilling the terms of reference, increasing choice due to the AV element, creating a more inclusive and consensual politics. Jenkins notes, 'AV counters one important objection to electoral reform. This is the tendency to transfer power from voters to the subsequent deals of politicians'[66] due to AV's ability to avoid coalitions and deliver majority governments. The accusation of two types of MP was considered unproblematic as there was a difference between borough and county MPs in the nineteenth century. Alexander added a note of reservation, arguing in favour of FPTP. Alexander's reservation was leaked to the *Financial Times* prior to the Commission's publication, at the behest of Lipsey, to avoid the accusation 'Jenkins divided'. Lipsey did not consider that Alexander's dissent had undermined the argument proposed by the Commission.[67]

In the same fashion as Plant, Jenkins did 'not recoil with horror from the very idea of coalitions, regarding them, on the basis both of British and of some foreign experience, as capable of providing effective and decisive governments' with the quality of the coalition depending on whether it was 'honest'.[68] Honest was defined by agreeing more with each other than those outside. This was qualified by distancing from permanent coalition, preferring and regarding it more compatible with the terms of reference, as 'when there is a strong surge in one political direction or the other, single-party governments, even if with somewhat under 50 per cent of the vote'.[69] However, it was considered unacceptable to have a 'hinge party' – similar to that of the FDP in Germany which had a perpetual grip on power even switching sides, or the New Zealand First Party – and it was not believed 'there is anything inherent in an additional member/top-up system which make it do so'.[70] A substantial degree of proportionality could be attained with a top-up of 15–20 per cent, elected through an 'open list' using the D'hondt method.[71]

The 'top-up' system would be unable to have a by-election. Instead, the next candidate on the list should be elected or, failing that, the position would remain unfilled until the next general election. This did draw some criticism. Gerald Bermingham, MP, asked, 'How are the electorate to overturn a Government in the middle of their term of office if they cannot boot out the Government party at a by-election?'[72] No threshold was to be imposed, unlike in Germany, but in order to win top-up MPs a party had to contest 50 per cent of the constituencies in the top-up region. Lipsey maintained the reason for a relatively small top-up element – a smaller percentage than either the Scottish Parliament or Welsh Assembly – was an attempt to avoid spooking MPs into thinking they will lose their seat and their own prospects.[73]

An interesting consideration is the extent to which those outside the Jenkins Commission influenced proceedings. Given Jenkins's longstanding commitment to 'breaking the mould' of British politics through electoral reform, it would have been in his interests to keep Blair informed in the hope that he would be sympathetic to the recommendations. This consequently raises the question of whether it was prearranged that Jenkins would recommend AV+?

Lipsey rejected claims that the recommendation was hatched in private between Blair and Jenkins: 'Any suspicion that our conclusion resulted from secret negotiations between Lord Jenkins, Tony Blair and Paddy Ashdown … is unfounded.'[74] Nevertheless, Blair is reported to have met with Jenkins during the lifetime of the Commission, discussing progression. Jenkins informed Ashdown that Blair listened to the suggestion of a decentralized AMS-based system. Blair and Ashdown also debated this issue of thresholds in private – a party that won 45 per cent of the vote or more should win over 50 per cent of the seats, with Ashdown claiming the Jenkins Commission proposals fell somewhat short of that. Blair did not think it was acceptable, as only one postwar government would have been able to form a majority.[75] This view is echoed in a note recapping a discussion between Lipsey and Pat McFadden, one of Blair's special advisors, in March 1998. According to McFadden, Blair was 'instinctively against PR' considering 'governments that win as big as in 45, 79, 97 should have overall majorities. He is happy with AV'. Although AV would not satisfy the Liberal Democrats, Blair 'does want to do something with the Liberal Democrats, and recognises that Paddy may need more than just AV'. Moreover, there was the problem of Party management. Fraser Kemp and Jim Murphy, both Labour MPs in Scotland, were planning speeches on the subject at the Scottish Labour Conference. 'Their theme is "enough is enough" after Scotland, Wales, London and Europe.'[76]

Margetts and Dunleavy claim there is evidence that at Easter 1998 Jenkins and Blair met to discuss the interim ideas of the Commission. At the time, the mixed system consisted of two-thirds constituency and one-third top up. However, Blair is supposed to have rejected this possibility, on advice given by Mandelson and Number 10 staff, who warned the PLP would not accept such a radical change. Consequently, Blair allegedly asked Jenkins to look again at a system with more constituency MPs, as this had greater feasibility.[77] Blair and Jenkins also met to discuss how best to incorporate top-up MPs, by reducing the number of constituencies or increasing the number of MPs. Both solutions contained problems. The former as sitting MPs would be concerned that they would no longer have a seat when the boundaries were redrawn, and the latter would have entailed informing the electorate that there should be 100 additional MPs would have been a hard sell. Lipsey realized that sitting MPs had a self-interested reason to reject the Commission's proposal.[78]

The *Ashdown Diaries* suggest Blair, prior to the formation of the Commission, indicated one possibility would be AV for the next election; the second, full proportionality after that. 'The Commission could recommend the ultimate destination but ought in our view to recommend the intervening staging-post of AV; as well using the phrase "The government may want to do this in two stages"'.[79] Stating categorically that this was the case is challenging to substantiate. Regardless, this was the course of action promoted by Lipsey, who privately pressed the matter with Jenkins.

The trick we missed was we should have recommended moving to AV and then considered the introduction of top-up lists as a second stage later on and then we might just have got AV through. This was a tremendous tussle within in the Commission as we had people who were more keen on proportionality, namely Bob Alexander.[80]

However, whatever approach the Commission and those sympathetic to reform advocated, they faced considerable opposition from within the PLP and the wider Labour movement. It is to that which we now turn our attention.

Reaction to Jenkins and Labour divisions over PR

In April 1998 the Labour government insisted the AV would fulfil the remit of the Jenkins Commission. Straw considered AV to be 'broadly proportional', adding that the government planned to hold a referendum on PR well before the next general election. Yet, the government was not bound by the Commission's recommendations, which would have to be subject to Cabinet consideration, and if a referendum were to be held it could choose an alternative to FPTP of its own liking.[81] In public, Blair remained 'unpersuaded' on the merits of PR. Supplementing his doubts may have been the strength of feeling within the PLP. Around eighty Labour MPs had joined 'Keep the Link', an anti-PR campaign group. As the name implies, the group wished to 'retain the all-important constituency link' between MPs and voters. The backbench group was led by Martin Salter, Labour MP for Reading West and included Dale Campbell-Savours – who proposed SV, which the Plant Report advocated – and Patricia Hewitt.[82] If change were to take place then the greatest concession should be AV.

The Amalgamated Engineering and Electrical Union (AEEU), led by the General Secretary Ken Jackson, sought to lead a trade union and grassroots revolt against PR and as a result place increased strain on Labour–Liberal Democrat relations. For Jackson, PR was the niche concern of metropolitan classes, having little traction amongst the working class, and would undermine Labour's ability to govern. He continued: 'No serious Labour party member could countenance a change which would take the party from majority government to a situation where it might be frozen out of government or to a situation where Labour could be held hostage by minority parties.'[83] Stuart Bell, chairman of the FPTP group, went further citing Labour's past sense of betrayal at the hands of the Liberals; the 1924 Labour government and David Steel withdrawing from the Lab–Lib Pact.[84]

Gordon Brown held significant influence in the Cabinet and wider PLP, but had kept his views on electoral reform private. However, Robert Peston, writing in the *Financial Times*, affirmed that Brown was strongly opposed to PR. Blair would on several occasions cite Brown as an impasse to electoral reform as Brown was in favour of FPTP and generally, bar Menzies Campbell and other individuals, the Liberal Democrats 'were not to be trusted'.[85] Brown did have a private meeting with Ashdown, stating that whilst he was not opposed to PR, the matter raised doubts and problems. 'I am really frightened about factionalism in politics and really frightened about running a Cabinet in which individuals would have to run back to their own sections or groups to get validation for what they are doing.' 'There are those in the Labour Party', continued Brown, 'who push for PR because they believe it will enable them to push Labour back on to a conventional left-wing agenda'.

Interestingly, Blair and Brown's thoughts on electoral reform differ on means but arrive at the same ends, namely keeping Labour on a centrist agenda. For Blair, he understood, although did not fully subscribe to the view that PR was the method that would permit a reuniting of the centre left, allowing him to marginalize the left wing of the Labour Party. Brown considered FPTP the best method of pursuing a centrist agenda, forcing the Labour Party to abandon a left-wing agenda by appealing to the median voter.

To risk Cabinet divisions over PR to keep alive the 'project', with no political necessity would have entailed Blair exercising his authority on a matter not deemed a priority, thus damaging his position and the standing of his government. In addition, Blair had to keep Prescott onside, understanding that whilst from different backgrounds and representing different wings of the Labour Party, he could only push his deputy so far. Prescott was immovable on PR for Westminster and coalition with the Liberal Democrats, reportedly telling one campaigner for constitutional change, 'I'm not in fucking favour of fucking PR for anything.'[86] In a meeting with Ashdown, Prescott expanded on his reservations. He was a 'Labour man to the core', not sharing Blair's and Ashdown's analysis of a schism on the political left, believing that it would 'break up my party' and if there was a push for PR, he would oppose Blair privately and publicly. He had 'no qualms about the Labour Party being in power time and time again, and in between taking our turn at defeat, too.'[87] As for having Liberal Democrts in the Cabinet, Prescott thought that Blair could not carry the Party on that matter. Prescott told Blair: 'If Ashdown walks in the back door and gets a Cabinet job, I'm straight out the front door. It's not a negotiable issue for me.' The reason for this was twofold. Ashdown was a Liberal and he didn't want anything to do with them and secondly, there was no need as Labour had a large majority.[88]

The 1998 Labour Party Conference saw the issue of electoral reform take centre stage. Edmonds, who had earlier in 1998 orchestrated a grassroots campaign to defend FPTP, considered 'arms had been twisted' and the Labour Party leadership had conducted a 'shabby little deal' to avoid a debate and vote on PR, which had been postponed as the NEC believed it would be 'premature' to force a vote before Jenkins had reported. AEEU leader Jackson had also been involved in the FPTP campaign but bowed to pressure from the Party leadership and had withdrawn a motion calling for FPTP to be retained. Jackson considered: 'There is genuine diversity of opinion in our party. PR cannot become Labour's EMU – a force for division, an excuse for open warfare.' Jackson then added a staunch defence of FPTP: 'We can only go on serving our people if we keep the system that delivered that historic [1997] victory. PR would mean permanent Liberal coalitions.' 'Think about the nightmare of Liberal Democrats calling the shots, and minority parties being able to veto parties on the back of a whim.' Stuart Bell asked delegates to 'Imagine, under PR, a deal with the Liberals, coalition government, Paddy standing in front of you speaking as Chancellor – that is not going to happen because under PR he could be at the Conservative party conference.'[89]

Blair delivered a riposte to those within Labour who opposed closer links with the Liberal Democrats, returning to a theme he had outlined in opposition. Fundamentally, deemed Blair, there was a bigger picture in which the people agree. He continued: 'We're all modern social democrats, a large part of the Liberal Democrats are in that position and where we do agree we should be working together. Let's not be tribal about all this.' Echoing his belief in reuniting the centre-left Blair considered, 'What is important is to recognise that politics has undergone a huge change, here and round the world, and I just believe in doing what is sensible. If people do agree then why not try to work together?' During his afternoon question and answer session,

Blair took a more conciliatory approach: 'I understand it is an important issue, but frankly schools, hospitals, crime, industry and jobs – these are also very, very important.' Blair said, 'There will be no decision taken on this unless the party is fully and completely involved. It is far too important a decision to be done in any other way. We will proceed with care once this report is published.'[90]

Minimizing divisions amongst Cabinet ministers and the wider PLP was the leadership's priority whilst also avoiding accusations of reneging on its commitment to hold a referendum on electoral reform. A conference vote against PR and in favour of FPTP would have been a repeat situation of 1995, allowing Blair to have his hands tied by conference, permitting him to drop a commitment which threatened to split his party and Cabinet. Yet, the bigger picture for Blair was keeping open the option of bringing Liberal Democrats into government, which would have been derailed if the referendum commitment had been dropped.

Margaret Beckett, the leader of the House and therefore in control of the government's legislative programme, poured cold water on the Commission and the wider 'project' a week before the publication of the Jenkins Report. Manifesto commitments were simply a 'declaration of intent and goodwill', not a list of what the government would deliver in Parliament. 'One cannot take manifestos as being a list for the Queen's speeches.'[91] Following the publication of the Jenkins Report, Blair issued a statement: 'I welcome it warmly. The report makes a well-argued and powerful case for the system it recommends. It's very much a modification of the existing Westminster system rather than any full-blown PR system as practised in other countries.' On the one hand, Blair's response was positive, recognizing the achievement of the Commission. On the other hand, if they were hoping for a personal endorsement, they may well have been disappointed, offering no guarantee of Blair's support for reform in a future referendum. Supposedly, Blair told Cabinet ministers that only he and Jack Cunningham, minister for the Cabinet Office, were empowered to speak at length on electoral reform. Cunningham was known to be keen on electoral reform, whereas others were allowed to 'give their views if asked' but were not to campaign. According to one unnamed Cabinet minister, this was 'unsustainable' and 'all the ingredients (were) in place for a cabinet revolt.'[92] For Campbell, once it became apparent the leadership were attempting to help

Ashdown and strike the balance Blair desired, the Cabinet 'basically knew it (PR) was for the long grass'.[93]

The Jenkins Commission proposals met with strong opposition from a cross-party group including Labour backbenchers, trade unionists, Conservatives and the Institute of Directors. A press release from Labour FPTP campaign group stated: 'The proposal that 15–20 per cent of MPs should be chosen by a list system breaks the constituency link between MPs and electors.' Bell continued: 'This recommendation would add to the volatility of the electoral system by institutionalising tactical voting and making coalition government inevitable.' Channel 4 conducted a poll of Labour's Campaign Group, finding four-fifths thought voting reform could produce a split within the Labour Party and the formation of a breakaway party. Ken Jackson considered Jenkins to be 'irrelevant' to the concerns of the British electorate. 'Labour will win the next election by delivering what it promised, not by appeasing the Liberals. The government was elected to reform the welfare state, improve our schools and rebuild the NHS – it must not allow Liberals to hijack its agenda for Britain.'[94] It was reported in the *Financial Times* that at least 100 Labour backbenchers were making common cause with the Tory party and trade unionists to block the changes,[95] highlighting a significant section of the Labour Party were manoeuvring to ensure the proposals were rejected.

A parliamentary debate took place in the House of Commons on 5 November 1998. Straw opened the debate and only offered faint-praise. The Report had 'a number of important points of detail … to be resolved', a task which 'would plainly take time'. Straw reiterated that 'the process certainly could not be completed before the next general election' and that the government 'will not rush into holding a referendum'. There was also the need to study the Neill Committee's report on Party funding and the wider constitutional changes enacted by the Labour government.[96] Straw's comments suggest that any government impetus for reform was on the wane, with the Home Secretary willing to bury PR behind other matters. Straw had damned Jenkins with faint praise.

Then followed the opportunity for Labour backbenchers to pass judgement: Gerald Kaufman considered the report to be 'glutinously euphuistic as well as being intellectually shoddy'; with the effect of AV+ being fewer Labour seats and 'Lord Jenkins's own party will enjoy the greatest enhancement.' In a referendum the Labour Party would be split. Kaufman offered eight reasons why the Jenkins Commission should be rejected: hopelessly complicated, complex and confusing ballot paper, self-contradictory report, arbitrary top-up mechanism, disparately sized and disparately elected top-up constituencies, potentially insoluble problem of filling vacant top-up seats, FPTP delivers on its professed benefits and the presence of an inbuilt bias against Labour in AV+.[97]

Giles Radice entered parliament as 'an unquestioning supporter of first past the post' yet changed his mind for three main reasons: the Thatcher government was elected on a percentage in the low forties, FPTP is unfair towards the Liberals and Labour's inability to win seats in the South of England.[98] Anne Campbell, MP for Cambridge, desired a 'fairer' voting system under which 'Parliament better represents the views of the voters' believing 'a large proportion of votes do not count'. This has resulted in tactical voting which was 'unfair to the Conservative Party' in 1997 but could 'equally be unfair to other parties' in subsequent elections. 'The adversarial system is extremely off-putting to a large proportion of the electorate, particularly women.' Moreover, 'There is no room in the system for taking on board someone else's view, or to consider a range of opinion.'[99]

Tony Benn MP affirmed:

> The idea that every Liberal or Labour voter supports every item of Liberal or Labour party policy is absolute nonsense. People want to be represented. Introducing proportionality completely destroys the idea of representation … (leading) to people being governed by a Government whom nobody had voted for, because nobody would know the basis of the coalition on polling day. At least the coalitions of the parties are transparent: people can see them developing and know what they are voting for and what their own Member thinks … The idea that the parliamentary Labour party would go through the Lobby to destroy 50 of its own Members … is ludicrous. People ask whether the proposals would lead to a coalition; but they are all about getting a coalition.[100]

Roger Godsiff supported the AV recommendation but not the top-up element as in Birmingham where the Liberal Democrats polled 11.8 per cent they would have won an extra seat. 'It is illogical. If one wants to give more seats to the Liberals, so be it … but it is nonsense to give them localised democratic legitimacy in this way.'[101] Martin Salter MP also supported electoral reform but wished to maintain the constituency link. Salter believed 'that the system is a recipe for civil war inside the Labour Party. The constituencies of many Labour Members are surrounded by those of other Labour Members. Will we spend the next three, four, five or eight years deciding which of our number will be chopped? I think not. This system is not a recipe for a cohesive parliamentary party'.[102] Bell considered Jenkins was 'trying to increase the number of Liberal Democrat Members of Parliament'.

> FPTP 'has given us stable government. It gives us the constituency link … it provides accountability. It also gives us the doctrine of mandate … Every party puts forward its proposals in a general election and the country votes on them. The manifesto is there; we are there to fulfil the manifesto commitments. If we fail, we should say why. If we are not successful, the public have a chance to turn us out'.[103]

Richard Burden, MP for Northfield, supported Jenkins arguing that the constituency link was maintained, the top-up list will empower voters and 'coalitions are good or bad depends not on the electoral system, but on whether the electorate gives a clear view and whether the coalitions are honest, open and transparent'.[104] Robert Wareing, MP, considered 'PR would mean coalitions being cobbled together in back rooms by politicians. It is an electoral system for politicians' whereas FPTP 'is an electoral system for the people of this country'. Furthermore, it would not be the case that the Liberal Democrats would support the Labour Party and he asked the question who would give way for Ashdown to have a seat in the Cabinet.[105] Claire Ward, MP for Watford, in all her years campaigning for the Labour Party had not come across a Labour voter who was voting Labour in order for them to change the electoral system. 'The electorate vote for a party and a candidate to form a Government' and people wanted a 'Labour government implementing their policies, not forming a coalition with the Liberal Democrats'.[106]

Jenkins for the 'long grass'

Over the thirteen years of a Labour government, no referendum on the electoral system materialized and Jenkins was 'kicked into the long grass'. The reasons for this are varied. Mandelson cites the example of the referenda in

Scotland and Wales as a cause of retreating enthusiasm. 'Both of which had been won' writes Mandelson, 'but by an extremely narrow margin in Wales, Tony's appetite for a further public vote was waning'.[107] Furthermore, the Labour Party was elected on a manifesto commitment to hold a referendum on the United Kingdom's adoption of the euro currency. If Blair was 'worried about the obstacles to holding and winning a referendum on the single currency', thought Mandelson, 'he knew that those to remaking Britain's voting system were likely to prove even more difficult'.[108] Moreover, if the Labour government were willing to hold a UK-wide referendum on the electoral system, then the calls to hold a referendum on the single currency would have likely increased, thus pressurizing the government into holding a potentially divisive referendum for both Party and country.

Blair had informed Ashdown prior to the publication of Jenkins that he would be unable to deliver PR before the next general election. Blair outlined his reasoning: 'there was so much constitutional change going through we had to watch out for overload, added to which we needed to see how it worked elsewhere', touching on the earlier theme that 'enough is enough'. Blair 'was not convinced and in any case could not get it through Cabinet' as he was isolated. Campbell also claims that the media 'thought we were going to kick it out'.[109] Opposition within the Cabinet and the wider PLP was considerable. Joining Prescott was Beckett, Straw and Blunkett. Exercising his authority as a high-profile Cabinet minister would have weakened Blair's position. At the Labour Party Conference in 2000, Prescott scorned links with the Liberal Democrats and attempted to bury PR. 'Put it [PR] in a boat and send it away with the Lib/Labs' and Prescott had 'seen nothing [in the 1970s] or nothing since that convinces me that PR is in the nation's interests of stable government'.[110]

The lack of support in the Cabinet and the dominance of those hostile to reform meant there was a lack of high-profile pro-reform ministers and MPs who could pressurize Blair, convince fellow MPs and build support for the movement away from FPTP. Robin Cook – famously described as being in 'a minority of one'[111] – had other PR sympathizers in the Cabinet, including Mo Mowlem, the Northern Ireland secretary, along with Chris Smith, the culture secretary, and therefore was not a lone voice. Baroness Armstrong deemed that although Cook was very knowledgeable and intellectual, he was never a 'clubbable person'. Therefore, he was 'not a good champion of the cause as he could not persuade his colleagues it was a good idea'. In addition, Armstrong, who joined the Cabinet in 2001, could not recall anyone else who shared Cook's enthusiasm for reform until Alan Johnson joined the Cabinet much later.[112] For Mandelson, Blair 'had not convinced enough people that this was a good thing to do in principle and therefore when the electoral need disappeared the support that existed for it disappeared as well'.[113] Colleagues, therefore, had not been convinced on an intellectual level. Moreover, with each Cabinet minister focusing on their own department and facing the practical constraints of holding high office, a limited amount of time could be spent promoting electoral reform.

At a Cabinet meeting in early 1999 Campbell recorded Dobson and Blunkett stating that 'people were not sure what the purpose of the Libs strategy was, and David was unsure our people meant it when they said they wanted a new politics'.[114] It was also 'incomprehensible' for some, deemed Mandelson, that after winning an historic landslide victory 'we should contemplate dealing away cabinet seats on the hypothesis that it might help keep the Tories from returning to power ten years down the road'. Having won such a big majority, and given the poor state of the Conservative Party, there was little prospect of defeat in the foreseeable future. Mandelson also places some of the blame on Ashdown, who overlooked a workable deal by insisting on increased seats in the Cabinet, coalition and a proportional voting system.[115]

Whilst Mandelson claims he was in favour of 'the project', a different picture emerges in the *Ashdown Diaries*. By July 1998 Mandelson expressed his two main concerns. Firstly, it will not be viewed as like-minded people coming together but as an attempt to create an even greater hegemony. Secondly, the Jenkins proposals will divide the Cabinet. In Mandelson's mind, there was the problem of how the British public would perceive coalition and how Blair would get this through the Cabinet, especially before the agreed November 1998 timetable. Furthermore, according to Roger Liddle, it was Mandelson who 'has been trying to persuade Blair that he can't win a referendum on PR' and had stated it could not be won in September.[116]

Mandelson replied in *The Times*, acknowledging that Ashdown blamed him for blocking the switch to PR. However, Mandelson was only prepared to support the switch to PR if this was the prime minister's will.

In the event it was not. To Ashdown this looked pusillanimous. But the problem was that Blair was far from convinced either that PR was desirable (because of the political instability it brings) or that the public would go for it in a referendum. A referendum vote lost would have meant losing the issue for a generation or more. Is this what Ashdown wanted to risk, we kept asking?

Blair maintained that if the Liberal Democrats were to become a party of government, they must have firm policies on economic and social issues, not just constitutional reform and PR. However, Blair continued to engage Ashdown in Blair's opinion of what the 'project' was about: 'An approach to politics based on co-operation and partnership rather than tribalism or electoral mechanics … Ashdown on the other hand, insisted that PR was the *sine quo non* of enduring co-operation.'[117]

Domestic and foreign affairs also prompted Blair to move away from PR. The Labour government had encountered difficulties with other European leaders whose coalition partners in their own country prevented them from taking a hard line over Kosovo. Campbell observed the problems facing Schroeder, the German chancellor, and how in part this was caused by their political system which was a recipe for weakened leaders. This view was reinforced every time Campbell met Schroeder.[118] Mandelson reflected on the importance of continental politics on Blair's attitude. Unlike Campbell, Germany provided a good example of coalitions working, but Blair pointed to other examples, such as Belgium 'which he thinks produces a complete mess'.[119]

Elsewhere across Great Britain, AMS in Scotland and Wales had denied the Labour Party a majority in both devolved assemblies. Blair was said to be annoyed by the behaviour of the Liberal Democrats in Scotland, particularly in relation to tuition fees in coalition talks.[120] This played into the hands of those who were already suspicious of the opportunism of the Liberal Democrats, witnessing first-hand their ability to hamstring the Labour Party, something in their mind would happen if PR was adopted at Westminster. Additionally, the European elections – the first UK-wide election to be held under PR – took place in June 1999, resulting in Labour's representation reducing from sixty-two to twenty-nine, an election in which the Labour Party had finished second behind the Conservatives. A poll of 150 Labour MPs for BBC One programme *On the Record* in September 1998 had shown 58 per cent in favour of the new European electoral system. The Sunday following the European elections, this had reduced to 43 per cent, with a majority now in favour of returning to FPTP.[121]

Internally, the opposition appeared to be mounting against abandoning FPTP. A consultation with rank-and-file Labour Party members had produced 1,800 responses; 75 per cent were in favour of retaining FPTP, while 25 per cent backed AV+. Margaret McDonagh, then Labour Party general secretary and known supporter of FPTP, believed that the Liberal Democrats were failing to woo Conservative supporters. Without the electoral benefit of Liberal Democrats undermining the Conservative Party the case of working with the Liberal Democrats was limited.[122] Therefore, the referendum pledge should be dropped. However, publishing the results was claimed to be disingenuous: many of the 1,500 submissions received were postcards printed by the AEEU, a trade union that backed FPTP, and officials had analysed not all submissions. In addition, McDonagh opposed PR, leading the *Guardian* to ponder whether it was a calculated leak by Labour.[123] Given the overall lack of responses, it could be argued the 'rank-and-file' had displayed apathy towards the issue. The GMB Union also attempted to thwart a manifesto commitment appearing at the 2001 general election by submitting an amendment to the National Policy Forum.[124]

The lack of enthusiasm for reform was such that the 2001 Labour Party manifesto commitment on proportional representation was buried behind other constitutional changes already made by the Labour government.[125]

Summary

Reforming FPTP had underlying importance for the relationship between the Labour Party and the Liberal Democrats, specifically Blair and Ashdown. PR was the mechanism, in Ashdown's opinion, that would ensure the Liberal Democrats could survive during unpopular periods for the junior partner in government, allowing for continued support towards a Labour government whilst also allowing for a more open and pluralistic British politics. Indeed, Ashdown emphasized the introduction of PR that his position as leader of the Liberal Democrats was reliant on Labour delivering such a pledge, providing him with a policy concession to appease both MPs and supporters.

For Blair, a coalition – whether a loose arrangement or with Liberal Democrats in the Cabinet – offered political and ideological benefits. Politically, Blair was unsure whether he would achieve a parliamentary majority – a view he held up to the last few days of polling – and wanted to be able to offer the Liberal Democrats something should a hung parliament emerge. Eighteen years of opposition had fuelled questions of whether Labour could ever win again. For critics of Blair's strategy, they sought to remind him of Callaghan's experience of the Lib–Lab Pact. Yet, Blair wanted to bind the Liberal Democrats into a position where they would back the Labour government on most policies, not just the constitutional reform agenda but health and education, thus preventing them peeling off and resorting to typical 'Lib Demery' and opportunism. Such a tactic would avoid the situation whereby both the Liberal Democrats and the Conservatives could attack the Labour government over the lifetime of the parliament, especially once the honeymoon period had worn off and the government was becoming unpopular. In addition, it would allow Blair to marginalize the left wing of the Labour Party and the trade union movement, showing the electorate that he was a 'centrist' and willing to work with the centre; a visible break from 'Old Labour'.

Theoretically, Blair saw merit in the 'progressive left' thesis, subscribing to a more pluralistic vision of the British left. Personally and politically, Blair aligned closely to the social-liberal wing of the Liberal Democrats believing their views overlapped, supporting a broadening of cooperation within Labour's 'big tent' of support in the country and Parliament. The project was worth pursuing for the reasons outlined above, yet Blair had reservations about PR. Whilst it opened up an avenue to the Liberal Democrats it was not a policy concession he was willing to make, due to a combination of political reservations and the influence of high-profile opponents of PR in the Cabinet and the wider PLP. PR and coalition with the Liberal Democrats was a minority pursuit, and while figures like Tony Wright thought it was an historic opportunity to forge a durable centre-left hegemony,[126] the existential reason for committing to one or both did not exist. With the Conservatives in disarray, it appeared Labour would remain in office for a prolonged period. The 1997 general election result had given the Labour Party no cause to seek the support of the Liberal Democrats, and after winning the greatest victory in

Labour Party history, Blair was not willing to push his party towards doing a deal with the Liberal Democrats.

Labour fulfilled their manifesto commitment insofar as a Commission was formed to examine the electoral system. Jenkins, unlike Plant, was from the outset an overtly political exercise, designed to keep the possibility of a coalition alive, delivering the commitments Blair had made to Ashdown in private. Baroness Gould thought, 'The Jenkins Commission was fundamentally different to the Plant Report. Whereas Jenkins started from the premise of change, Plant did not.'[127] The differing objectives of the reports and backgrounds of the two men influenced their findings. Plant with his academic expertise in political philosophy sought to address questions of representation and democracy, whereas Jenkins was concerned with arriving at a political end, namely an alternative electoral system.

The decision to appoint Jenkins – who had a personal relationship with Blair – was a political move designed to reach out beyond 'tribal' Labour. From the outset, it left many in Labour uncomfortable as a politician who had broken away from them in the 1980s had now been charged with devising a system that would, in all likelihood, reduce the number of Labour MPs. Indeed, Jenkins continues to divide opinion. The academic, Kevin Hickson, writes that the Labour Party moved over time in the direction of Jenkins, embracing pro-Europeanism, constitutional reform and cultural liberalism, all of which have not done the Party any electoral favours.[128] From within Labour, Spellar urged those to reject Jenkins's view of realignment, reminding readers that whilst Jenkins wrote a biography of Gladstone, Crosland wrote *The Future of Socialism*.[129]

Straw's terms of reference for the Commission were irreconcilable, and although little attention was paid to these once the Commission had embarked on its work, it suggested the government had asked the Commission to deliver the impossible. As Lipsey affirmed, the Commission was not there to 'square the circle' and address theoretical issues, but to devise a system that could be put before the British people in a UK-wide referendum. Indeed, it was hoped the system chosen offered the greatest chance of success, rather than being the 'best' form of PR. The system devised was AV+, a variation of AMS, with only a small number of top-up seats based on a county system. It was not wasted on Labour's supporters of FPTP that the main beneficiary of the new system would have been the Liberal Democrats.

Whilst much discussion took place on the prospects of closer relations between the two parties after May 1997, both the 'project' and the introduction of the Jenkins proposals disappeared into the 'long grass'. Had Blair chosen to pursue his relationship with Ashdown and introduce PR, it risked splitting the Cabinet, the wider PLP and the trade unions for the sake two issues that many in the Labour movement did not much care for. In the process, Blair risked damaging his position over an issue which was not deemed a priority and for which there was no political necessity. Consequently, as Labour and the Liberal Democrats drifted apart throughout the parliament, the possibility of a realignment of the British left faded along with the prospect of PR at Westminster.

5

The end of New Labour

The Labour Party won a historic third successive general election victory in 2005. However, Labour's third term in office would be marked by a change in leadership, with Gordon Brown replacing Tony Blair. Having long desired to become prime minister, Brown endured a challenging three years as leader, facing Cabinet resignations and in-fighting, as the Party became increasingly unpopular with the electorate in the face of the 2008 financial crash. Electoral reform returned to the fore towards the end of Labour's third term, an issue which for much of the decade had become an increasingly marginal concern, at least at Westminster. As such, this chapter charts Brown's conversion to electoral reform having long been considered a supporter of FPTP, and the five days of coalition negotiations that followed the 2010 general election, specifically Labour's attitude towards electoral reform and the idea of coalition government.

Labour's continuing scepticism

The 2005 Labour Party Manifesto stated the Party remained 'committed to reviewing the experience of the new electoral systems – introduced for the devolved administrations, the European Parliament and the London Assembly'. It also noted that the Labour Party's view remained that a referendum was 'the right way to agree any change for Westminster'.[1] The result of the 2005 general election saw the Labour Party win a majority on only 35 per cent of the vote across Great Britain and therefore a historic third-successive general election. However, in England, the Conservatives were experiencing a revival; outpolling Labour by 50,000 votes, although Labour won 286 seats to the Conservatives' 194, partly due to the smaller urban constituencies favouring

Labour. A brief outpouring emanated from electoral reformers in the weeks following the election, but many of Labour's 'big hitters' sought to dispel calls for PR.

Straw dismissed those in the days following the 2005 general election, particularly the Liberal Democrats, calling for PR as it was not the panacea for all ills and the Labour Party had won the 2005 general election 'fair and square.' Whilst there had been a decline in the vote share for the two major parties and a case for AV could be made, FPTP was still preferable with the alternative being small parties on a considerably smaller vote share wielding disproportionate influence. The winner in any system necessarily gains much more power than those in opposition, and FPTP had two major strengths: the constituency link and the 'contract' between electors and parties in the form of the manifesto. 'Our people want strong majority government', wrote Straw, 'not the mush of PR.'[2] Elsewhere Straw affirmed PR would allow 'weak governments with limited mandates to hold on to power for decades and takes away the fundamental power of ordinary people to remove them'. Consequently, 'PR for the Commons would undermine our democracy, the effectiveness of our government and the relationship between electors and elected.'[3] Lord Falconer, the Lord Chancellor, also dismissed calls for reform, as there was no groundswell for change. Furthermore, 'the consequences of change would be significant for the way we are governed without the clarity of who is in power', a result of politicians becoming preoccupied with establishing coalitions.[4]

Yet in Scotland, Labour had been navigating coalition with the Liberal Democrats since 1999, and this continued after the 2003 Holyrood election. The stronger showing for the Scottish Liberal Democrats in 2003 brought the matter of electoral reform for Scottish local government to the fore. It had been raised after the devolution referendum in 1997; there was a Commission led by Sir Neil McIntosh which reported in 1999, and a working group led by Richard Kerley on 'renewing local democracy' was setup by the Labour-Liberal Democrat coalition, publishing its report in June 2000. The group recommended STV as it met the two key criteria of proportionality and councillor-ward link. However, the increased pressure and presence of the Scottish Liberal Democrats after 2003 and their influence over Scottish Labour meant that legislation was passed in the new parliament with local government elections to be held under STV in 2007. Following these elections, Labour retained overall control of two councils – Glasgow and North Lanarkshire – whereas it had had overall control of thirteen of Scotland's thirty-two councils before the election.[5] John Spellar later reflected that the change had led to 'damaging consequences', surrendering control to the advantage of the SNP, ruing the lack of thought about the impact that such systems have on the Party in reality.[6]

In January 2008 the Labour government, as promised, produced its review of the electoral systems used in the UK. This largely factual report drew attention to the problems associated with each electoral system and did not make any firm recommendations for reform.[7] The House of Lords debated the review and the government response did not suggest that change to the method of electing the House of Commons was imminent. The minister, Lord Hunt of Kings Heath, recognized the advantages of PR but added, 'The disadvantages seem to be pretty fundamental as well.' He acknowledged that the existing electoral system delivered 'core accountability' and was believed to deliver a legitimate outcome.[8]

A noteworthy aside is Hattersley's reasoning for coming out in favour of PR during the Labour government. During Labour's first term Hattersley continued to profess the virtues of FPTP, dismissing Ashdown and the Liberal Democrats as 'redundant'.[9] On the matter of the electoral system, the oft mentioned claim of 'fair voting' was 'inaccurate, impertinent and an arrogant attempt to end the argument before it begins'. He rubbished the claim that democracy depends on parliament becoming a mathematical reflect of the percentage of votes cast as a 'simplistic absurdity'. Moreover, 'the notion that the smallest party, in a three-party system, should decide which of its more popular competitors forms the government is equally indefensible'.[10] Notably, 'for Labour it would only mean the loss of what remains of its socialist identity' keeping 'Labour in the soggy centre for ever'.[11]

However, Hattersley warmed to PR, a result of Blair and the policies of New Labour. He believed it would allow a more social democratic party to flourish, not to replace the Labour Party but to pull it to the left. 'The attraction of a new voting system is the effect that new parties would have on Blair and his successors', allowing 'one or two new parties to flourish might produce what I hope is still possible in this country – a genuine social democratic government'.[12] Additionally, as the country had become more fractured and the political system had become multi-party, 'whether I liked it or not, the future of this country would be coalition government'. It would be 'better for people to know there was going to be a coalition government to begin with'. Under PR, the electorate would understand from the outset that 'they were not voting for a party that would win the election, they were voting for a part of a government'. Importantly, PR was a signalling that this country now accepts coalitions, making clear the 'limitations on our power before we started'.[13] Hattersley's change of mind emphasizes how fluid attitudes towards electoral reform are.

Brown's 'death-bed' conversion to electoral reform

Having long been considered a FPTP supporter, Brown announced that he would pursue electoral reform as prime minister. Consequently, it prompted questions of whether the basis for the reform was damascene or political expediency, genuinely convinced on the merits of reform or looking ahead towards a potentially difficult general election, hung parliament and coalition bargaining.

From the beginning of his premiership, Brown displayed an interest in constitutional reform. In his inaugural speech as leader of the Labour Party, he declared he wanted a new constitutional settlement for Britain, granting more power to parliament, local communities and the people. This, at least in part, was designed to please the Liberal Democrats. The reforms ranged from limiting the executive's royal prerogative powers, including the decision to declare war, making the executive more accountable, increasing public participation and considering a British Bill of Rights and Responsibilities. The ideas were to be found in a document called *The Governance of Britain*, with the foreword speaking of an intention to forge 'a new relationship between government and the citizen, and begin the journey towards a new constitutional settlement'.[14] There was only a brief mention of electoral reform, claiming that the government was still reviewing the different voting systems introduced for regional elections following devolution, all of which would contribute to the debate on electoral reform.

However, as a gesture reminiscent of the Labour–Liberal Democrat talks in the 1990s, Brown talked of a 'government of all the talents' offering Ashdown the position of secretary of state to Northern Ireland. Indeed, Brown's attempts to 'reach out' included the suggestion of coalition to the then leader of the Liberal Democrats, Sir Menzies Campbell. Three Liberal Democrat peers – Lord Lester, Lady Neuberger and Baroness Williams – accepted advisory posts, whilst retaining their independence and keeping the Liberal Democrat whip.[15] Ashdown records that he could not observe collective responsibility in a Brown Cabinet and without the promise of PR the Liberal Democrats were being offered a 'deadly suicide pill'. Brown thought such a move would pave the way for Liberal Democrat–Labour relations in the future, while on the matter of opposing this kind of government in 1997 it was because he could 'not trust the Lib Dems in government then'.[16]

Brown mooted the idea of electoral reform in June of 2009 in a statement to the House of Commons containing other constitutional reforms. In the Commons, Brown affirmed that he still valued the constituency link and change should only be pursued if there was broad agreement in the country, 'that it would strengthen our democracy and our politics by improving the effectiveness and legitimacy of both Government and Parliament and by enhancing the level and quality of representation and public engagement.'[17]

The commitment to hold a referendum on AV was made at the Labour Party Conference in September 2009.[18] In a speech to the Institute for Public Policy Research (IPPR) Brown made the case for AV, arguing that it would re-engage the public, enhance the mandate of MPs and provide greater choice. Brown committed to arguing and campaigning for such a change, and in 'moving towards a more democratic form of election' the hope was 'making parliament itself better reflect the people it serves.' AV 'offers a system where the British people can, if they so choose, be more confident that their MP truly represents them, while at the same time remaining directly accountable to them'. The referendum – should a Labour government be elected – was to be held before the end of October 2011.[19] However, at the meeting of the PLP, the veteran left-wing MP, Chris Mullin, records how there was opposition not just to incorporating a referendum into the Bill, but 'a host of objections to any change whatsoever', it was an irrelevance and 'stinks of desperation and self-interest'. Mullin concluded: 'The Parliamentary Labour Party is really a most conservative institution.'[20]

The commitment was in part a response to the revelations released in the *Daily Telegraph* about MPs' expenses which was 'a godsend for electoral reformers'.[21] FPTP, it was argued, had led to a culture of distant and remote MPs, a consequence of safe seats, leading MPs to assume immunity from criticism and wrongdoing. On the other hand, a proportional electoral system would make MPs more accountable to their constituents. However, not all members took so kindly to the suggestion that they were corrupt and that corruption resulted from the electoral system. Clive Betts, MP, rejected the argument that there was any clamour for reform amongst the electorate. Whilst voters wanted expenses to be cleaned up, they did not think PR was the answer.[22] Tom Harris, then Labour MP for Glasgow South asked rhetorically whether the 'stainless reputation of Italian politicians to the fact that the Italians have proportional representation?' Harris thought it was 'utter nonsense' and a 'complete myth to think the answer to the expenses scandal was changing the electoral system'.[23]

Ed Balls, a key Brown ally, was unconvinced on adding the AV referendum amendment to the Bill. He was concerned about the level of support and its benefit for the Party in the lead up to a general election.[24] Balls, whilst claiming to have advocated reform since 2005 for reasons to do with turnout and participation, was thought to be a sceptic on electoral reform. One senior minister outlined the 'credibility' problem facing Labour. 'How do you think it's going to look if we are fiddling the rules on how to get rid of us just weeks before an election?'[25] In an interview with the *New Statesman* in the days before the 2010 general election Balls dismissed PR, in what was thought to be a direct riposte to other Cabinet ministers, including Ben Bradshaw, Alan Johnson and John Denham. 'PR leads to a politics of behind-closed doors deals after elections. It makes it harder to make long-term decisions and it gives more power to small parties.' As a matter of principle Balls did not think 'coalition governments are better' as they are 'not the British way of doing government'. Importantly, he could still work with the Liberal Democrats although a realignment of the left was not the correct course for the Labour Party. 'Some people have said that it would be the fulfilment of New Labour to enter a coalition with the Liberals.' Yet for Balls, 'the whole point of New Labour was to show we could govern for the whole country ... as the Labour Party'[26] returning to themes outlined by Blair's dismissal of PR in the 1980s and early 1990s.

Pressure from within

Alan Johnson, a vocal advocate of electoral reform, wrote that there should be a referendum on the same day as the next general election with the electorate asked whether they want AV+, the system proposed by Jenkins. Furthermore, it was reported that Johnson would trigger a by-election and stand on a platform in favour of PR. Johnson's position was partly influenced by the 'safe seat' mentality, which, in his opinion, ought 'at least be an aspect of the accusation that MPs became careless in their expenses claim and dismissive of their electorate.'[27] Johnson admitted he had visited Brown and the prime minister was 'seized by AV+' with the matter being discussed on a subcommittee. However, the consensus that emerged was due to the influence of 'people like Peter Hain, [who] thought that it should be AV, without the Plus'. AV+ would have involved a redrawing of the boundaries and a reduction in constituencies, consequently '*real politik*', which led to a coalescing 'around what was possible and that was AV'.[28]

Ben Bradshaw recalls there 'being widespread support for it as a policy' around the Cabinet.[29] Seldon and Lodge record that within the Cabinet, Jim Murphy and Andy Burnham were against, whereas those in favour included Ed and David Miliband, Johnson, Hain, Bradshaw and Andrew Adonis. Consequently, Bradshaw's assertion that there was widespread support for AV appears questionable. Seldon and Lodge list only six members of the Cabinet who were willing to support the proposal, suggesting that only a minority of Cabinet ministers backed AV and therefore Bradshaw overstated the level of support. Straw reportedly took soundings of the PLP and found that all the Scottish MPs totally against as electoral reform would damage Labour in Scotland. By this point, Labour's dominance in Scotland had come under threat from the SNP, who had formed a minority government in Holyrood in 2007, the same year STV was introduced for Scottish local government.

As for Johnson's idea of holding a referendum on the same day as the general election, the Cabinet office informed Brown that there was not the parliamentary time to make that possible. Furthermore, there was doubt a referendum could be won, and 'no' votes could harm Labour support. Nick Brown, the chief whip, steered Labour's Constitutional Reform and

Governance Bill through the Commons with only three Labour MPs voting against. Allegedly, Nick Brown informed sceptics not to worry as it would not be enacted before the general election.[30] For critics, the Act contained little in the way of a 'more participatory, pluralistic form of politics' as it sought to address specific issues and was overtaken by high-profile events. 'Cumulatively, these reforms did little to challenge the continuing asymmetry of centralised power that the core executive commanded.'[31]

Johnson rejected the accusation that the policy change on electoral reform was based on political calculations and the desire to secure the support of the Liberal Democrats. Instead, Johnson was 'simply a supporter of getting rid of a system that does not empower the voter'. Straw was said to support AV, although not PR which would lead to backroom deals; and Alistair Darling was said to be open to the idea.[32] Legislating in 2010, considered Bradshaw, would 'expose the Tories for what they are – the no change status quo party', allowing for policy differentiation between Labour and the Conservatives. Legislating for AV now, according to the *Guardian*, was a move backed by Denham and Hain as it would attract the support of the Liberal Democrats, providing practical electoral benefits.[33] Interestingly, Bradshaw, who would lead Labour Yes to AV in 2011, stated he also favoured AV+, as it synthesizd the constituency link and greater proportionality. In addition, it would restore trust, make MPs more accountable, empower citizens, produce a representative system, all things that AV fails to do.[34]

Progress, the Blairite wing of the Labour Party, along with Labour's Campaign for Electoral Reform (LCER), gathered the signatures of thirty-five prospective parliamentary candidates (PPC) in a letter to Brown expressing their belief that Labour will only win if a referendum on electoral reform was offered on the same day as the general election. A 'referendum on polling day on a system that delivers real voter choice', it was claimed, 'would see hundreds of Liberal Democrats switching to Labour, hundreds more stay-at-home Labour supporters coming out to vote for the government and every Tory opponent on the back foot'.[35] Compass, the cross-party anti-Conservative think tank, deemed that a referendum on FPTP contained many advantages for the Labour Party: Cameron would represent the status quo, be on the defensive, help build a progressive coalition, voters would be more likely to turn out and vote Labour, and it could be Brown's 'Clause IV' moment.[36]

The attempt to win support of wavering Liberal Democrat voters was, as the academic John Curtice claimed, the more instrumental reason behind Brown's conversion to electoral reform. For all the talk about political reform and changing the way politics is conducted, the opinion polls were pointing towards a hung parliament and the Conservatives were starting from a low point, requiring a significant swing to achieve a majority of one. Therefore the Labour Party, by bringing forward legislation on AV and making a manifesto commitment, had laid down a marker.[37] Furthermore, polling conducted by YouGov for the Electoral Reform Society in August 2009 had showed that one in three Liberal Democrat voters would be willing to consider switching his or her vote to Labour if the Party delivered on an electoral reform referendum[38] suggesting this policy change could win essential votes. Mullin recorded in his diary that the policy won't save the Party from defeat but might save it from ruin.[39]

Therefore, a commitment to a referendum on AV entailed practical political benefits by attracting wavering Liberal Democrat voters, placing the Conservatives on the back foot and preventing a landslide defeat. Charles Clarke considered that Brown 'wanted to hold it over as a point of negotiation with the Liberal Democrats' implying he was already looking to a post-election situation where coalition-building was necessary. However, 'all the measures he announced in terms of constitutional reform when he became Prime Minister, almost all, just faded away'.[40] Mandelson, who Brown had brought back into government, outlined Brown's issues over these constitutional matters. Firstly, 'the conversion looked a little belated, a little shallow'. Secondly, 'there was a feeling that it would be difficult to get the Party to campaign enthusiastically on these issues'. Thirdly, 'there was the issue of how that would leave his position if he were defeated in the referendum, either on all the issues or on one or two of them. Would he then need to resign?'[41]

Nick Clegg, the leader of the Liberal Democrats, dismissed Labour's commitment to AV. Given the underlying reasons were to appeal to the Liberal Democrats and the likelihood of a hung parliament in 2010 – making Clegg kingmaker – it somewhat failed in its objective. The NOtoAV campaign would tirelessly repeat his response in the *Independent* during the AV Referendum, 2011, namely that he was 'not going to settle for a miserable little compromise thrashed out by the Labour Party'.[42] Clegg had to consider the pressures facing his own party and he was not the first leader of the Liberal

Democrats to be approached by Labour with promises of electoral reform. Had he been seen to be aligning with the Labour Party, it had the potential to lose right-leaning Liberal Democrats to the Conservatives. On the other hand, had Clegg been perceived to be aligned with the Conservatives he risked losing the Labour-leaning voters willing to support the Liberal Democrats. Additionally, electoral reform was a key policy for the Liberal Democrats and, with the Labour Party moving on to Liberal Democrat territory, AV had to be dismissed as an insignificant reform, to ensure that the Liberal Democrats retained their 'radical' stance on electoral reform by offering more than any other mainstream party.

Prior to the general election there had been indications that Clegg wished to keep his distance from the Labour Party. He had written an article in 2009 for *Demos* claiming that this was the 'Liberal moment', Labour was out of touch and morally bankrupt and all 'progressives' should fall under the Liberal Democrat banner,[43] a stance unlikely to have endeared him to Labour. Importantly, with the polls pointing to a hung parliament, Clegg affirmed in that situation he would consult with the largest party first, in all likeliness the Conservative Party. Moreover, he did not 'think at a time when people will have voted for massive change it would be acceptable to the public to have no change at all, to have the same person in Number 10'.[44] Clegg was implying either Brown had to step down for the formation of a Lab–Lib Pact or a complete change of government was required, namely a Conservative or Conservative-led government.

Adonis – a former Liberal Democrat councillor, parliamentary candidate and importantly for Brown, someone who maintained good relations with his former party – wrote in the *Independent* at the start of the general election campaign that Labour and the Liberal Democrats were 'united by a common antipathy to Conservative values'. Indeed, Labour and the Liberal Democrats shared several policies on public services, constitutional reform, equal rights, fair taxation and Europe, and 'philosophically it was nonsense to pretend that the Lib Dems ... are equidistant between left and right'. Only a Labour government could implement Liberal Democrat policies with policy disagreements revolving around PR for the House of Commons. However, Labour's commitment to a referendum on AV was a case of 'the nature of reform rather than the principle'.[45] Two journalists, Adam Boulton and Joey

Jones, view this as Adonis laying out Labour's agenda for coalition negotiations with the Liberal Democrats.[46]

The 2010 Labour Party Manifesto, written by Ed Miliband, included a manifesto commitment to hold a referendum on AV.[47] Placing the issue in the hands of the electorate, rather than a firm commitment to reform, was a useful party management tool particularly considering the impending general election, a tactic deployed by previous Labour leaders. Harris thought this a mistake, deeming electoral reform a 'complete red herring' and 'one motivation for having constitutional reform should never be electoral gain'. The people will 'not believe that the only chance of winning the next election is to promise some form of electoral reform'. The Labour Party after thirteen years of a government 'should be able to stand on its own platform, own policies and win a fourth election'.[48] Having spent thirteen years in government, Harris considered, the Labour Party had a record of achievement it could defend on social and economic matters – the 'bread-and-butter' concerns of voters – rather than seeking to muster a few extra votes on a niche issue.

The 2010 general election and coalition negotiations

It was widely predicted from inside and outside of Labour that it would be a very poor night for the Party. Labour had accepted it would lose the general election, with the question being 'by how much'. The Brown government had become increasingly unpopular due to the financial crash, in-fighting with Cabinet resignations and rumours of leadership coups, and the alleged tiredness produced by thirteen years of government. Brown's ratings as prime minister were poor. Despite these beneficial factors for the Conservatives, their low starting point required them to achieve a significant swing across Great Britain to achieve a majority of one. Indeed, an 11-point lead was required for a bare majority and if the Labour Party could have been on the same vote share as the Conservatives, they would have returned to Westminster with more MPs.[49] The 7-point lead left the Conservatives shy of a majority and produced the first hung parliament since February 1974.

The 29 per cent of the vote received by the Labour Party was the second lowest since 1918 and compared to 2005 was a loss of 6 per cent of the national vote, resulting in a significant reduction in votes and seats. In the south, outside London, the Labour Party held only 10 out of 197 seats, described as the 'dismembering of New Labour's electoral triumph.'[50] Labour had been pushed back into its heartlands. Worryingly, since 1997 Labour had lost five million voters. The bias in the electoral system had seen the Labour Party win a majority of sixty-six in 2005 on 35 per cent of the vote, whereas the Conservatives on 36.1 per cent fell short of a majority in 2010. Yet, the Conservatives on a small increase of the vote had managed to significantly increase its number of MPs. The 65.1 per cent combined vote of Labour and the Conservatives was the lowest since 1918, beating the previous low of 67.6 per cent of the vote set in 2005. Only 210 out of the 650 MPs in 2010 secured 50 per cent of the vote or more in their constituency, 67.7 per cent had been elected on a plurality compared to 1955 when only 5.9 per cent of MPs were elected on a plurality.[51] Whilst FPTP had all but 'kicked' Labour out of office – one of the professed benefits of the system – it had not clearly facilitated a new government.

A simulation by the Electoral Reform Society predicted the Conservatives under AV would have won 281 seats (down 26), Labour 262 (up 4) and the Liberal Democrats 79 (up 22). The British Election Study simulation calculated the Liberal Democrats would have won 89 seats.[52] Such an outcome would have changed the nature of the coalition negotiations, strengthening the bargaining hand of the Liberal Democrats. Thus, the Liberal Democrats could have formed a coalition with Labour as a potential Lab–Lib coalition would have had 341 seats. Rallings and Thrasher argued that under AV many British voters would only indicate one preference, known as 'plumping' and think the Liberal Democrats would only have won fifteen more seats. Curtice maintains that the electoral benefits of AV for the Liberal Democrats would be 'modest', with 'the prospect of the occasional Conservative or Labour landslide.'[53] Yet 'modest' gains still had the potential to increase the likelihood of a hung parliament in the future and make the Liberal Democrats kingmakers. Harris raised this point during the AV referendum in 2011. Although Labour and the Liberal Democrats would have had the numbers to do a deal and therefore 'remain in power – despite losing to the Conservatives', Harris questioned, 'How can that possibly be fair or democratic?'[54]

The Liberal Democrats decision to 'go right'

The result of the general election put the onus on the Liberal Democrats to choose which of the two major political parties it would support in government. Brown, as the sitting prime minister, had the constitutional right to remain in Downing Street until the political situation became clear; either the Liberal Democrats along with the smaller parties would sustain a Labour government, or the Conservatives would form a minority government or seek to govern in coalition with the Liberal Democrats.

Supporting either party posed problems for the Liberal Democrats. Backing Labour would have meant propping up a 'tired' and defeated party, allowing an unpopular prime minister to stay in office and, due to the numbers, offered little prospect of stability. On Channel 4 News on the Monday after the election, Peter Hennessy deemed that a rainbow coalition 'would have too many moving parts'. Many within Labour were hostile to a Lab-Lib coalition, sceptical about its longevity, the high price in buying Liberal Democrat support and the concessions that would be made to minor parties. Supporting the Conservative Party – considered by many in the Liberal Democrats to be 'toxic' – would mean being in government with a party with whom they are in direct competition for votes and seats in the southwest of England and alienating many voters who had voted for the Liberal Democrats believing them to be on the 'progressive' side of politics. In the north of England – where the Liberal Democrats had replaced the Conservatives as the main opposition to Labour – they would take the punishment for government policies.

Ashdown remarked that the voters at the 2010 general election seemed to have 'invented a deliciously painful torture mechanism for the Liberal Democrats because our instincts go one way (Labour) but the mathematics go the other (Conservatives)'.[55] Whilst Ashdown considered the 'instincts' of the Liberal Democrats leant towards Labour, the years of opposition to a Labour government should not be underestimated in encouraging the Conservatives and Liberal Democrats together. Previous leaders such as Ashdown, Kennedy and Campbell may have been inclined towards Labour, yet the 'modern era' of Liberal Democrats had been upset by Labour's record on civil liberties, the environment, constitutional reform and the Iraq War. Clegg, David Laws, Jeremy Browne and Danny Alexander were part of the *Orange Book* Liberals, moving away from social liberalism towards classical liberal positions, professing the benefits of the free market rather than the state. The shift at the top of the Liberal Democrats coincided with the 'compassionate conservatism' advocated by Cameron, resulting in a policy and ideological crossover on the centre right of British politics.

Adonis later recognized the ideological overlap, considering the decision of Clegg and Laws to enter a coalition with Cameron and Osborne was not simply a matter of parliamentary arithmetic and building a coalition that could survive the full parliament, but 'was a marriage of neo-liberal minds'.[56] The influence of ideology is highlighted by the Liberal Democrats' acceptance of faster and deeper public spending cuts, a policy they had opposed during the election campaign. 'Clegg and Laws did not lead their party into coalition with the Conservatives despite Osborne austerity', wrote Adonis, 'but because of it'. Other areas of agreement included education reform, allowing parents greater influence over state school provision; public sector reform; localism; and devolution. 'It was therefore not pre-ordained that Britain should have taken the Tory road in 2010 ... the critical determinant was Nick Clegg's instinct to go Right rather than Left.'[57]

As shown, the Liberal Democrats' movement away from Labour was a process that began many years before Clegg's leadership, regularly voting against Labour and voting with the Conservatives. Notably, in 2009, the Conservatives and Liberal Democrats worked together to defeat the government over the settlement rights of the Gurkhas. Stuart states: 'It seems that long before the 2010 General Election, the Liberal Democrats had progressively fallen out of love with the Labour Party and were far more favourably predisposed towards the Conservatives.'[58] Kavanagh and Cowley argue that Labour 'underestimated the extent to which there had been a generational shift at the top of the Liberal Democrats'.[59] However, Baroness Armstrong deemed any thought of a Lab–Lib coalition ended upon Clegg winning the leadership. The divisions within the Liberals, clear to her, supplemented the belief that they would rather deal with the Conservatives.[60]

Other factors decreased the likelihood of coalition: the strained personal relationship between Brown and Clegg. Brown viewed Clegg's politics and ideological beliefs as 'largely Conservative': English, affluent public school boy and not belonging to the same political wing of the Liberal Democrats as Ashdown and Kennedy. Disparagingly, Brown had always referred to the Liberal Democrats as the 'Liberals', refusing to dignify them with full use of their name. Such difficult personal relations between the two men posed the issue of whether a government in the short term could survive with evident acrimony between the two leaders of the two parties in government.

Edgar wrote: 'The conventional wisdom about the five days is that Cameron and Clegg played their hands better than Labour.' Labour was unprepared for talks, coming to the negotiating table with the Liberal Democrats with few agreed positions. Moreover, 'the reality of the election result was that, together, the Tories and the Liberal Democrats commanded a comfortable Commons majority over all other parties, while a Labour-Lib Dem coalition would have had to rely on the fickle support of smaller parties to get its legislation through'.[61] A coalition between the Conservatives and the Liberal Democrats would produce an overall majority of eighty-three seats. For those negotiating, knowing such numbers would allow a Conservative–Liberal Democrat Coalition to pass its legislative programme for the duration of the parliament whilst allowing for rebels and marginalizing the more controversial wings of both parties. Coalition also offered the Conservative Party the route back into government after thirteen years of opposition, having not won a general election since 1992, allowing Cameron to promote a new type of open and pluralistic conservatism, representing how the party had changed from the dogmatism of the Thatcher years and was willing to listen to ideas from outside the party.

Jones deems the account given by Adonis can be termed the '"bad faith" thesis'[62] as the numbers, contrary to Edgar's view, did add up for a Labour–Liberal coalition. Gordon Brown had thought 'the key numbers were these: Labour plus Lib Dems 315; Tory 307; other parties, almost all of them more anti-Tory than anti-Labour – 28'.[63] The Social Democratic and Labour Party (SDLP) from Northern Ireland was a natural ally, so was the Green MP Caroline Lucas who would not vote for a Conservative government. There was also an Alliance MP, an ally of the Liberal Democrats and an independent Unionist, bringing a potential Lab–Lib coalition very close to the 323 mark. Furthermore, the nationalist parties could not risk a repeat of 1979 when they brought down the Labour government and ushered in a Conservative government. Additionally, triggering another election risked the electorate blaming the smaller parties for failing to act in the 'national interest' and provide the stable government the country required. Fighting another general election raised the practical issue of cost and campaign funding. Having already fought one general election and the costs incurred, parties would have been reluctant to fight a second in a short space of time.

For Brown, the prospect of doing a deal with the Liberal Democrats and relying on the support of smaller parties held out the prospect of remaining in power. He told the Cabinet which met on Monday, 11 May: 'It (was) to be an enduring progressive alliance … leading naturally to an electoral pact at the next election, with the two parties standing down in favour of each other in some seats. "This is an historic opportunity for progressive politics which may not come back for fifty years." '[64] The account given by Adonis claims that the Cabinet overwhelmingly backed Brown's plan to seek to form a coalition with the Liberal Democrats. The trade unions were also supportive: 'They are absolutely clear that we should govern with the Liberals rather than let them put the Tories in, with all that would mean for the public services and union members'.[65] David Miliband is quoted as saying there were 'grave risks – no one won, but we lost'. Nonetheless, Cameron had 'legitimised coalition government by offering one to the Lib Dems rather than just saying "I've won, you've lost" '[66] – something Salmond had done in 2007 for the Holyrood election – and as such, the Labour Party was entitled to seek to govern in coalition.

Denham considered coalition was in the best interests of the Labour Party and should be presented as 'the best attainable government'. Otherwise, the 'Tories could lock us out of power for a generation'.[67] Bradshaw concurred thinking power should not just be handed to the Tories, for Labour as the second-largest party could govern in the same fashion as Brandt and Schmidt, the 'great historic progressive German Governments'.[68] The issue of the Liberal Democrats was then raised. Mandelson, whilst supporting Brown's plan, affirmed 'the Lib Dems will need to stop being normal opportunist Lib Dems'.[69] Liam Byrne thought: 'Many of the PLP think it better to renew in opposition and they positively relish the idea of the Liberals doing a deal with the Tories.'[70] Only Burnham clearly opposed coalition. 'While we might be able to stitch something together, it won't be "renewal" and the country won't listen to us,' he said. 'The public will find it a surprise; it will build up resentment and we will find ourselves punished in an election in twelve to eighteen months' time.'[71] Burnham became the first senior minister to publicly express opposition when on *The World at One*, he declared that the Party had to 'respect the result of the general election and we can't shy away from the fact that Labour didn't win.'[72]

The other 'evident sceptics' in the Cabinet were Darling and Straw. There was the 'spectre of real problems in working with the Lib Dems in practice'. For Straw, 'We have been fighting the Lib Dems like cats and dogs.'[73] Straw fleshed out his objections in *Last Man Standing*. Brown, whilst advocating an alliance with the Liberal Democrats, was not at ease with the idea like Mandelson and Adonis. Brown 'went through the dangers to the country, and the Party, if the Tories were to take power, whether in a coalition or as a minority government, claiming that "15 million people had voted for the progressive majority"'. Yet, for Straw, Brown 'hadn't quite come to terms with the fact that we had lost the election, comprehensively, even if we'd done a lot better than most of us had feared'. Having witnessed how the Liberal Democrats 'operated institutionally', Straw was unable 'to trust them as a party'. Moreover, the numbers did not add up, having sixty fewer seats than the 'hand-to-mouth existence' of the 1974–9 Labour governments enjoyed.[74]

Straw is reported to have told Brown on Sunday, 10 May, that a period in opposition might not be bad for Labour as 'we have to accept that we lost. We need time in opposition.'[75] On the Tuesday, Sadiq Khan, Andy Burnham and Bob Ainsworth gathered in Straw's Commons room. 'We were all of one mind. A Lib-Lab coalition would not work.' Straw sent Brown a note outlining his reservations on why 'coalition with the Lib Dems would be doomed – on grounds of legitimacy, stability, and the management of the economy and public finances'. Importantly, Straw succinctly rejected the progressive-left thesis. 'The fanciful notion of a "progressive alliance"' was, in Straw's opinion, nothing more than 'arrogant nonsense' as 'there was no "Progressive Alliance" on the ballot paper'. Many of those who voted Lib Dem would have done so tactically to stop Labour, despite, not because of, the Lib Dems' policy offer.[76]

Darling questioned whether there could be an agreement on the economy, rejecting the view that Labour could put something together with the Liberal Democrats. Moreover, there was both a principled and practical objection. The principled objection was a result of Labour losing the election. 'We did not have the moral right or the high ground needed to form a government and then embark on highly contentious and deeply unpopular measures as we set about cutting borrowing.' The practical objection was

> that the numbers did not add up. Even adding the Liberal to the Labour MPs, we would still be short of a majority in the House of Commons. We would be at the mercy of the minority parties from Northern Ireland and the Scottish and Welsh Nationalists, who would be able to extract what they wanted on a daily basis.[77]

There was no harm in Labour talking to the Liberals in case their deal with the Conservatives unravelled, thought Darling, 'not being against coalitions in principle'. However this was qualified: 'In practice one involving the Labour Party was dead in the water.'[78]

Bradshaw debated who had won the election and who had legitimacy to govern with Boulton on *Sky News*. Boutlon claimed that Labour had lost the election and if the result was done on a points system – points won for votes and seats gained, points lost due to seats and votes lost – only a Conservative–Liberal Democrat coalition had the moral authority to govern. The parliamentary numbers meant only a Conservative–Liberal Democrat government could offer stability. Bradshaw rejected this view, claiming the combined Labour and Liberal Democrat vote share had five million more votes than the Conservatives and no one had won the election. Regardless that the Conservatives could make the same argument about combining vote shares and therefore the 'legitimacy' to govern. Yet, Bradshaw reasoned on policy issues – the economy, electoral reform, Europe, securing the recovery and paying down the deficit – concluding that a 'much more sustainable potential coalition between us and the Liberal Democrats and the other progressive parties'.[79] Bradshaw developed his position: 'I've always thought it tragic and made more tragic by FPTP that we have been lumbered with majority Conservative governments for most of our modern history because the progressive centre and left are divided.'[80]

John Reid publicly opposed a deal with the Liberal Democrats, telling the BBC a Lab–Lib pact would be 'disastrously wrong for the country and the Labour party'. In terms of the country, 'I fail to see how trying to bring together six different parties – and even then not having a majority – will bring the degree of stability we need.' Furthermore, 'it doesn't match up from the point of view of the electorate for the two losing parties to cobble together a deal'. Relying on the nationalist parties, who would demand extra spending for their respective parts of the UK, would result in an English backlash which would suffer the brunt of spending cuts. 'From the point of view of the Labour Party, if we look as if we are "cocking a snook" at the electorate when we have lost more MPs than at any time with the exception of 1931, they will wreak revenge on the Labour Party at future elections.'[81] Reid told *Sky News* he feared a Lab–Lib Pact would result in 'mutually assured destruction' and that it was the responsibility of the Conservatives as the biggest party to form a stable government.[82]

David Blunkett not just opposed coalition but openly damned the Liberal Democrats on BBC Radio 4 questioning what was in the best interests of the British people and 'our future democracy'. Blunkett stated: 'We see now what it would be like with fully fledged PR, don't we? We see what we would have to put up with. Secondly, can we trust these people? Can we trust the Liberal Democrats? They're behaving like every harlot in history.' Thirdly, what were the thoughts of the British public, 'not what a small group on each side feel but how we put together something that people in this country can respect as part of our living democracy?' Blunkett, in the same fashion as Reid, outlined the potential political damage: 'A coalition of the defeated, cobbled together, uncertain whether it can carry anything night by night', what it 'would do to the Labour Party and its vote'. Blunkett questioned how the nation would have felt if having rejected Heath in February 1974 he'd remained in power through a deal with Jeremy Thorpe.[83]

Brown's position as prime minister and behaviour towards the Liberal Democrats were considered a block to a Lab–Lib coalition, initially refusing to give a specific date for when he would step down. This caused angst amongst the Liberal Democrats, who did not want to be seen as propping up a defeated prime minister. Brown announced on Monday, 10 May, that he would step down by September 2010, a move that paved the way for negotiations with the Liberal Democrats. Their precondition of Brown standing down, in Straw's opinion, 'could only add to the instability of any arrangement with them, and provoke scorn from the electorate that they were being foisted off with a new prime minister who had been untested at the election'.[84] For Harris, who had along with colleagues, told Brown during his premiership that he should stand down, it reinforced his opposition to electoral reform. After all, it should be the electorate who decides who governs, not the actions of one person, in this case, Clegg.[85] On the matter of electoral reform, Harris blogged that Labour MPs will not vote for the replacement of FPTP with AV, or for a referendum on further change after that towards PR. Moreover, the word 'progressive' has now been redefined as 'willing to barter away everything you campaigned for in return for the chance to be in government, albeit at the beck and call of a party that has spent its entire existence trying to wipe you off the political map'.[86]

In the cities of northern England the Liberal Democrats had become the main opposition to Labour, as the Conservatives had still not recovered from their electoral decline in industrial areas since the 1980s. In Liverpool and Sheffield, for example, the Liberal Democrats had gained control of the city councils for periods of the Labour government. Bradshaw considered that the 'historical and geographical context determined the attitude towards the Liberal Democrats'; therefore, the hostility in those areas was understandable. However, in other parts of Britain, Labour and the Liberal Democrats had a common enemy in the Conservatives.[87] Johnson reiterated the geographical dimension, as some opposition to coalition stemmed from local government. 'You read a Lib Dem focus leaflet with them being all things to all people, some of the terrible things they put out if they thought they had a chance of beating the sitting Labour MP, leading to an understandable offence.' Johnson believed this caused an 'inability' for some Labour MPs 'to look at the bigger picture'.[88]

Mandelson remarked in *The Third Man* that during the days following the 2010 general election he reminisced about the Lab–Lib talks in the 1990s. Mandelson 'did not see them so much as a missed opportunity as an opportunity that was never really there to be grasped'. There were strong forces against a deal 'in both of our parties ... and the circumstances were never propitious enough to overcome them'. Whilst not an excuse for not working towards cooperation, something could have been put together 'at any time during the previous thirteen years. When the circumstances changed with the hung Parliament in 2010, both the electoral arithmetic and the lack of an established rapport between our parties and their leaderships militated against any serious prospect of a progressive alliance'.[89]

For Labour MPs two immediate issues were influencing their decision. Firstly, did the Labour Party have the 'moral authority' to govern and, secondly, did the numbers stack up for a coalition with the Liberal Democrats? A 'coalition of losers' would have faced questions of legitimacy – denying the biggest party in terms of votes and seats the right to govern – especially from an unsympathetic press. Longer-term issues can be added: firstly, looking forward, the electoral consequences for Labour if it were to enter a coalition with the Liberal Democrats and minor parties. By remaining in office there was a fear the electorate would wreak revenge and do considerable damage to the Labour vote, its representation in parliament and its standing as a national party. Secondly, a period back in opposition would allow Labour to regroup, whilst it was hoped that the coalition government took the electoral punishment for introducing the deep economic cuts forecast in the parliament, providing an opportunity to return to office in 2015. Thirdly, the problems of sharing office with the Liberal Democrats with whom Labour had a strong dislike and mistrust. This was succinctly outlined by one Liberal Democrat who thought a Lab–Lib coalition would be primarily a Labour government with one or two Lib Dems – 'a continuation of the current government, just with a few irritants added in'.[90]

Labour's offer on electoral reform

The negotiations provide an example of the length that Labour was willing to go to tie in the Liberal Democrats and remain in office. Considerable opposition to coalition and electoral reform existed within the PLP, yet the Cabinet was willing to countenance the idea. Mandelson considered the disagreement on electoral reform 'was never properly tested in the coalition negotiations'.[91] However, during the five days following the election, electoral reform was one of the key determinants. On Friday, 8 May, the day after the election, an hour before Cameron made his 'big, open and comprehensive offer' to the Liberal Democrats, Brown made a statement on the steps of Downing Street. He spoke of his 'plan to carry through far-reaching political reforms, including changes to the voting system', believing that the 'British people should be able to decide in a referendum what the system should be'.[92] Although unspecific, Brown appeared to be willing to consider going further than the manifesto commitment already made on AV. In support of this view, the Liberal Democrat draft coalition agreement with Labour referenced in Adonis's *5 Days in May* suggested an agreement to bring forward a post-legislative multi-option referendum on alternate voting systems, to include the option of STV, no later than May 2011.[93]

Boulton and Jones record a meeting on Saturday, 9 May, between Mandelson and Danny Alexander, a key ally of Clegg and member of the Lib Dem negotiating team. During the meeting, Alexander floated the idea of Labour and the Liberal Democrats imposing AV without a referendum. According to Mandelson, the worry was that a 'referendum would be lost because voters might see a Lib-Lab pact as a self-interested stitch-up on both sides, so it might be better to avoid such a test'. Alexander pointed out that the Lib Dems had no such manifesto commitment, simply a commitment to deliver it. Reportedly, legislating for AV without a referendum was due to the Lib Dem fear that a 'coalition of the losers' would find it hard to sell anything to the British public let alone a new voting system.[94] This was not the first time Mandelson had affirmed he thought a referendum on changing the voting system would be lost. Mandelson had told Blair that a referendum on the Jenkins's proposal might not be won.

According to the journalist Michael Crick, Brown held two secret meetings with Clegg on Sunday, 10 May. The suggestion of AV without a referendum was made at their first meeting. Qvortrup suggests at these talks that it might be possible to go ahead with AV without a public vote and then have a referendum at a later stage on more radical and proportional electoral reform.[95] After the Cabinet had met on Monday, 11 May, news broke that Cameron had offered AV with a referendum to the Liberal Democrats. Brown told Adonis to move as quickly on AV, with a referendum, to avoid the Lib Dems claiming that there was nothing to choose between the two parties.[96]

Laws, a Lib Dem negotiating team member, recorded the first negotiating meeting on Monday, 11 May, between Labour and Liberal Democrats. Adonis reiterated Labour's commitment to a referendum thinking 'most Labour MPs will support AV but vote against proportional representation'. Harriet Harman emphasized the opposition to AV: 'Most Labour MPs will grit their teeth and vote for AV, but let's be clear that many of my colleagues are not exactly champing at the bit!' – implying a referendum on AV would not be easy to implement. When the Lib Dem negotiating team questioned further, Laws writes, Labour 'cracks opened up'. Alexander asked: 'Can we rely on Labour MPs supporting an AV referendum?' Adonis said, 'That is what is guaranteed in our manifesto.' Yet Balls intervened to say: 'AV would not be at all straightforward' and 'the chief whip thinks it would be difficult to get the AV referendum through. Many of our colleagues are opposed to it. It cannot be guaranteed.' It was, for Laws, a 'deadly intervention'. The prospect of a Lab–Lib coalition rested on delivering a referendum on AV, which it had in its manifesto, but could not guarantee to deliver.[97]

Laws records that electoral reform was discussed at the second meeting. Mandelson thought there were three main issues: political legitimacy, policy agreement and deliverability. However, Adonis affirmed the AV Referendum would be a 'confidence issue for the government', implying that the government would challenge its own backbenchers to vote down the government. Adonis reiterated that Labour could 'certainly agree to a post-legislative referendum on AV'. However, if STV or AV+ was put into the Bill it raised problems of timing and deliverability. 'Labour would support AV but we would have to oppose PR.' Mandelson agreed with Adonis, arguing that it would be best if a Lab–Lib coalition coalesced around AV, to avoid dividing the coalition and presumably to present a united front in the referendum. Balls, as in the first negotiations, was sceptical, deeming, 'Getting our people to support AV is going to be quite hard. There are a lot of Labour MPs opposed.'[98]

Ed Miliband's account of the first meeting of the two teams maintains that Brown was not willing to offer AV without putting it to the people. At this meeting, it emerged that the Liberal Democrats might push for AV without a referendum. All those on the Labour side thought that this was not possible. At another meeting, the discussion was 'consumed by whether or not we could have AV without a referendum … or have it for by-elections. We didn't want it without a referendum but they said as a compromise, "well, let's just have it for by-elections." We thought that was just for the birds, frankly.'[99] The influence of political ambition for both Ed Miliband and Ed Balls cannot be underestimated. Remaining in government with Brown as prime minister – to stand down at 'some point' in the future – would have meant a leadership contest whilst in government, potentially during a time of unpopularity for the government due to spending cuts, in coalition government and without having been tested at a general election. Therefore, a lack of enthusiasm for the Liberal Democrats and scepticism towards electoral reform hampered the likelihood of a Lib–Lab deal, increasing the likelihood of Labour moving into opposition and conducting a leadership election.

Johnson claims that he 'had a role with Chris Huhne talking about PR as part of the deal'. According to Johnson, the deal on offer from Labour was either 'genuine PR, AV Plus or something similar' placed in front of the people in a referendum. However, the Liberal Democrats asked for 'AV without any reference to the British people, no referendum introduced through Parliament, and then further down the line a referendum on a much more proportional electoral system'. This was not acceptable as the prevalent belief in the Labour Party was that a constitutional change requires going 'back to the British people'. Accordingly, this is 'what the negotiations floundered on'.[100] Seldon and Lodge support this view, writing that Brown was willing to assent to a multi-question referendum allowing for a choice between FPTP, AV or a proportional system, going beyond AV. The government would make this an issue of confidence to ensure its passage through the Commons, yet the Liberal Democrats demanded AV without a referendum.[101]

Cameron and the Conservative leadership team were under the impression that the Labour Party was willing to offer AV without a referendum. Whether Cameron foisted his doubting backbenchers into coalition with the Liberal Democrats, based on fallacious rumours about AV without a referendum, is a contentious matter. During a debate on the British constitution and Home Affairs, early in the lifetime of the coalition government, Dr Julian Lewis, the Conservative MP for New Forest East, asked Straw if the Labour Party had offered the Liberal Democrats AV without a referendum. Straw rejected this claim, citing the opposition to the proposal within Labour ranks.[102] Later in the same debate, Lewis would raise the same issue with Clegg who responded that the Labour Party did not offer this in those discussions.[103] Clegg repeated his position in Nick Robinson's *Five Days That Changed Britain*. Instead, there was plenty of toing and froing around different electoral systems and the appropriateness of referendums, but he received no formal offer.[104]

The journalist Crick offers a persuasive overview of events. Based on conversations he had held, he considered the Liberal Democrats asked Labour for AV without a referendum and at some point Brown may have discussed it without making a formal offer; the Liberal Democrats then over-egged this in their conversations with the Conservatives. Cameron did not probe deeply enough, and perhaps did not want to, knowing he could use this to cajole his MPs into accepting AV with a referendum.[105] Tellingly, Laws admitted to a select committee that Liberal Democrat talks with Labour were, in part, a device to ratchet up concessions from the Conservatives. 'Coalition with the Labour Party was certainly something we were willing to consider and we would have been mad not to because it would have weakened our negotiating position in terms of delivering as many of our policies as possible.'[106]

Summary

Electoral reform featured heavily at the end of New Labour, just as it did at its beginning. Yet, the scepticism evident at the beginning of New Labour was just as pronounced at the end, and Labour's pronouncements in support of AV appeared belated and insincere. Indeed, support within the Cabinet was lukewarm at best, as the electoral reformers in the Cabinet preferred some form of PR, and sceptics preferred the present system. Perhaps only Peter Hain and Jack Straw advocated AV out of a belief in its intrinsic merits. Whilst Brown linked the arguments in favour of AV to a more pluralist conception of politics, it was also part of a political strategy to entice the Liberal Democrats in the event of a hung parliament, something that irked much of the PLP who were prepared to take their turn in opposition. After all, any incoming government faced significant economic pressures which encouraged thoughts that victory was possible in 2015, and taking a turn in opposition was simply playing by the rules of the game.

The 2010 general election result had all but removed the Labour government – a point not missed by Blunkett, Reid and Burnham – but not completely inserted a new Conservative administration. While some considered that the result displayed a progressive majority, making possible a realignment of the left, negotiations between Labour and the Liberal Democrats were unsuccessful. There was considerable opposition within the PLP and sections of the Cabinet for a deal with the Liberal Democrats, a point not missed by the latter. Moreover, Labour appeared to be unprepared for the negotiations compared to the Conservatives, and unwilling to make as many policy concessions. Specifically for Labour, AV was a means of tying the Liberal Democrats into government not an end in itself, doubtful of even making it onto the statute due to opposition within the PLP. On the other side, the Liberal Democrats were now led by those sympathetic to the *Orange Book*, ideologically closer to Cameron's liberal conservatism. They understood that by negotiating with Labour they could gain more concessions from the Conservatives, 'stringing along' Labour to strengthen their hand.

The five days that followed the 2010 general election were important for it exposed two tensions: Labour's antipathy towards electoral reform and its attitude towards coalition, the likely consequence of PR. Electoral reform was a key policy that the Liberal Democrats had long desired and to which Labour had a manifesto commitment. Yet negotiations floundered, in part due to Labour's scepticism towards entering a coalition with the Liberal Democrats, and although PR was mooted it was never formally offered. As Balls stated in the negotiations, AV, let alone PR, would have struggled to pass through the House of Commons given the opposition within the PLP. Elsewhere, high-profile Labour figures were openly damning the idea of coalition, which added to the Liberal Democrats' belief that whatever Labour offered was not deliverable. However, the failure of 'realignment' and the fulfilment of the 'progressive-left' was influenced by factors other than electoral reform: ideological overlap between the *Orange Book* liberals and 'compassionate conservatism', parliamentary arithmetic and the political stability of coalition with the Conservatives, and the gradual 'falling out of love' with Labour over the course of thirteen years of government. The 'bad-faith' was apparent on both sides and the political will was therefore lacking.

Attitudes to coalition were, to some degree, influenced by the heavy electoral defeat and the desire to renew in opposition, allowing the Conservatives to take the electoral punishment for unpopular public expenditure cuts. However, the arguments put forward by the likes of Blunkett, Reid and Straw went beyond one solitary general election defeat, to the heart of Labour's thinking about coalition government at Westminster. There was the question of how a 'coalition of the losers' reliant on the potentially fickle support of the minor parties would survive from day to day. Moreover, how would the electorate and the media perceive such a government, what would this do to the standing of the Labour Party as a national party of Great Britain, and if it was perceived negatively, what would be the electoral backlash at future elections and would this do irrevocable damage to the Labour vote? Whilst Adonis might have viewed such an attitude as 'defeatist', it was the more realistic and politically acceptable decision to make.

6

Debating the electoral system in opposition, 2010–21

Since 2010, the Labour Party has faced a series of significant political, social and ideological challenges. Austerity saw a further retrenchment of the welfare state and the Conservative–Liberal Democrat coalition successfully pinned blame for the financial crash, 2008, on the Labour Party. To move on from the New Labour era, Labour sought to redefine itself under the leadership of Ed Miliband and then Jeremy Corbyn. While the latter outperformed expectations in the general election in 2017, he led the Party to its worst result since 1935 in 2019. Corbyn was replaced by Sir Keir Starmer, a figure from the right of the Party. Electorally, the SNP has become the major party in Scottish politics, following the Scottish Independence referendum in 2014, and the 'red wall' in the North of England turned blue by voting Conservative in 2019, partly a consequence of Labour's second referendum policy on EU membership. In sum, Labour has not won a UK-wide election since 2005, and is faced with a significant electoral challenge to gain even a small majority at the next general election.

The problems identified above are, in some ways, like the issues faced by the Party in the 1980s, a period in which interest in electoral reform, proportional representation and electoral pacts grew. While there has been some talk in the aforementioned, the scale of the result of the Alternative Vote (AV) Referendum, 2011, took the wind out of the sails of the electoral reformers within and without the Labour Party, and for much of the period analysed, electoral reform has been a minority interest. Yet, the 2019 general election result and the opportunities presented by the Starmer leadership – although it is far from clear that he is a reformer – have renewed interest in whether Labour should advocate a move away from FPTP.

We begin this chapter by charting Labour's approach to the AV Referendum. Despite being only the second UK-wide referendum, its importance has seemingly been dwarfed by the referendums on Scottish Independence and continuing British membership of the European Union. From there, we look at how electoral reformers sought to keep the issue alive under Miliband and Corbyn. We finish, by assessing how debates over electoral reform have played out under Starmer's leadership. First, we turn our attention to the AV Referendum.

The Alternative Vote Referendum, 2011

The AV Referendum meant that after many years of discussing electoral reform and manifesto commitments to hold a referendum the Labour Party was faced with a UK-wide vote. Rather than viewing the AV Referendum as an individual event it is best viewed as part of a wider interest in AV, starting with Gordon Brown becoming prime minister and the ensuing coalition negotiations after the 2010 general election. Indeed, taking a longer historical view, AV has often been put forward by reformers within Labour as a 'half-way house', accepting the principle of reform but rejecting PR. The early polling evidence suggested there was a considerable chance that there would be a movement away from FPTP, but the two-to-one margin of victory for the 'No' campaign ensured that FPTP was retained.

The AV Referendum in 2011 came about as a result of the coalition negotiations between the Conservatives and Liberal Democrats. Neither the Conservatives nor the Liberal Democrats had a manifesto commitment. The Conservatives were committed to FPTP and the Liberal Democrats committed to STV. Therefore, the referendum was a result of political bargaining. One member of the Liberal Democrat Federal Executive summed up the attitude on AV after the 2010 general election, stating: 'This is as good as it's going to get, we can't get any better,'[1] understanding the limitations of pursuing PR. For Labour, whereas the Plant Report and Jenkins Commission had been theoretical and political exercises conducted on the whole behind closed doors, the referendum openly and publicly pitted Labour politicians against one another.

The response of the Labour Party was vital to the overall outcome of the referendum as the Party had the ability to influence key sections of the electorate who would determine the outcome of the referendum, a point not missed by either side of the divide within Labour. From the outset the divide was apparent as in campaigning and financial terms Labour did not register as a permitted participant, and as a party did not spend anything on the campaign. On the other hand, the Conservatives spent £660,785 and the Liberal Democrats spent £62,782. Instead, Labour split into two campaign groups: 'Labour No to AV' and 'Labour Yes'. The former spent £192,084 whereas the latter, like the Party itself, did not spend anything, and was therefore outspent by the 'Conservative Yes' campaign.[2]

In comparison, the stance of the coalition parties was clear. The Conservative Party was overwhelmingly against, whilst the Liberal Democrats were overwhelmingly in favour. Cameron and Clegg had to respond to different pressures and consequently the result mattered for the coalition partners; Cameron had to deal with his backbenchers, disgruntled at being in coalition with the Liberal Democrats and opposed to AV believing it could prevent the Party from winning a parliamentary majority in the future. Although it was claimed that Cameron had assured Clegg he would not campaign hard against AV, he would duly make several high-profile statements in favour of the status quo. On the other hand, Clegg, whose ministerial oversight included constitutional reform, had to provide something substantial for his own MPs, party members and electoral base to show that the Liberal Democrat participation in government with the Conservatives was worthwhile. Many Liberal Democrats from across the Party felt uneasy about being in coalition with the Conservatives, thinking it was damaging aligning with a party that they had spent their entire existence fighting.

The Coalition: Our Programme for Government bound the issue of AV with a reduction in the number of constituencies across the United Kingdom, an act which was believed to be in the electoral interests of the Conservative Party. This was designed to satisfy the separate demands of the coalition partners: electoral reform, a longstanding policy commitment for the Liberal Democrats and, as a quid pro quo, the Conservatives could nullify the Labour Party's advantage in small urban constituencies by reducing and therefore redrawing the constituency boundaries. Furthermore, the Conservatives had two insurances for either winning or losing the referendum: if the referendum was lost the reduction in the number of parliamentary constituencies would help mitigate the bias towards Labour; should the referendum be won, the Fixed Term Parliament Act would prevent the Liberal Democrats withdrawing from the coalition.

However, the Parliamentary Voting System and Constituencies Bill 2010 did not sit well with Labour MPs and peers, who deemed it an act motivated by the electoral interests of the Conservative Party. The Labour Party would have been affected by the reduction of MPs, particularly in its industrial heartlands where constituencies tend to have fewer electors, along with Scotland and Wales, and a number of Labour MPs would have had to find different constituencies to contest. Additionally, a considerable number of voters – estimated to be 3.5 million – were missing from the electoral register, many of whom would be in urban areas; poorer, working class, or students more inclined to support Labour. Several Labour peers sought to wreck the Bill in the House of Lords by imposing a 40 per cent turnout threshold, proposed by Falconer. Only at the last minute did the Bill pass in the Lords, by 224 votes to 210. Other Labour peers indicated that they would let the referendum clauses pass if they were decoupled from the constituency redistribution parts of the Bill.[3]

Lipsey wrote that for reformers, ideally a Liberal–Labour government would have enthusiastically brought forward electoral reform, presenting a united front. However, the Conservative–Liberal government meant that one party favoured reform, and the much larger party wholly opposed it. Consequently, the makeup of the government limited the openness to reform. As we have seen, Lipsey argued for AV during the Jenkins Commission as he thought it had a greater chance of coming to fruition. Also, he thought it in the political interests of the Labour Party as it would lead to more Labour or Labour-led governments in which the Liberal Democrats would support Labour. Yet, by 2011 Lipsey had growing concerns about AV as it could lead to the multiplications of fringe parties, a further fracturing of the Party system, and vote shares for governing parties so low that it brings into question the legitimacy of the democratic system. Lastly, it was far from clear that the Liberal Democrats would post-2010 ally with the Labour Party.[4]

For Harris, the holding of a referendum highlighted the rotten nature of coalition government, taking place not because there was the demand for any reform, but the consequence of horse trading behind closed doors. As such, 'it wasn't at all democratic or transparent', for the Coalition Agreement had no mandate, drafted after the general election, influenced by a handful of politicians at the top of the Conservative and Liberal Democrat parties. Harris continued: 'The Lib Dems themselves never supported AV. We had a referendum on a system proposed by a government, neither of which the two parties in the government supported. The only party that had proposed a referendum on AV was the Labour Party. We were against having a referendum … on a system that nobody wanted.'[5] Falconer was also critical of the cause of the referendum. Not only did he think it a complicated system, but there was no groundswell of support and it was a concoction of the politicians.[6]

Burnham, who had stood Labour's 2020 leadership contest, raised opposition to AV. It was an 'irrelevant' issue, the 'fringe pursuit for *Guardian*-reading classes' implying that it might be a concern of the liberal middle classes, but it is not a dispute that has any traction amongst working-class Labour voters. Burnham went on to say it was not his job to 'prop up the Liberal Democrats by helping them win a referendum that is important to them.' The Liberal Democrats at the time were languishing in the opinion polls around 10 per cent down from 23 per cent in the general election. The Labour Party could not officially take sides in the referendum, according to Burnham: 'The party nationally couldn't campaign for any one position.' Furthermore, 'those who are calling for retention of first past the post are making an incredibly important and legitimate argument.'[7]

In July 2010 Burnham continued to express doubts on the merits of AV in the *New Statesman*. Although Burnham did not want to dismiss the importance of the debate, he was asking Labour to keep it in perspective. 'I don't believe any of my constituents would put it in their top ten most important issues.' Focusing on the matter of electoral reform could 'cement an impression Westminster and the Labour Party is out of touch and talking about things that are not the everyday concerns of people'. The coalition government had embarked on a course of deep spending cuts, meaning there were more urgent and pressing issues. Although he was 'tending towards AV', questions remained what the reform meant for 'our political system and Labour's place within it'. Coalition government 'could be attractive and it would be wrong for Labour to snigger or dismiss coalition'. Yet, Burnham stated his reservations as 'this country has been served well by majority government over the years; that clarity helps drive social change when it's necessary. You have to look carefully at what kind of political system you want.'[8]

Burnham was appointed as Labour's election campaign coordinator and reiterated in November 2010 that the Labour Party would not campaign in favour of AV in the referendum, as it would be concentrating on the Scottish, Welsh and local elections on the same day. Therefore, AV was not the priority and allowed Labour to avoid the potentially divisive issue as the party machine and activist network could not help the 'YES! To Fairer Votes' campaign. Lipsey considered that this was Clegg's biggest blunder as it split the two leaders who were sympathetic to reform.[9] For Burnham, the referendum campaign was distinct from the local election campaign, and Clegg had been outmanoeuvred by Cameron.[10]

Joan Ryan, who had lost her seat in the 2010 general election was deputy campaign director of the cross-party NOtoAV, was pleased to see support from across the Party. Tom Watson, reportedly switched from FPTP to AV, thought it was hard to analyse any pattern in how Labour members thought. 'New intake MPs, MPs in safe or marginal seats, northern MPs or whatever – it is an issue that divides all the Labour tribes, groups and regions.'[11] In addition, trade unions joined the NOtoAV campaign, including the GMB, Community, Alliance, Aslef and the Prison Officer's Association. Unite, although not officially part of No2AV, campaigned against reform and Unison remained neutral. Billy Hayes of the Communication Workers Union supported AV, arguing that the MP has to get 50 per cent of the vote, and only Cameron would benefit from the retention of FPTP.[12]

Labour's 'Yes to AV' campaign wrote a letter to the *Guardian* in December 2010, claiming that elections are decided by a handful of swing seats and Labour is the party of fairness and change.[13] Present at the launch of the Labour 'Yes to AV' campaign were Johnson, Denham, Bradshaw, Livingstone, Oona King, Kinnock and the Labour leader Ed Miliband. Yet, some of the aforementioned had varied history with electoral reform: Kinnock became convinced of the need for reform. Johnson and Denham both supported AV+, with the latter believing AV 'would have given us an even bigger majority in 1997 and it would have given the Tories an even bigger majority in 1983 and 1987 as well'.[14] Bradshaw became the front of the Labour Yes to AV campaign.[15]

Johnson, on reflection, considered AV to be a 'sop' as it was missing the 'Plus bit' meaning electoral reformers 'were not enthused by it'.[16] Given that AV was not the preferred choice of a number of electoral reformers, it was perceived as a 'Trojan horse'. Harris deemed AV to be 'seen by reformers as a stepping stone to something else, not an end in itself', something he thought 'was very cynical and dishonest'.[17] Beckett concurred, deeming the 'people who wanted AV wanted it as a stepping stone, they did not want it as a system in itself'.[18]

Nevertheless, Denham stressed AV to be fairer, making each MP work harder, having to 'gain the support of a greater group, the support of half the people who voted'. As a result, voters would no longer believe that they have to 'vote tactically or their vote will be wasted, it's more democratic, it's fair and it will produce a better type of politics'.[19] However, there was a backlash against the accusation of 'lazy' MPs from Labour figures, including Ian Murray, Jeremy Corbyn and Kerry McCarthy, called on the Yes campaign to name the MPs who were supposedly not working hard enough.[20]

Denham, along with Chris Huhne, a Liberal Democrat MP, and Caroline Lucas, the sole Green MP, explained why party difference must be put aside to change British politics. Britain, the article claimed, 'votes as a centre-left country and yet the Conservatives have dominated our politics for two-thirds of the time since 1900'. Progressives, tactical voting and safe seats were all mentioned as AV would be the 'dawn of an honest age', creating a 'system that reflect how Britain actually votes, the progressive majority will be one step closer to reality'.[21] Given that Britain was a year into a Conservative–Liberal Democrat coalition government, the 'progressive majority' argument had been shaken and the refutation offered in Healey's autobiography appeared increasingly relevant.[22]

Harris rejected the argument that it was FPTP that had delivered Conservative governments for much of the twentieth century. Blaming FPTP for Labour's electoral defeats was fallacious. The Conservatives had governed for most of the twentieth century 'because they were more popular, because they won more votes, because they had more popular policies and because they won the argument'. Passing judgement about events post-1992, Harris affirmed that the Labour Party faced two different options: either to stop trying to connect with the voters and seek to 'change the electoral system so we could achieve government by changing the rules' or do as Tony Blair did and propose 'new, attractive policies and messages, broadening our appeal beyond our traditional base'. For Harris the correct course of action was the one pursued by Blair, as elections are won, 'by appealing to more voters, not by changing the system'.[23] Denis MacShane submitted written evidence to the House of Commons Constitutional Reform Committee. FPTP in the post–Second World War era had facilitated an almost even split of Labour and Conservative governments. Moreover, he rejected the 'once a fashionable view that coalitions in and of themselves produce good government' as there are 'plenty of examples of coalition governments being complete disasters'.[24]

Tessa Jowell supported AV considering preferential voting would force politicians to look beyond 'what might be defined as a core vote' and put the 'voter first'. Jowell extended the argument of making more votes count, estimating on BBC *Daily Politics* that 'at the last election the focus was on 460,000 swing voters. We should be looking to involve the whole country in electing our government'.[25] The number referenced by Jowell was supposedly the number of voters who determined the outcome of the 2010 general election, targeted by the Conservatives and Labour in marginal constituencies, in order to win a parliamentary majority. Consequently, only a fraction of the electorate determines who forms the government. However, as Harris noted, such an argument fails to consider the clear majority of voters who have participated in the election and how they have decided to vote. 'Everyone's vote matters', stated Harris, 'even those who are committed to voting one way at every election have the same right to have their voices heard. Elections are won, yes, by persuading part of the electorate to change their minds. But they are also won by persuading an even larger proportion of the electorate not to'.[26]

Indeed, the fundamental reason why Harris was in favour of FPTP was that 'it gives the people of this country something extremely valuable: the ability to sack a government'.[27] The argument that the purpose of elections was to elect a government was regularly used by supporters of FPTP during the AV Referendum. Prescott deemed: 'It is what government does that is the important thing about elections ... Government is the most important decision people can make', adding that trust in government is based on governments delivering on what they've promised.[28] Blunkett, in the NOtoAV campaign, video-released the day before the referendum, echoed Prescott's sentiments, ending the campaign broadcast stating FPTP was 'a system that elects a government rather than having decisions taken after the election about policies and programmes'.[29]

Conversely to Miliband's refusal to share a platform with Clegg, Reid shared a platform with Cameron – an unholy alliance that cut across party and class lines – humorously pointing out he had yet to see any of those MPs advocating AV step forward to say they are the ones who are not working hard enough. Reid continued: 'It would be an outrage to try and secure a change in our electoral system for tactical party advantage.' This was the aim of the leadership of the Liberal Democrats, yet what they had to realize was 'every system has its losers as well as its winners, which is the nature of elections; it is the nature of the contest'. Consequently, 'the answer for losing parties is to work harder to win the confidence of the electorate'. Reid's statement correlated with his attitude towards coalition after the May 2010 general election when he proclaimed that Labour must accept defeat. 'What you don't try and do is try and change the rules of the game to suit yourself" as the British way is not for the 'Government to sack the electorate, or change the electoral system just because they, the politicians, don't like the result. In a democracy it works the other way round'.[30] The objective of reaching out across class and party lines worked, as the *Guardian* published a poll the following day highlighting how support for AV had plummeted. According to Dan Hodges, a communications consultant for NOtoAV, it was the moment when the referendum campaign was, to all intents and purposes, over.[31]

Advocates of AV criticized those within Labour who opposed AV, arguing it was the same system used for electing the leader of the Labour Party, a pertinent point as Ed Miliband had narrowly been elected only nine months prior to the referendum. The argument put forward by No campaigners within Labour was the same as the argument made in the Plant Report: different institutions depending on their function could use different electoral systems. Beckett thought that electing a government and electing a leader of a political party were 'two completely different things', a view shared by Prescott.[32] Harris fleshed out the position adding that choosing the leader of the Labour Party is 'choosing amongst people who are members of the same party as me, who have the same set of values and principles as I do. In a general election you are not.' Thus, AV is 'sensible for you are giving second or third preference to other

Labour candidates'. In a general election Harris didn't 'have a second or third preference', only one preference which was the Labour Party.[33]

Ed Miliband supported AV, albeit unenthusiastically. Miliband found himself in the minority in the PLP, and faced dissent from a number of high-profile Labour politicians. The referendum put into focus Miliband's political judgement and had AV won the referendum, he risked being on the 'wrong' side of the PLP. Should FPTP be maintained it had the potential to lead to the perception that Miliband was an electoral underachiever. However, Miliband's objective was attracting disaffected Liberal Democrats into the Labour fold. Therefore, the act of coming out in favour of AV would have appealed to former Liberal Democrat voters, regardless of the overall outcome of the referendum. It was in many ways a 'win-win' situation for Miliband, who could present himself as a modernizer if the public supported AV whilst privately relishing the predicament in which Clegg and the Liberal Democrats would find themselves should a key Liberal Democrats coalition policy be rejected by the electorate. Equally, a Yes vote would have caused difficulties for Cameron. Conservative backbenchers, many disillusioned with 'compassionate conservatism' compounded by the inability of Cameron's rebranding to win a majority, would have blamed him for conceding permanent coalition government with the Liberal Democrats or the Opposition should the Liberal Democrats join forces with Labour.

Miliband wrote in the *Guardian* that AV offers an 'opportunity for political reform, ensuring the voice of the public is heard louder than it has been in the past'. He gauged the matter 'not to be at the top, or even near the top, of many people's lists of concerns', being a matter not often raised in his constituency or any other, implying a lack of enthusiasm. However, the reform was still necessary due to the low current standing of politicians in the eyes of the public, and therefore the opportunity should be taken to make politics more relevant to people. AV 'combined the direct representation of first-past-the-post with one that will make the votes of more people count' and breaking that link would be a mistake. AV would not alone bridge the disconnect between people and politicians, as House of Lords reform was also necessary, but AV had the benefit of increasing political accountability, forcing 'parties to admit where there is agreement between them, prising open our confrontational system'.[34]

At the launch of 'Labour Yes to AV', Miliband claimed that the great tragedy in British politics has been the split in the progressive vote. Whilst Clegg's decision to go into coalition with the Conservatives had made this less obvious, it should not be assumed that is 'going to persist forever because that would be a cardinal mistake when we look back at our history'. In a direct approach to those disaffected by the coalition government, Miliband claimed the Tories were against reform because 'they fear the creation of a progressive majority in this country'.[35] He returned to the split in the progressive vote in the days leading up to the referendum, reiterating his belief that AV would reflect confidence and express the anti-Conservative and progressive majority in Britain. Moreover, FPTP had enabled Thatcher to enact her policies and somewhat dubiously and disingenuously added: 'Labour has always been a force for political reform'.[36] Basing his argument on the 'progressive-left' thesis, yet refusing to share a platform with Clegg, the leader of the other 'progressive' party, was contradictory and a 'tribal approach'. Although Miliband could point to sharing a platform with other Liberal Democrats, to not share with Clegg, arguably, undermined his professed belief in the progressive left.

The *Financial Times* reported that in the event of a 'No' vote, Miliband wished to retain a commitment to electoral reform in the next Labour manifesto, keeping the possibility of a pact with the Liberal Democrats alive. According to one unnamed Labour insider, 'if there is a No vote, it's important that the margin of defeat is as narrow as possible to keep the reform agenda alive'.[37] If correct, it infers the Labour leadership were keeping their options open to a potential deal with the Liberal Democrats in 2015, suggesting even as early as 2011 they were unsure of outright victory and desired an 'insurance' policy.

The 'No' campaign focused on the issue of coalition government and the role of the Liberal Democrats within it, particularly on what were perceived as broken promises. The coalition government was one year into the parliament, and the Liberal Democrats were becoming increasingly unpopular. Students were particularly upset due to the volte face on tuition fees amongst other Liberal Democrat policies that failed to make it into the Coalition Agreement. Tom Watson had always expected a majority of Labour MPs to oppose AV, a position determined by the attitude towards Clegg.[38] Clegg had become the persona non grata, symbolic of the broken promises, and whilst the 'Yes' campaign chose to focus on other figures, he was part of the reason why the referendum was taking place. When Clegg insisted on attending a "YES! to Fairer Votes' event Miliband withdrew because Clegg represented the 'old politics; of breaking your promises'.[39]

Clegg played directly into the hands of the 'NOtoAV' campaign, who could tap into Labour voters' dislike of the Liberal Democrat leader, with posters appearing of 'No to President Clegg'. Indeed, the scathing attacks on Clegg in the campaign literature were, according to the journalist Matthew D'Anconna, pushed by Labour people in the 'No' campaign.[40] Hodges supports this view, writing how Joan Ryan pushed for the twin attack of the £250 million cost of the AV referendum and the personal attack on Clegg. Indeed, it was Ryan who met one of Cameron's close aids, Stephen Gilbert, and advocated Cameron and Reid making a joint statement to avoid accusations of NOtoAV being a 'tory front'. Reportedly, Cameron and Conservative HQ did not wish to attack Clegg when he was already down, yet to motivate Labour voters, it was agreed to emphasize how the referendum was an opportunity to punish Clegg and the Liberal Democrats for letting the Conservatives in.[41] 'Labour No to AV' also attacked Clegg mercilessly, associating him with all the pledges he had failed to keep and utilizing 'pictorial narratives', one of which was a mock *Guardian* front page with the headline: 'New voting system saves President Clegg'. Other images included Clegg walking into Downing Street with his hand on Cameron's back after the formation of the coalition government and Clegg holding the tuition fees pledge.

As such, Labour was pinning the blame on the Liberal Democrats for propping up the Conservatives, rubbishing any suggestion that the Liberal Democrats were on the 'progressive' side of British politics and holding them equally responsible, if not more so than the Conservatives, for the coalition's economic reforms. For some within the Labour Party, a No vote offered the opportunity to inflict damage on the Liberal Democrat and give Clegg a 'bloody nose'. Baroness Armstrong shared Blair's desire to bring about progressive centre-left politics, and was personally 'ambivalent towards the huge anti-Liberal factor in the Labour Party'. However, the referendum was 'a means of kicking the Liberals', something they deserved for all their compromises with the Conservatives.[42] Harris echoed Armstrong's sentiment: 'The hatred of the Liberals and the belief that they had betrayed all their principles was a factor throughout 2010–15 and I have no doubt impinged on the AV debate.'[43] Indeed, a post-referendum analysis by the Liberal Democrats considered the whole exercise and campaign tactics were designed 'to kick the party twice'.[44]

While Clegg and the actions of the Liberal Democrats were important in shaping attitudes towards AV, other issues were in play. Whitty deemed the referendum took place too early in the lifetime of the coalition. The Labour Party had 'been defeated; so the thinking was we'd better let the other lot run it for a bit. The perceived wisdom was to work out how to get back into power on the traditional method.'[45] Therefore, gains that could be made by disrupting the workings of the coalition – particularly damaging Cameron who would be held responsible for the change to the electoral system by his backbenchers – was not the preferred option. Instead, Labour was prepared to 'wait their turn' to resume office under the current system. Harris affirmed that most of the Party 'understood the debate was about more long term important issues rather than getting short term political advantage over another political party'.[46] In this case, the other political party was the Conservatives, and the vehemently anti-Liberal section in the Labour Party was more than happy to gain an advantage over the Liberal Democrats.

The result and its implications

On 5 May 2011 the electorate went to the polls to vote in only the second UK-wide referendum. The question put to the British electorate was whether the alternative vote system should replace FPTP. The outcome was unanimous, with the electorate rejecting AV by a majority of 2:1 with only ten counting areas across the UK voting in favour of AV.

Baston and Ritchie analysed the result, and deemed the scale of the defeat for reformers a 'disaster'. Only a further eleven counting areas returned a Yes vote above 45 per cent and all eleven shared similarities with the ten counting areas that did return a Yes vote: 'highly educated, youthful, liberal and cosmopolitan areas'. Areas which had a 45 per cent yes vote shared these characteristics, and also places where local competition was between Labour and the Liberal Democrats, Labour and the SNP or Labour and the Green Party.[47] Tellingly, Baston and Ritchie conclude that the Yes campaign 'had made the reforming vote a stereotype of itself, the domain of the metropolitan liberal middle classes – a potentially broad coalition had been whittled down to its hard core'.[48]

Lipsey, who had taken a back seat during the referendum campaign, was even more damning. While he sat on the steering committee for the Yes campaign, it was 'dominated by constitutional reform fanatics who lived on a different political planet' to the one he inhabited. Moreover, the Yes campaign was hampered by internal divisions. David Owen argued for a more proportional system, not just AV, whereas some Labour electoral reformers argued for SV, believing that was superior. Either way, 'banging on about systems, they damaged the case for the only alternative system on offer'. In addition, the 'Make your MP Work Harder' slogan was incomprehensible to the public, as was using celebrities, as the public wanted to hear from trusted politicians. The anti-politics thrust caused a basic strategic error: it stopped the 'yes' campaign dominated by Liberal Democrats from directly appealing to Labour voters.[49]

Polling conducted on behalf of YouGov on election day found 47 per cent of Labour voters backed Yes and 53 per cent voted No. Fifty-three per cent of those belonging to ABC1 voted Yes whereas 60 per cent of C2DE voted No.[50] Whilst the Yes campaign may have thought little of the Labour 'old guard' – Beckett, Reid, Blunkett – labelling them 'dinosaurs', traditional Labour voters may have looked more kindly upon these experienced politicians. Electoral reformers' claims that public demand for reform was proved doubtful due to the magnitude of defeat in terms of votes and the widespread rejection across the UK.

The defeat of AV in the referendum and the Conservative–Liberal Democrat coalition challenges the progressive left thesis. Adonis, who joined the Labour Party in the mid-1990s from the Liberal Democrats, was originally in favour of a coalition between Labour and the Liberal Democrats. He was influenced by the work of Roy Jenkins, who advised: 'The only real difference is that Labour is now the larger party of social democrats, the Lib Dems are the smaller; and in our political system, it is generally wise to support the larger party if they are on the same page.'[51] Additionally, believers in the social market economy and liberal society are spread across all three major parties 'having more in common with progressives in other parties than with the extremes of their own party. Coalitions might therefore promote consensus behind mainstream social market policies, and make governments stronger and better.'[52]

However, in practice such an arrangement is only superficially attractive and considering the 2010 Conservative–Liberal coalition his opinion had changed. Adonis lists four lessons he has learnt about coalition, of which two are of specific interest: 'It is possible to make coalitions work in modern Britain, and for them to be as stable as single-party governments' but qualifies this point, affirming 'coalition is not a superior form of government to single-party majority government … Labour must seek to win on its own, and to do so as an effective progressive coalition within itself.'[53] He continued, reflecting on the transformation of the Labour Party from the mid-1980s onwards under Kinnock, Smith and Blair. Transformation was achieved by 'leadership from within, not by coalition from without', meaning the 'extremists had become the prisoner of the moderates, not the other way around'.

> In reality, the best way to advance mainstream progressive politics is to organise, lead and win from inside the major parties. It is a chimera to regard coalition as a means of securing 'external' victory after 'internal' defeat. Coalition may be a necessity where there is no Commons majority for a single party; but it is no more than that.[54]

After the 2015 general election result, Bradshaw shared Adonis's preference 'for them [progressives] to all join the Labour Party so we have one centre left progressive party that can fight more effectively and beat the Conservatives'.[55] Lipsey lamented the prospects of a progressive alliance: 'It is hard to see the progressive alliance, once dreamed of by Blair and Jenkins, re-emerging.'[56] Given that Adonis, Bradshaw and Lipsey have, at different times, seen merit in a realignment, it reveals how attitudes towards coalition, electoral strategy and the role of the Labour Party are fluid, shaped, by events and experience. Indeed, moving forward, the impact of the Conservative–Liberal Democrat coalition will, in all likelihood, have a significant baring on Labour's approach to electoral reform and coalition. Throughout, it has been shown that supporters of the present system argue that the progressive left thesis is based on a misreading of British political history. The 2010–15 Conservative–Liberal Democrat coalition strengthens their argument, building on other critical events including the first and second minority Labour governments, the Lib–Lab Pact 1977–8, the 1979 vote of no confidence and the SDP breakaway.

The scale of defeat for AV also raises problems for electoral reformers within and without the Labour Party. The comprehensive victory for the 'No' campaign suggests that there is little appetite for reforming the Westminster electoral system. Interestingly, there was a 'No to AV, Yes to PR' campaign, which enjoyed support from figures such as David Owen and, the academic, Robert Skidelsky. The group understood that many of those in favour of AV desired some form of PR but rejected that AV could be a steppingstone as this would cause instability and be seen as a cynical attempt for partisan advantage.[57] However, it seems unlikely that the bulk of the electorate voted 'No' to AV as they wanted PR. In addition, if another referendum on voting reform took place, then the 'halfway' house of AV is no longer an option, and perhaps by extension, neither is SV. This leaves hybrid systems or proportional representation, two types of systems which as has been shown would struggle to make any headway within the Labour Party for Westminster elections. Moreover, as Beckett emphasized, if another referendum was held, 'It would look as if the people spoke but they got it wrong, so let's ask them again, which is not a wise thing for any government to do.'[58]

Despite the blow that electoral reformers within and without Labour experienced in the AV Referendum, the matter persists, and it is, according to reformers, still Labour holding 'the trump cards' on electoral reform.[59] Paul Blomfield, the Labour MP for Sheffield Central, argued that it was Labour's tribalism that came to the fore during the referendum. However, a different, pluralistic, approach to politics was needed, forcing the Party to find agreement and achieve progressive goals with those outside the Labour movement.[60] As early as 2013, reports emerged that the Liberal Democrats would be open to doing a deal with the Labour Party, based on a range of constitutional reforms including electoral reform for local government.[61] Harris retorted, reminding the Party that talk of coalition and deals with the Liberal Democrats gives the impression that the Party is planning for failure, rather than majority rule.[62] It was reported in the run up to the 2015 general election that senior trade union leaders were urging Ed Miliband to offer electoral reform to the Liberal Democrats in return for supporting a Labour government. While this was not tested due to the surprise Conservative victory, Miliband's support for electoral reform had waned. A year earlier, he had argued that 'electoral reform was not the answer to disengagement with politics', a view supplemented by the decisive result of the AV referendum and how the issue had divided the Party.[63] On the other side, some Conservative figures such as Francis Maude hoped that the Conservative–Liberal Democrat coalition would continue after the 2015 general election.

Post-May 2015, Jonathan Reynolds, MP, and the now former Labour MP Chuka Umunna critiqued the workings of the electoral system, with reformers emphasizing that 2015 was the most disproportionate result yet. They argued that under FPTP 'too many people feel remote and unrepresented' as it forces 'the major parties to overwhelmingly devote their resources on just a handful of constituencies, because they believe these are the ones that might change hands. It therefore fails to treat voters equally.' Most of all, 'it creates false electoral deserts where whole regions of the country are dominated by one party despite their opponents recording substantial numbers of votes'.[64] John McDonnell from the left of the Party, wrote: 'The stark reality is that most voters explicitly rejected the Conservative manifesto last year, and yet we all must suffer a majority government as it tries to force these extreme measures upon an unwilling country.'[65]

In addition, a cross-party group of MPs and pressure groups was formed in 2016 to build a consensus in favour of PR and introduce PR by 2021.[66] This was echoed by the party leaders of the SNP, Plaid and Greens, who wished to see all the parties of the centre-left unite around PR. Indeed, it was claimed that Corbyn, the then newly elected Labour leader, was open to reform and dealing with the Liberal Democrats. However, any reform had to maintain the constituency link. Talk of reform drew criticism from John Spellar. Any deal was 'fundamentally undemocratic', entailing 'politics by the back door', 'transferring power from communities to a coterie of elites' and a 'concern of the metropolitan elite' whereas 'ordinary people have more sense'. He continued, arguing that the people had spoken in 2011 and clearly did not support electoral reform – they did not have to keep voting until they gave the 'right' answer for the metropolitan intellectual cultural elite – and was dismayed at the defeatism that had taken over the Party.[67]

In 2016 Lisa Nandy coedited *The Alternative* with Caroline Lucas and Chris Bowers, advocating cross-party cooperation among 'progressives' in light of the 2015 general election result and the 2016 Brexit vote. The editors advocated political pluralism, claiming it 'delivers better answers and better government'. A progressive alliance based on a shared agenda would rebuild democracy and have a 'political reach that no one party alone could have today' rather than narrow tribalism under the present system. FPTP no longer accurately mapped British society and its fluidity, with people demanding greater choice and control, yet the political system denies them a voice.[68]

Neal Lawson, the commentator and director of the cross-party campaign group Compass, echoed these sentiments. For him, the 'good society' entailed neither the free market, nor big state as this meant politics was done *to* people, not *with* people. Social class was no longer the agent of change, but by being a 'networked citizen' in cooperative, the sharing economy, the world of peer-to-peer activity, in civil society and purposeful companies, social enterprises and NGOs. Consequently, the differences between Labour, the Liberal Democrats and Greens needed to be put aside, as no one party could resolve today's problems.[69]

Despite some newspaper talk about electoral reform and Corbyn's supposed openness to doing a deal with the Liberal Democrats and the nationalists, the matter took a backseat during his leadership. It was far from clear that Corbyn favoured reform, merely stating that he was 'open' to the idea. Moreover, the 2017 general election result in which Labour, much to the surprise of many commentators, exceeded expectations by polling over 12.8 million votes, resulting in a net gain of thirty seats. A popular post-election refrain was that had 2,000 votes across marginal constituencies gone to Labour, then they could have formed a government. In addition, with deep divisions within the Conservative Party over May's Brexit deal and their reliance in the House of Commons with the Democratic Unionist Party (DUP), it perhaps appeared that victory at the next election was in reach. Yet, internal divisions within Labour over Brexit, Corbyn's leadership, infiltration of the 'hard left' and accusations of antisemitism, led seven Labour MPs – Luciana Berger, Ann Coffey, Mike Gapes, Chris Leslie, Gavin Shuker, Angela Smith and Chuka Umunna – to form Change UK along with three pro-European Conservative MPs – Sarah Wollaston, Heidi Allen and Anna Soubry. The departure of the seven Labour MPs was another example of the ruptures evident within Labour's history, sharing similarities with those who left to form the SDP in 1981.

The issue of electoral reform returned to the fore during the 2020 Labour leadership contest. The contest came after Corbyn announced he would stand down as leader following Labour's worst electoral result since 1935. While Clive Lewis MP was the first candidate to drop out of the contest, he argued that Labour must work with other 'progressives' if it was to win.[70] The other candidates were also encouraged to give their opinion; Starmer called for a constitutional convention to address issues including 'the fact that millions of people vote in safe seats and they feel their voice doesn't count', Rebecca Long-Bailey also backed a constitutional convention without explicitly backing PR, while Emily Thornberry opposed the idea, arguing against moving to a system that is not based around constituency MPs.[71] Nandy's support for electoral reform is less clear, and she has not argued for it in general elections.

The journalist Polly Toynbee asserted that thanks to the efforts of Lewis, electoral reform is 'mainstream Labour'.[72] The 2021 Labour Party Conference witnessed a motion submitted by 153 CLPs in support of proportional representation, and a poll of the Party membership revealed that 83 per cent favoured reform. Interestingly, figures from the left and right of the Party championed its cause, for instance, Nadia Whittome and Laura Parker from the left, and Luke Akehurst and Ben Bradshaw from the right. Lawson returned to the themes he outlined in 2016, when he criticized the Party leadership and the trade unions for blocking PR at Labour Party Conference, 2021 – Starmer had also ruled out a deal with the SNP – for continuing to accept a top-down view of politics and the electoral system rather than embracing pluralism.[73]

On the flip side, the Labour supporting academic Richard Johnson wrote a piece that explored the philosophical arguments against PR, and reminded the Party that it would be electorally catastrophic, meaning the end of majority Labour governments and potentially the Labour Party itself. The eco-socialist political programme envisioned by some reformers was fantasy, and the obsessions with PR 'fetishes process and ignores the importance of outcomes'.[74] From within Labour, Spellar dismissed electoral reform as an 'inner city London media issue'. He said: 'If it happened the party would split within a year between a Corbynite and a traditional Labour party. It would be the Tories and the Greens who would benefit.' For Spellar, it was laughable that reformers had resorted to hysterical claims that British democracy had led us to a climate breakdown and a second gilded age of hoarded wealth and power – in part, a response to those within Labour who had set up 'Labour for a New Democracy' – and that PR was the answer.[75]

Summary

It would be the Conservative–Liberal Democrat coalition who would deliver Labour's referendum manifesto pledge. Burnham had made clear in 2010 that Labour would campaign neither for nor against, instead focusing on the different elections taking place across Great Britain. The matter was deemed secondary to the primary concern of winning seats in local government and the devolved assemblies. During the AV Referendum, the newly elected Labour leader Ed Miliband found himself in the minority view of the PLP, supporting a switch to AV. Miliband, having only narrowly beaten his brother months earlier in a tight leadership contest, had little political capital to use and although he campaigned in favour, it was not considered a priority like the other elections taking place across Britain. Labour duly split.

Many of the Labour politicians who were openly opposed and expressed reservations of coalition with the Liberal Democrats in 2010 were most opposed to AV, including Reid, Blunkett, Falconer, Harris and Beckett. Clegg was attacked mercilessly and provided a figurehead to point out all that was wrong AV and coalition government. Yet, underpinning the referendum was a traditional defence of FPTP: broadly, arguments centred on the purpose of voting is the creation being a single-party government, the electorate's ability to sack a government and the rejection of hung parliaments and coalition government as it would lead to broken promises and the trading away of manifesto pledges. For the Yes side, whilst they could call upon the support of high-profile Labour figures such as Ed Miliband, Johnson and Bradshaw, the refrain of 'fair voting' lacked traction as did the belief that AV would clean up politics, create greater choice and increase accountability. Whilst pro-reform politicians, commentators and academics talked about the split on the British left and how AV would foster 'progressive' politics, the creation of the coalition government suggested such a notion was illusory.

While the sheer scale of the defeat for AV led some supporters of FPTP to believe that the cause of electoral reform, whether it be a different majoritarian system or proportional representation, had been set back a generation, voices from within and within the Party have continued to argue their case. In fact, these voices represent a range of traditions from across the Labour movement and they consider that their argument has been strengthened by the electoral difficulties faced by the Party in the period assessed. As with the 1980s and 1990s, reformers claim that only through electoral pacts, coalition and PR can the Labour Party return to government. They continue, arguing that FPTP and Britain's constitutional setup supposedly operates in the electoral and political interests of the Conservative Party, not Labour, who must embrace a more pluralistic approach to politics. This has been countered by defenders of FPTP, who point to the formation and policies of the Conservative–Liberal Democrat Coalition, the scale of defeat for AV in 2011, the belief that only through the right policies, leadership and organization will Labour attract support, and the underlying belief that a general election is concerned with the creation of a single-party government.

Conclusion

The electoral reform debate is of fundamental importance, generally for British politics and specifically for the Labour Party: its place within the British political system, its unique objective of bringing about a social democratic Britain through parliament and how it relates and behaves towards other political parties. An alternative electoral system is likely to impact how Labour operates within the political system and has consequences for its desire to form single-party governments, transform society and defeat its political opponents.

By drawing out the ideas in the narrative, Labour's attitude towards the electoral system, as this book makes apparent, is primarily based on two competing views and approaches: elitism and pluralism. The former has emphasized the need for a parliamentary majority, delivered by FPTP, allowing the Party to enact its vision of socialism, or more accurately *Labourism*, from the centre. The latter has stressed consensus, cooperation and dialogue, ideas which, according to its proponents, are marginalized within the Westminster model of politics, and within Labour's 'tribal' approach to politics. Marxism has rarely influenced Labour's attitude towards the Westminster electoral system, instead finding favour with those outside the Party and movement. However, it would be a mistake to dismiss Marxism as its importance can be viewed in its critique of the Labour Party's acceptance of parliamentary orthodoxy.

The Party, as the political wing of the Labour movement, has considered parliamentary representation the priority, delivering socialism through the parliamentary method. Popular movements have been sidelined in favour of elections, with Labour attempting to capture the state and utilize the power invested in a parliamentary majority to reform and ameliorate capitalism. The Attlee governments highlighted the benefits of a single-party majority in the House of Commons, convincing the Party that the state could be used to meet

Labour's ends. The state was there to be captured, and Britain's constitutional arrangements, including the workings of FPTP, was deemed the best attainable method to produce Labour governments. From there, it could implement its distinct socioeconomic agenda, symbolized by the introduction of the welfare state. The objections raised by Labour's political opponents within and without Parliament could be countered by a parliamentary majority, with the oft-repeated achievements of Labour governments used to defend FPTP. Despite the raft of constitutional changes introduced by New Labour, critics claimed that Labour's commitment to this top-down view of politics and policy continued. During the days following the May 2010 general election, Labour's behaviour and attitude displayed a clear and unfailing constitutionalism, abiding by the 'rules of the game', and in some cases, gladly accepting defeat and entering opposition.

Both the Marxists and pluralists critique *Labourism* and what they see as its conservative ethos. For the former, the Labour Party is not an effective vehicle to introduce socialism as it is wedded to the parliamentary method, reluctant to challenge the entrenched power of capital found within the British state. Labour's acceptance of FPTP is unsurprising, for it aligns with its belief in moderation and gradualism. Proportional representation would permit a realignment in British politics. The Labour Party would be pulled to the left by the emergence of a fully avowed socialist party, exposing the class divisions within society. Alternatively, Labour would split with the right of the Labour Party joining the centre party, and the left of the Party – freed from constitutional and economic orthodoxy of Labour – able to join or become a Socialist party truly representing the interests of the working class. Consequently, the compromises Labour makes with capital in order to win elections – necessary through the workings of FPTP forcing Labour to attract and win the votes of non-socialists and Conservatives – would cease.

Such a view contradicts Labour's principles and objectives, which, as outlined, is concerned with parliamentary representation and the formation of a government operating in the interests of working people. For this end to be realized Labour must build broad electoral coalitions, attracting support from different classes and regions of Great Britain. Therefore, Labour becomes not just a class-based party but a national party and, importantly, desires to be perceived by the electorate as a national party. Consequently, the Labour

Party is a broad church in relation to its electoral base, membership and parliamentarians, including trade union members, the working-class and middle-class intellectuals, all from across the regions of Great Britain.

Here, we can see something of Labour's ethos. The Labour Party, having in large part developed out of the working class movement, considers itself to be the sole defensive agent of the working class. The Labour Party has, what it sees, as a unique socioeconomic ideology committed to furthering the interests of the working class and bringing about a social democratic Great Britain. FPTP encourages the Labour Party to come together, fusing a coalition of people who broadly share the same principles, deeming it better to work within one party than with those who may or may not agree in a different party. An electoral system that causes division, such as STV where Labour candidates would compete against one another, would harm Labour as Labour's factions from left, centre and right would be exposed. Prevalent amongst the FPTP supporters during the Plant Report was the recent memory and trauma of the SDP and, more generally, Labour's history of ruptures. An electoral system which had the potential to foster further splits was to be opposed.

However, the pluralists object to what they see as Labour's conservative and defensive ethos, deeming it limiting, restrictive and preventing it from reaching out beyond 'the tribe'. Healing the historic schism on the British left between Labour and the Liberal Democrats through PR would permit Labour to create a greater electoral coalition which otherwise would remain out of reach. They argue that Labour on its own is incapable of attracting the support of social groups required to deliver a parliamentary majority due to its 'tribalism' and belief that only it is capable of defeating the Conservatives. Through political engagement, a renewed interest in politics would ensue, allowing Labour to gain from those who deem constitutional reform to be important.

According to its proponents, this entails several benefits for the Labour Party, for instance, making it 'safe' in the eyes of the electorate and therefore electable. In the 1990s, figures like John Denham argued that it was an indispensable part of Labour's modernization,[1] evidence that the Party was 'New Labour', rejecting the politics of the Old Left and Old Right. The Labour left would be silenced by the moderating influence of the centrist MPs. The centre party would also ensure a Labour government would remain in office for a prolonged period of time, working in unison in parliament, creating both a united front against the Conservatives at Westminster and in the country. This would prevent a Conservative government, perhaps for a generation, allowing for the implementation of, to some degree, a social democratic policy agenda. Unlike the twentieth century which was dominated electorally by the Conservative Party, the 'progressive' forces in British politics could ensure a 'progressive' twenty-first century. Consequently, PR and coalition would transform Labour politics, creating a truly 'progressive' Party and movement.

Whilst the pluralist analysis has its supporters within the Labour Party, and has experienced times of prominence, the elitists have remained dominant. Consequently, many in the Party have rejected the 'progressive left' thesis put forward by Marquand and others. Firstly, they have treated the professed benefits of pluralism with caution. Throughout, Labour figures have expressed concern about the consequences of PR and coalition. For some, it would signal the end of the Party – shedding what is left of its working-class origins, or splitting the Party into two – encapsulated by Harold Wilson's comment that 'this Party is not for burning'. Secondly, because it runs counter to Labour's objective of having sole control over the levers of power, it would entail watering down policies designed to ameliorate capitalism. Thirdly, the likely introduction of PR, often thought of as a method to aid realigning the British left, would be an acceptance that Labour is no longer capable of governing without the support of others. The electorate would question Labour's resolve and standing as a national party, a sure sign of defeatism.

Moreover, the Marquand view has been dismissed, for it has been based on a misreading of twentieth-century British politics. Far from Labour and the Liberal Party – in all its various guises – complementing one another, sharing the same history, ideology and policies, they are in direct competition for votes, seats and power and have different views on the direction in which socially and economically they desire to take the country. Whenever Spellar heard talk of healing the schisms between liberalism and socialism, his thoughts turned to Hattersley, who would point out that it assumed that the creation of the Labour Party was a historic mistake, implicitly criticizing social democracy from breaking with liberalism, with its emphasis on collective action and provision.[2]

Realignment of the left is also rejected by Labour politicians through appeals to Labour history, recalling how the Liberals voted with the Conservatives to oust James Callaghan in 1979, beckoning in eighteen years of Conservative government. The SDP split in which Labour MPs left the Party – comparable to MacDonald forming the 'National Government' – was intent on replacing Labour as the main opposition to the Conservatives. At a local level the Liberal Democrats fought and beat Labour, for example, the city councils in Liverpool and Sheffield. The campaigning and electoral tactics deployed by the Liberals on the ground, in election material and general demeanour, has led some in Labour to view them as untrustworthy, duplicitous and opportunistic. Consequently, they are viewed as having no firm principles and beliefs.

Plant broke with Labour orthodoxy when he stated it is far better that Labour implemented some of its manifesto in coalition with a like-minded partner than remain impotent in opposition, thus rejecting the doctrine of the mandate and the manifesto. No longer did a single policy document and the general election, in an era of declining class and political loyalty, with voting now taking place on instrumental lines and electors thinking of their own interests in deciding how to vote, sufficiently represent the views and changing nature of British society. Many of the arguments in Plant in favour of electoral reform continue to be utilized to the present day by pluralists within the Party, suggesting a continuity of rationale.

For Plant, FPTP supporters wanted to resist the idea of people voting instrumentally. The idea of class identification and the more cultural identification of working people led Labour FPTP supporters to conclude that the working class should vote Labour however hopeless it might seem, rather than tactically or instrumentally. Consequently, an election is partly about expressing loyalty to a set of ideas.[3]

Primarily, Labour politicians have viewed a general election to be about the creation of a government. Importantly, it was accepted that different institutions had different purposes and, therefore, alternative electoral systems were permissible. However, it should have been no surprise during the AV Referendum that the majority of Labour MPs backed FPTP, continuing Labour opposition to electoral reform also seen at the time of Plant and Jenkins. Labour has continued to support FPTP at Westminster despite the ideological shifts within the Party and the acceptance in the latter part of the twentieth century of much of the New Right agenda. Healey's dismissal of the 'progressive left' and PR, based on his experience of the Lib–Lab Pact, summarizes Labour's prevalent attitude: FPTP produces the best form of government; compromising on policy does not better represent the views of the electorate; Labour cannot escape its problems through PR and coalition; there is an anti-Labour majority just as large as the anti-Conservative majority due to the centre parties being deeply divided; and the benefits of PR in terms of aiding the Labour Party in forming a government are unlikely to materialize.[4]

The actions of the Parliamentary Labour Party and Labour leadership have reinforced this view. Labour's scepticism of coalition at Westminster has been commonplace through much of the twentieth and into the twenty-first century. Whilst the Lib–Lab Pact was born out of necessity, the aftermath of the 2010 general election clearly revealed Labour's reluctance to embrace coalition with the Liberal Democrats fully. Whilst the scale of the 2010 election defeat is significant, prominent Labour figures damned coalition with the Liberal Democrats. The events of May 2010 exposed the failings of the 'progressive left' thesis, and vindicated those in the Labour Party who had opposed realignment. Beckett considered that the 'progressive left' was 'a leap of faith without any concrete evidence which supports the claim'. For her, the 'assumption was the Liberal Democrats would always go with the Labour Party never seemed accurate'.[5] Consequently, the rejection of the 'progressive left' thesis is based on historical as well as theoretical grounds.

Whilst the pluralist analysis outlines the overlapping policies and shared values between the two parties – especially the right of the Labour Party and the Liberal Democrats on issues such as nationalization, welfare, the economy, taxation and Europe – support and opposition towards PR does not fit comfortably into a 'Left–Right split'. Not all those on the right of the Labour Party support PR just as not all those on the left of the Party support FPTP. Therefore, the matter is best viewed as an issue based on competing governing strategies and perceived self-interest. Tom Harris, on the right of the Party, is staunchly in favour of FPTP having little time for the Liberal Democrats. On the other hand, Ben Bradshaw, MP, supports a move away from FPTP to PR. During Blair's premiership, a figure on the left of the Cabinet such as John Prescott damned the notion of PR, vetoing Blair's overtures towards the Liberal Democrats. On the right of the Cabinet, Jack Straw also dismissed PR. On the left of the Party, John McDonnell, MP, is in favour of PR, whereas Denis Skinner remains wholly opposed.

However, attitudes towards the electoral system in the Labour Party are fluid. Roy Hattersley changed his mind, having led the arguments against PR in the 1980s and 1990s, he then accepted PR. Collectively, the Labour Party in the 1920s moved away from PR towards FPTP, a position it has maintained ever since with fluctuating confidence. Baroness Armstrong moved towards FPTP and her comments encapsulate Labour's broader thoughts on PR and its consequences:

> The longer I was on the Working Party the less convinced I became about change. I went on as an agnostic but came off thinking the sacrifices we would have to make from losing our system were greater than what we would gain, largely because of one person and the identification with constituents.[6]

Between the polarized views is a cohort of MPs who are agnostic on the matter of electoral reform, deeming it not to be a burning issue. Mandelson neatly summarized the view, stating, 'It's not a passionate view of mine and it's not the highest priority issue for me.'[7] Hattersley deemed, 'There is no point the Labour Party tearing itself apart over a Liberal issue … an issue that is somewhat marginal'.[8] Labour politicians perceive liberal issues to be of no concern to the electorate and working class, reminiscent of Gilbert Gray's quip 'they speak of little else in Barnsley'. Whilst PR might be an urgent issue for the liberal intelligentsia and north London dinner table sets, the working class – as far as the dominant view in the Labour Party is concerned – are interested in the economy, health service and education, not the mechanisms that send representatives to Parliament.

PR becomes a distraction from the task of winning the general election, which is to be fought under FPTP against the Conservatives. Advocating electoral reform is a sure sign of defeatism, pandering to the Liberal Democrats rather than appealing to the electorate through credible and sensible policies and displaying confidence in your own ability to win. Moreover, the electorate did not vote Labour to introduce PR but to build hospitals and schools, and it is on these issues that the electorate will judge the Party. The 1992 general election was a case in point. Although Labour had been discussing constitutional issues including PR for several years, ambiguity over PR was blamed for defeat, creating a distraction from the *serious* business of governing. Whilst competing views on the electoral system are sincerely held, unity is required in the Labour Party. The matter becomes – as far as the leadership is concerned – one of party management, a position adopted by John Smith who thanked the Plant Commission for its deliberations, before committing the Party to a referendum on the electoral system to sidestep a divisive issue. A referendum commitment found favour with Blair and Brown, both of whom acknowledged the divisions in the Cabinet, the PLP and wider Labour movement.

Looking ahead, the referendum tool is more problematic now than it was for previous leaders. Firstly, the scale of defeat over AV would make it look as if the Labour Party thinks that the electorate got it wrong in 2011. Secondly, finding agreement on an alternative electoral system to be presented to the electorate is not straightforward. AV was put forward as a 'halfway' house as it maintained the constituency link and held out the prospect of majority governments, whilst also accepting the principle of reform. However, it was defeated by a considerable margin and its close relation, SV, could be dismissed because it is a preferential system. Proportional systems that break the constituency link – something politicians of all parties value – is unacceptable, leaving some type of hybrid system. When the Jenkins Commission raised this prospect, it was damned by large parts of the Labour Party. Its adoption in Scotland has proved to be an unhappy one for Scottish Labour.

Interest in PR has remained within the Labour Party despite thirteen years of government between 1997 and 2010. Towards the end of the Brown government, electoral reform returned to the agenda, hoping they could hold it over into the coalition talks with the Liberal Democrats. A historic three successive election victories, of which 1997 and 2001 were landslide victories, may have justified those who rejected PR during the eighteen years in opposition. But as the AV referendum and subsequent events have highlighted, a significant minority of the PLP consider electoral reform to be a worthwhile pursuit. Pressure for reform will grow under the Starmer leadership, with calls for Labour to embrace pluralism, the bleak electoral prospects, and a way of displaying that Labour has moved on from both Corbyn and New Labour. Put another way, there will be those who argue that the only way to make Labour safe again is if it embraces PR.

However, reformers in the Labour Party are hindered by a lack of agreement on the type of electoral system they wish to see implemented and faced by a unified bloc of FPTP supporters. Besides, they often resort to extravagant claims about how PR will transform democracy, treating PR as if it is the panacea to the nation's ills, claims that do not hold up under scrutiny. Importantly, Labour must win under the present system and while the Party faces considerable obstacles, the pendulum will eventually swing back to Labour. Elsewhere, attempts to realign the left may result in asymmetrical benefits, in which the minor parties benefit much more than the Labour Party. Indeed, there is no guarantee that the methods to realign the left will work, and there is plenty of evidence at all levels of governance in the UK of the so-called progressive parties siding with the Conservatives. Today, in all likelihood, any deal would have to involve the SNP. Not only would this be ideologically incoherent, but it would prompt an English backlash. In short, it is wrong to dismiss supporters of FPTP within the Labour Party. They make a vitally important contribution to the debate over Britain's constitutional settlement understanding that the most crucial power the people have is the power to choose their government.

As this book has shown, attitudes towards the electoral system are both matters of principle and perceived self-interest. Given the sincerely held views on both sides, PR will continue to cause division as long as the Labour Party exists.

Notes

Introduction

1 https://www.politicshome.com/news/uk/social-affairs/politics/news/69720/union-bosses-tell-ed-miliband-give-lib-dems-election (accessed 15 December 2016).

2 *Guardian*, 'Labour Should Fight for Electoral Reform', Thursday, 15 November 2019.

3 A. H. Hanson, 'The Labour Party and House of Commons Reform – I', *Parliamentary Affairs*, vol. 10, no. 4 (1956), p. 456.

4 A. Wright, 'British Socialists and the British Constitution', *Parliamentary Affairs*, vol. 43 (1990), pp. 323–45.

5 See J. Miles, 'Harold Wilson and the British Constitution', in A. Crines and K. Hickson (eds), *Harold Wilson: The Unprincipled Prime Minister?* (London: Biteback, 2016).

6 D. Marquand, 'Democracy in Britain', *Political Quarterly*, vol. 71, no. 3 (2000), p. 269; V. Bogdanor, *The New British Constitution* (London: Hart, 2009), p. 231.

7 *Observer*, 'The Great Democrat Must Keep His PR Pledge', 13 July 1997.

8 Quoted in J. Morrison, *Reforming Britain: New Labour, New Constitution?* (London: Reuters, 2001), p. 263.

9 R. McKibbin, *Parties and People: England 1914–1951* (Oxford: Oxford University Press, 2010), pp. 159–60.

10 H. J. Hanham, *The Reformed Electoral System in Great Britain, 1832–1914* (London: Historical Association, 1968), p. 7.

11 G. D. H. Cole, *Social Theory* (New York: Frederick A. Stokes, 1920).

12 T. Wright, *Citizens and Subjects: An Essay on British Politics* (London: Routledge, 1994), pp. 71–2. Mark Evans also argues that for much of the twentieth century, the Labour Party adopted a 'High Tory' approach to the constitution. See 'New Labour and the New Constitutionalism', in M. Beech and S. Lee, *Ten Years of New Labour* (Hampshire: Palgrave Macmillan, 2008), p. 71.

13 Wright, *Citizens and Subjects*, p. 75.

14 H. Drucker, *Doctrine and Ethos in the Labour Party* (London: George Allen & Unwin, 1979), pp. 91–6.

15 See A. Gamble, 'The Progressive Dilemma Revisited', *Political Quarterly*, vol. 88, no. 1 (2017), p. 136.

16 Drucker, *Doctrine and Ethos in the Labour Party*, pp. 1–21.

17 Quoted in K. O. Morgan, *Labour in Power* (Oxford: Oxford University Press, 1985), p. 85.

18 M. Evans, 'New Labour and the New Constitutionalism', in M. Beech and S. Lee, *Ten Years of New Labour* (Hampshire: Palgrave Macmillan, 2008), p. 71.

19 R. Crossman, *The Crossman Diaries* (London: Mandarin, 1966), p. 247.

20 D. Blunkett and D. Richards, 'Labour in and Out of Government: Political Ideas, Political Practice and the British Political Tradition', *Political Studies Review*, vol. 9 (2011), p. 179.

21 J. Schumpeter, *Capitalism, Socialism and Democracy* (London: George Allen & Unwin, 1976), p. 295.

22 R. Barker, *Political Ideas in Modern Britain*, 2nd edn (London: Routledge, 1997), pp. 111–12.

23 G. Foote, *The Labour Party's Political Thought: A History* (Kent: Croom Helm, 1986), p. 24.

24 R. Miliband, *Parliamentary Socialism* (London: Merlin Press, 1961), p. 13.

25 Ibid.

26 T. Cliff and D. Gluckstein, *The Labour Party – A Marxist History* (London: Bookmarks, 1988), pp. 319, 388.

27 A. Gamble, *Britain in Decline*, 1st edn (Hampshire: Macmillan Education, 1981), p. 232.

28 Ibid.

29 H. Wainwright, *Labour: A Tale of Two Parties* (London: Hogarth Press, 1987), pp. 281–2.

30 K. Hickson, *Britain's Conservative Right since 1945: Traditional Toryism in a Cold Climate* (Hampshire: Palgrave Macmillan, 2020), p. 1.

1 Labour and the electoral system in historical perspective, 1900–31

1 H. Pelling and A. J. Reid, *A Short History of the Labour Party* (11th edn) (Houndmills: Macmillan, 1996), p. 7.

2 See V. Bogdanor, *Politics and the Constitution: Essays on British Government* (Aldershot: Dartmouth, 1996), p. 121; N. Blewett, *The Peers, the Parties and the People: The General Elections of 1910* (London: Macmillan, 1972, pp. 241, 262.

3 See D. Butler, *The Electoral System in Britain since 1918* (2nd edn) (Oxford: Oxford University Press, 1963), pp. 6–7.

4 *Labour Party Conference Report*, 1909, p. 87.

5 *Trades Union Congress Annual Report*, 1908, pp. 155–6.

6   *Trades Union Congress Annual Report*, 1909, p. 163.

7   *Labour Party Conference Report*, 1910, pp. 75–7.

8   J. R. MacDonald, *Socialism and Government* (London: Independent Labour Party, 1909).

9   Ibid., pp. 150–3.

10 *Labour Party Conference Report*, 1911, pp. 103, 105.

11 *Labour Party Conference Report*, 1913, p. 108.

12 G. H. Roberts and W. C. Anderson, 'The Case for Proportional Representation', in J. R. MacDonald, G. H. Roberts and W. C. Anderson (eds), *The Labour Party and Electoral Reform: Proportional Representation and the Alternative Vote* (London: The Labour Party, 1913), p. 7.

13 Ibid., p. 8.

14 Ibid., pp. 10, 13.

15 Ibid., p. 14.

16 Ibid., p. 17.

17 MacDonald, 'The Case against Proportional Representation', in MacDonald, Roberts and Anderson, *Proportional Representation and the Alternative Vote*, p. 26.

18 Ibid., p. 27.

19 Ibid.

20 Ibid., p. 28.

21 Ibid.

22 Ibid., p. 27.

23 Ibid., p. 28.

24 Ibid., p. 30.

25 *Labour Party Conference Report*, 1914, 27 January 1914, p. 105; *Justice*, 1 February 1914.

26 M. Pugh, 'The Background to the Representation of the People Act of 1918', PhD Thesis, University of Bristol, United Kingdom, 1974, p. 73.

27 M. Steed, 'The Evolution of the British Electoral System', in S. Finer (ed.), *Adversary Politics and Electoral Reform* (London: William Clowes & Sons, 1975), pp. 44–5.

28 Wilson, *Political Diaries of C. P. Scott, 1911–1928*, pp. 316, 317.

29 Butler, *The Electoral System in Britain since 1918*, p. 43.

30 D. Marquand, *Ramsay MacDonald* (London: Jonathan Cape, 1977), p. 289.

31 J. R. MacDonald, *Diary*, Entry 1st May 1923; J. R. MacDonald, *Parliament and Democracy* (London: Leonard Parsons, 1920), pp. vi–vii.

32 'Socialist Review' and 'New Leader' quoted in *Manchester Guardian*, 'Labour Party Leaves Its Members a Free Vote', 2 May 1924.

33 C. Cook, 'Labour's Electoral Base', in C. Cook and I. Taylor (eds.), *The Labour Party: An Introduction to Its History Structure and Politics* (London: Longman, 1980), p. 86.

34 R. W. Lyman, *The First Labour Government: 1924* (London: Chapman and Hall, 1957), p. 89.

35 Quoted in T. Wilson, *Downfall of the Liberal Party 1914–1935* (London: Collins, 1966), p. 289.

36 Ibid., pp. 290–2.

37 T. Wilson, *The Political Diaries of C. P. Scott 1911–1928* (London: Collins, 1970), pp. 460–1, 15 July 1924.

38 House of Commons Debates, vol. 169, col. 773, 12 February 1924.

39 D. Marquand, '1924–1932', in D. Butler (ed.), *Coalitions in British Politics* (London: Macmillan, 1978), pp. 53–4.

40 *Manchester Guardian*, 'Premier's Doubts of PR', 17 May 1924.

41 *Manchester Guardian*, 'Labour Party Leaves Its Members a Free Vote', 2 May 1924; *The Times*, 'The PR Bill', 2 May 1924.

42 *Manchester Guardian*, 'Commons Reject PR: Majority of 94 against Liberal Measure', 3 May 1924.

43 Wilson, *Downfall of the Liberal Party*, p. 296.

44 *The Times*, 3 May 1924.

45 *Labour Party Conference Report*, 1926, p. 273; Butler, *The Electoral System in Britain since 1918*, p. 47.

46 Labour Party, *Annual Conference Report*, 1923, p. 178, quoted in Foote, *The Labour Party's Political Thought*, p. 28.

47 S. Webb, 'Historic', in G. B. Shaw (ed.), *Fabian Essays* (London: George Allen & Unwin, 1962), pp. 66–7.

48 G. B. Shaw, *Report on Fabian Policy and Resolutions, Fabian Tract No. 70* (London: Fabian Society, 1896).

49 *Fabian News*, November 1896, p. 35, quoted in Foote, *The Labour Party's Political Thought*, p. 29.

50 H. Finer, *The Case against Proportional Representation*, Fabian Tract 211 (London: Fabian Society, 1924), p. 7. PR has always recommended itself to men with a mission, but without much visible evidence of popular support, p. 3.

51 Ibid., p. 5.

52 Ibid., pp. 5–6.

53 Ibid., p. 7.

54 Ibid., pp. 1–17.

55 A. J. P. Taylor, *English History 1914–1945* (London: Penguin Books, 1970), pp. 342–3.

56 J. R. MacDonald, *Diary*, 19 December 1929.

57 Pethick-Lawrence to MacDonald, 2 June 1929, MacDonald Papers, Public Record Office, PRO 30/69/1300, quoted in J. D. Fair, 'The Second Labour Government

and the Politics of Electoral Reform, 1929–1931, *Albion: A Quarterly Journal Concerned with British Studies*, vol. 13, no. 3 (Autumn 1981), p. 278.

58 House of Commons Debates, vol. 229, cols. 49, 64–5, 73–4, 2 July 1929.

59 Fair, 'The Second Labour Government', pp. 279–81.

60 Quoted in J. F. S Ross, *Elections and Electors* (London: Eyre & Spottiswoode, 1955), p. 319.

61 MacDonald to Ullswater, 25 and 30 July 1929, MacDonald Papers, PRO 30/69/1300, quoted in Fair, 'The Second Labour Government', p. 280.

62 *The Times*, 'Liberal Party Policy', 14 June 1929; *The Times*, 'The Coal Bill', 6 January 1930.

63 J. R. MacDonald, *Diary*, 3 February 1930.

64 Note dates 4 February 1930, MacDonald Papers, 5/171, quoted in Marquand, *Ramsay MacDonald*, pp. 529–30.

65 Ibid.

66 'Memo by J.R.M.', MacDonald Papers, PRO 30/69/5/166, quoted in Marquand, *Ramsay MacDonald*, pp. 531–2.

67 Quoted in J. Campbell, *Lloyd George: The Goat in the Wilderness* (Chatham: W&J Mackay, 1977), p. 264.

68 'Further Developments of Electoral Reform', 23 May 1930, Templewood Papers, V1, 2, quoted in Fair, 'The Second Labour Government', p. 287.

69 Butler, *The Electoral System in Britain Since 1918*, pp. 60–1; Fair, 'The Second Labour Government', p. 287; R. Skidelsky, *Politicians and the Slump: The Labour Government 1929–1931* (London: MacMillan, 1994) p. 164; P. Snowden, *An Autobiography* (London: Ivor Nicholson and Watson, 1934), p. 887; Marquand, *Ramsay MacDonald*, p. 533.

70 Quoted in *Manchester Guardian*, 'Electoral Reform Bill: Second Reading Carries Majority of 65', 4 February 1931. Kenworthy, quoted from House of Commons Debates, vol. 249, 4 March 1931, cols. 495–6.

71 *The Times*, 6 March 1931; *Manchester Guardian*, 'The Alternative Vote: Rejection Motion Defeated Majority of 26', 5 March 1931.

72 Skidelsky, *Politicians and the Slump*, pp. 328–31.

73 F. Owen, *Tempestuous Journey: Lloyd George, His Life and Times* (London: Hutchinson, 1954), p. 717. Thorpe references Lloyd George to Lansbury, 16 February 1931 (Lansbury Paper, 10). A. Thorpe, *The British General Election of 1931* (Oxford: Clarendon Press, 1991), p. 56.

74 R. Miliband, *Parliamentary Socialism* (London: Merlin Press, 1961), p. 234.

75 R. Eatwell and A. Wright, 'Labour and the Lessons of 1931', *History*, vol. 63, no. 1 (1978), p. 40.

76 Drucker, *Doctrine and Ethos in the Labour Party*, pp. 119–20.

2 Labour and the electoral system in historical perspective, 1931–87

1 J. Hart, *Proportional Representation, Critics of the British Electoral System 1820–1945* (Oxford: Clarendon Press, 1992), p. 248.

2 M. Beech and K. Hickson, *Labour's Thinkers* (London: Taurus Academic Studies, 2007), pp. 58–77.

3 J. Callaghan, 'Fabian Socialism, Democracy and the State', in G. Duncan (ed.), *Democracy and the Capitalist State* (Cambridge: Cambridge University Press, 1989), pp. 173–7.

4 H. Laski, *The Crisis and the Constitution: 1931 and After* (London, 1932), p. 44, quoted in R. McKibbin, *Parties and People: England 1914–1951* (Oxford: Oxford University Press, 2010), p. 160.

5 *Manchester Guardian*, 'Electoral Reform: All-Party support of PR', 8 July 1943.

6 *Manchester Guardian*, 'Unjust Election System: Labour Member Criticises Party Attitude to PR', 12 September 1936.

7 R. Crossman, *How Britain Is Governed* (London: Labour Book Service, 1939), p. 29.

8 Ibid., p. 31.

9 R. Crossman, 'Introduction', in W. Bagehot (ed.), *The English Constitution* (Glasgow: Fontana/Collins, 1963), p. 10.

10 V. Honeyman, *Richard Crossman* (London: I.B. Tauris, 2007), p. 96.

11 *Manchester Guardian*, 'Electoral Reform Problems: Mr. Morrison and "Tricky" Questions of Redistribution', 2 February 1944.

12 Butler, *The Electoral System in Britain since 1918*, p. 91.

13 *Conference on Electoral Reform and Redistribution of Seats* (Cmd. 6543), 1943–4, p. 8.

14 Pugh, *The Electoral System in Britain 1918–1951*, p. 92.

15 Quoted in S. Beer, *Modern British Politics* (London: Faber & Faber, 1982), pp. 179–83.

16 H. Dalton, *High Tide and After: Memoirs 1945–60* (London, 1962) p. 40.

17 D. Butler, '1945–1977', in Butler, *Coalitions in British Politics*, p. 95.

18 Quoted in P. Catterall, 'The British Electoral System, 1885-1970', *Historical Research*, vol. 73 (2000), p. 171.

19 K. O. Morgan, *Callaghan: A Life* (Oxford: Oxford University Press, 1997), p. 362.

20 C. Cook, 'Labour's Electoral Base', in Cook and Taylor, *The Labour Party: An Introduction*, p. 99.

21 H. Morrison, 'Our Parliament and How It Works', Labour Party Educational Series, no. 4, January 1953.

22 H. Morrison, 'British Parliamentary Democracy', *Parliamentary Affairs*, vol. 4, no. 2 (1949), pp. 356–8.

23 H. Morrison, *Our Parliament and How It Works* (London: Labour Party, 1953), pp. 10–12, 27–8.

24 H. Morrison, *Government and Parliament* (Oxford: Oxford University Press, 1954), pp. 98, 161–2, 165.

25 M. De Wolf Howe, *Holmes-Laski Letters: The Correspondence of Mr Justice Holmes to Harold J Laski* (London: Oxford University Press, 1953), p. 494.

26 H. J. Laski, *Reflections on the Constitution* (Manchester: Manchester University Press, 1951), pp. 55–6, 59.

27 A. H. Birch, *Representative and Responsible Government* (London: Allen & Unwin, 1964), p. 227.

28 D. Butler and A. King, *The General Election of 1966* (London: Macmillan, 1966), p. 2; J. Kirkup, 'The Parliamentary Agreement between the Labour Party and the Liberal Party 1977–1978 "The Lab-Lib Pact" ', PhD Thesis, Cardiff University, United Kingdom, 2012, pp. 29–30.

29 P. Ziegler, *Wilson: The Authorised Life* (London: Weidenfield & Nicolson, 1993), p. 207.

30 LSE Archives PARKER 4/2 A, House of Commons Mr Speaker's Conference on Electoral Law, Wednesday, 9 November 1966, p. 3.

31 Ibid., Wednesday 9 November 1966, p. 5.

32 Ibid., Wednesday 16 November 1966, p. 9.

33 Ibid., Wednesday 16 November 1966, p. 8.

34 Ibid., Wednesday 16 November 1966, p. 10.

35 Ibid., Wednesday 16 November 1966, p. 10.

36 Ibid., Wednesday 16 November 1966, p. 15.

37 Ibid., Wednesday 22 November 1966, p. 16.

38 Ibid., Wednesday 22 November 1966, p. 16.

39 *Conference on Electoral Law* (Cmnd. 3202), 1966–7, p. 5.

40 House of Commons Debates, vol. 770 (14 October 1968), col. 39 and 775 (11 December 1968), col. 462.

41 M. Taylor, 'Labour and the Constitution', in D. Tanner, P. Thane and N. Tiratsoo (eds) *Labour's First Century* (Cambridge: Cambridge University Press, 2000), p. 166.

42 C. A. R. Crosland, *Can Labour Win?* (London: Fabian Tract 324, 1960), p. 22.

43 Norton, *The Constitution in Flux* (Oxford: Martin Robertson, 1982), p. 264.

44 Quoted in D. Coates, *The Labour Party and the Struggle for Socialism* (Cambridge: Cambridge University Press, 1975), pp. 142–3.

45 J. P. Mackintosh, *People and Parliament* (Hampshire: Saxon House, 1978), p. 177.

46 J. P. Mackintosh, 'What Is Wrong with British Parliamentary Democracy?', 'The Declining Respect for the Law', in D. Marquand, *John P. Mackintosh on Parliament and Social Democracy* (London: Longmans, 1982), pp. 77–90, 143–4.

47 Shore papers, Nye Bevan Memorial Lecture, Bromsgrove, 5 December 1976, SHORE/11/22, LSE, quoted in K. Hickson, J. Miles and H. Taylor, *Peter Shore: Labour's Forgotten Patriot* (London: Biteback, 2020), p. 104.

48 Quoted in Norton, *The Constitution in Flux*, p. 240.

49 *Observer*, 'Callaghan: Coalition Is a Pipe Dream', 17 March 1974.

50 B. Castle, *The Castle Diaries 1974–1976* (London: Weidenfield and Nicolson, 1980), pp. 69–70.

51 *Guardian*, 'Wilson Rules Out Deal with "Liberal Tories"', 4 October 1973.

52 Quoted in Bogdanor, *The People and the Party System* (Cambridge: Cambridge University Press, 1981), p. 153.

53 Castle, *The Castle Diaries 1974–1976*, p. 554. Interestingly, those whom Castle listed as 'Jenkinite' coalitionists did not all go on to join the Social Democratic Party (SDP). Lever was made a Life Peer in 1979 and Prentice was deselected for his constituency in 1977 and stood for the Conservative Party in 1979. Williams, would be one of the 'Gang of Four', a founding member of the SDP.

54 Quoted in V. Bogdanor, *The People and the Party System: The Referendum and Electoral Reform in British Politics* (Cambridge: Cambridge University Press, 1981), p. 55.

55 *Scotsman*, 'Liberals and Social Democrats', 28 March 1977; *The Times*, 'The Case for a Realignment of the Left', 22 July 1977.

56 J. Callaghan, *Time and Chance* (London: William Collins Sons, 1987), pp. 445–56.

57 NA, CAB 128/62 CM (77): Cabinet Conclusions, 17 November 1977. Quoted in Kirkup, 'The Lab-Lib Pact', p. 286. See also M. Hagger, 'The United Kingdom: The Reluctant Europeans', in V. Herman and M. Hagger (eds), *The Legislation of Direct Elections to the European Parliament* (Hampshire: Gower, 1980), pp. 204–38.

58 M. Pugh, 'Political Parties and the Campaign for Proportional Representation', *Parliamentary Affairs*, vol. 33, no. 1 (1980), p. 294.

59 Kirkup, 'The Lab-Lib Pact', pp. 285–91.

60 'Home Thoughts from Abroad', Roy Jenkins, Dimbleby Lecture, Royal Society of Arts, London, 22 November 1979.

61 D. Healey, *The Time of My Life* (London: Penguin Books, 1990), pp. 458 and 582–3.

62 R. Hattersley, *Choose Freedom: The Future for Democratic Socialism* (London: Penguin Books, 1987), p. 18.

63 T. Ellis, R. Hughes and P. Whitehead, *Electoral Reform*, Fabian Tract 483 (London: Fabian Society, 1982) .

64 See Hickson, Miles and Taylor, *Peter Shore: Labour's Forgotten Patriot*, pp. 132–3.

65 P. Anderson and N. Mann, *Safety First: The Making of New Labour* (London: Granta, 1997), p. 294.

66 V. Bogdanor, *What Is Proportional Representation?* (Oxford: Martin Robertson, 1984), p. 21; J. Curtice and M. Steed, 'Appendix 2', in D. Butler and D. Kavanagh, *The British General Election of 1983* (London: Macmillan, 1983), p. 259.

67 *Tribune*, 20 December 1985. Quoted in A Conservative Research Department Paper, 'Proportional Representation', *Politics Today*, no. 12, 19 September 1991, p. 214.

68 H. Wainwright, *Labour a Tale of Two Parties* (London: Hogarth Press, 1987), pp. 281–2.

69 A. Scargill. 'Proportional Representation: A Socialist Concept', *New Left Review*, vol. 1, no. 158 (July–August 1986), p. 80.

70 Ibid.

71 Ibid.

72 Ibid.

73 Ibid.

74 Interview with Baroness Gould, 3 March 2015.

3 The slow rise and quick fall of the Plant Report

1 P. Hirst and K. Khilnani, 'Introduction', in *Reinventing Democracy* (Oxford: Blackwell Publishers, 1996), p. 2.

2 *Guardian*, 9 January 1989.

3 B. Jones and M. Keating, *Labour and the British State* (Oxford: Clarendon Press, 1985), p. 195.

4 D. Marquand, 'Spot the Radical', *Marxism Today*, July 1988.

5 T. Davis and D. Green, 'Labour's One Hope: Labour Cannot Win the Next Election', *Marxism Today*, February 1989; Hirst, *After Thatcher*, pp. 230–1.

6 P. Norton, *New Directions in British Politics?* (Aldershot: Edward Elgar, 1991), pp. 148, 168.

7 *Guardian*, 'The charter of despair', 12 December 1988.

8 M. Evans, *Charter 88: A Successful Challenge to the British Political Tradition* (Hampshire: Dartmouth, 1995), pp. 205–12.

9 Quoted in Anderson and Mann, *Safety First*, p. 429.

10 M. Linton, *Labour's Road to Electoral Reform?* (Guildford: Labour Campaign for Electoral Reform, 1993), p. 17.

11 Interview with Lord Hattersley, 17 November 2014.

12 *Samizdat*, September/October 1990.

13 Interview with Margaret Beckett MP, 26 March 2014.

14 *Labour Party Conference Report*, 1989.

15 See A. Heath, R. Jowell and J. Curtice, 'Can Labour Win?', in A. Heath et al. (eds), *Labour's Last Chance? The 1992 Election and Beyond* (Aldershot: Dartmouth, 1994), p. 291.

16 *The Times*, 29 October 1989.

17 *Guardian*, 29 September 1989.

18 Interview with Lord Rosser, 28 March 2014.

19 *Guardian*, 'A People's Bill of Reform Fare', 30 November 1988.

20 *Guardian*, 'Leading Kinnock Ally Calls for Labour Electoral Pact with the Democrats', 5 December 1988.

21 Interview with Charles Clarke, 21 May 2014.

22 Interview with Baroness Gould, 3 March 2015.

23 Linton, *Labour's Road to Electoral Reform?* p. 16.

24 Quoted in *Guardian*, 'Centre Boost on PR for Labour'; *Financial Times*, 'Labour Group Calls for Electoral Reform'; *The Times*, 'MP Claims Support for Voting System Reform', 29 September 1989.

25 *Guardian*, 'Poll Find Labour MPs Reject PR', 16 November 1989.

26 M. Linton and M. Southcott, *Making Votes Count: The Case for Electoral Reform* (London: Profile Books, 1998), p. 98–1987 – 25 Resolutions and Amendments; 1988 – 7 Resolution; 1989 – 37 Resolutions and 6 Amendments; 1990 – 31 Resolutions and 6 Amendments; 1991 – 35 Resolutions (30 in favour, 5 against).

27 *Labour Party Conference Report*, 1987, pp. 130–3.

28 C. Hughes and P. Wintour, *Labour Rebuilt* (London: Fourth Estate, 1990), p. 162.

29 Ibid., p. 163.

30 Ibid.

31 *Guardian*, 'The Centre Cannot Hold', 19 December 1988.

32 H. Emy, 'The Mandate and Responsible Government', *Australian Journal of Political Science*, vol. 32, no. 1 (1997), p. 70; R. Hofferbert and I. Budge, 'The Party Mandate and the Westminster Model: Election Programmes and Government Spending in Britain, 1945–85', *British Journal of Political Science*, vol. 22, no. 2 (1992), p. 157.

33 Interview with Lord Hattersley, 17 November 2014.

34 *The Times*, 'Adopting PR "Would Constitute Act of Historic Folly"', 6 October 1989; *Guardian*, 'Hattersley Says PR Reduces Democracy', 6 October 1989.

35 T. Benn, *The End of an Era – Diaries 1980-90* (London: Hutchinson, 1992), pp. 577–8.

36 *Meet the Challenge, Make the Change: A New Agenda for Britain* (London: Labour Party, 1989).

37 B. Gould, *A Future for Socialism* (London: Cape, 1989), pp. 177–8.

38 BBC Radio, *The World This Week*, 5 January 1992. Quoted in Evans, *Charter 88*, p. 234.

39 Interview with Lord Whitty, 31 March 2014.

40 Interview with Margaret Beckett MP, 26 March 2014.

41 P. Gould, *The Unfinished Revolution: How the Modernisers Saved the Labour Party* (London: Abacus, 1998), p. 150.

42 D. Butler and D. Kavanagh, *The British General Election of 1992* (London: MacMillan Press, 1992), pp. 89–90, 129.

43 *Labour Party Conference Report*, 1990, p. 268.

44 *Sunday Times*, 'Labour to Woo Owen with Electoral Reform', 10 June 1990.

45 Linton and Southcott, *Making Votes Count*, p. 99.

46 See *Guardian*, 'Hattersley Beaten on Voting Reform'; *Financial Times*, 'Leadership Resigned to Internal Debate on Proportional Representation'; *The Times*, 'Kinnock Welcomes Electoral Reform Talks but Warns against Coalition Government', 5 October 1990.

47 *Financial Times*, 5 October 1990.

48 R. Plant, 'Criteria for Electoral Systems: The Labour Party and Electoral Reform', *Parliamentary Affairs*, vol. 44, no. 4 (1991), p. 550.

49 Interview with Dr Tim Lamport, 14 July 2014.

50 Interview with Margaret Beckett, 26 March 2014.

51 Interview with Lord Rosser, 28 March 2014; interview with Dr Tim Lamport, 14 July 2014.

52 Interview with Charles Clarke, 21 May 2014.

53 Interview with Richard Rosser, 28 March 2014.

54 Interview with Margaret Beckett, 26 March 2014.

55 Interview with Lord Hattersley, 17 November 2014.

56 Interview with Lord Plant, 14 September 2016.

57 Quoted in K. Best, 'Plant: A Conservative View', *Representation*, vol. 31, no. 116 (1993), p. 80; C. Milton, 'Knee Deep in Mush', in Potted Plant, *New Statesman & Society*, 18 June 1993, p. 3.

58 Interview with Charles Clarke, 21 May 2014.

59 Interview with Lord Hattersley, 17 November 2014.

60 *Democracy, Representation and Elections, First Interim Report of the Labour Party Working Party on Electoral Systems* (London: Labour Party, 1991), p. 22.

61 Ibid., p. 37.

62 Ibid., pp. 37–8.

63 Ibid., p. 23.

64 Ibid., p. 52.

65 *Democracy, Representation and Elections, Second Interim Report of the Labour Party Working Party on Electoral Systems* (London: Labour Party, 1992), p. 3.

66 *Report of the Working Party on Electoral Systems*, 1991, p. 22.

67 Ibid., p. 26.

68 Plant, 'Criteria for Electoral Systems', p. 552.

69 *Second Interim Report of the Working Party on Electoral Systems*, 1992, p. 2.

70 R. Plant, 'The Plant Report: A Retrospective', *Representation*, vol. 32 (1995), pp. 12–13.

71 *Report of the Working Party on Electoral Systems*, 1991, p. 99.

72 Interview with Lord Plant, 14 September 2016.

73 Interview with Lord Whitty, 31 March 2014.

74 Interview with Lord Rosser, 28 March 2014.

75 *Report of the Working Party on Electoral Systems*, 1991, pp. 99–100.

76 *Second Interim Report of the Working Party on Electoral Systems*, 1992, pp. 6–7.

77 Bryan Gould, Personal correspondence, 26 February 2014.

78 *Report of the Working Party on Electoral Systems*, 1991, pp. 46 and 51.

79 Ibid., p. 96.

80 Labour Party Press Conference, 2 April 1992; Quoted in Blackburn, *The Electoral System in Britain*, p. 389.

81 Interview with Margaret Beckett MP, 26 March 2014.

82 Interview with Charles Clarke, 21 May 2014.

83 M. Westlake, *Kinnock: The Biography* (London: Little, Brown, 2001), p. 522.

84 *Newsnight*, BBC2, 3 April 1992.

85 Butler and Kavanagh, *The British General Election of 1992*, p. 253.

86 Interview with Charles Clarke, 21 May 2014.

87 Interview with Lord Hattersley, 17 November 2014.

88 *Guardian*, 'Love Affairs of the State', 10 January 1997.

89 Based on the calculations of P. Dunleavy, H. Margetts and S. Weir, *Replaying the 1992 General Election* (LSE Public Policy Paper No. 3, 1992) and (on SV) of Dale Campbell-Savours, *Independent*, 21 April 1993.

90 See G. Evans, 'Tactical Voting and Labour's Prospects', in A. Heath et al. (eds), *Labour's Last Chance?*, pp. 68–9; *Sunday Telegraph*, 5 April 1992.

91 *Tribune*, 5 March 1993. Quoted in M. Stuart, *John Smith: A Life* (London: Politico's Publishing, 2005), p. 293.

92 *Tribune*, 'Easy Does It?', 19 June 1992. Quoted in Stuart, *John Smith*, p. 294.

93 *Scotland on Sunday*, 10 March 1991. Quoted in A. McSmith, *John Smith* (London: Verso, 1993), p. 240

94 Interview with Lord Whitty, 31 March 2014.

95 *Report of the Labour Party Working Party on Election Systems* (London: Labour Party, 1993).

96 M. Duverger, *Political Parties*, 3rd edition (London: Methuen, 1992), p. 205.

97 *Report of the Labour Party Working Party on Electoral Systems*, 1993, p. 12.

98 Interview with Lord Plant, 14 September 2016; this view was shared by both Lords Rosser and Whitty, although the latter was unsure at 'what level between 35 and 50 it becomes an issue'.

99 *Report of the Labour Party Working Party on Electoral Systems*, 1993, p. 13.

100 A. Downs, *An Economic Theory of Democracy* (New York: Harper & Row, 1957), pp. 54–5.

101 *Report of the Labour Party Working Party on Electoral Systems*, 1993, p. 13.

102 Ibid.

103 Ibid.

104 Ibid., pp. 14–15.

105 Ibid.

106 Ibid., pp. 15–16.

107 Interview with Dr Tim Lamport, 14 July 2014.

108 *Report of the Labour Party Working Party on Electoral Systems*, 1993, p. 25.

109 Ibid., p. 26.

110 Ibid., p. 25.

111 Ibid., p. 28.

112 Ibid., pp. 28–9.

113 Ibid., p. 30.

114 Ibid., p. 18.

115 *The Report of Hansard Society Commission on Electoral Reform*, June 1976, pp. 37–40.

116 *Financial Times*, 'Labour Moves to Support Change in Voting System', 1 April 1993; *The Times*, 'Enquiry Puts Smith under Pressure on Electoral Reform', 2 April 1993. Evans also supports the claim that ten members supported the move away from FPTP and the six others the status quo. M. Evans, *Charter 88: A Successful Challenge to the British Political Tradition?* (Aldershot: Dartmouth, 1995), p. 234.

117 *Report of the Labour Party Working Party on Electoral Systems*, 1993, p. 4.

118 R. Plant, 'Proportional Representation', in R. Blackburn and R. Plant (eds), *Constitutional Reform: The Labour Government's Constitutional Reform Agenda* (London: Longman, 1999), p. 71.

119 Interview with Lord Plant, 14 September 2016. Plant considers that Alistair Darling was in favour of a move away from FPTP, only at the last minute to change his mind.

120 Interview with Dr Tim Lamport, 14 July 2014.

121 Interview with Plant, 14 September 2016.

122 Stuart, *John Smith*, p. 294.

123 Interview with Margaret Beckett MP, 26 March 2014.

124 *The Financial Times*, 'Beckett's Vote Reform Move Is Disallowed', 18 March 1993; *The Times*, 'Beckett Threatens to Oppose PR Report', 20 April 1993; Plant recalls Beckett in one of her 'rhetorical flights' suddenly said to Plant, 'You're a fucking wanker.' Ben Pimlott retorted: 'Isn't that a contradiction in terms?' Interview with Lord Plant, 14 September 2016.

125 Bryan Gould, Personal correspondence, 26 February 2014.

126 Interview with Baroness Armstrong, 16 July 2014.

127 T. Lamport, 'The Plant Report Two Years On – Some Reflections', *Representation*, vol. 33, no. 3 (1995), p. 19.

128 Interview with Dr Tim Lamport, 14 July 2014.

129 Interview with Baroness Armstrong, 16 July 2014.

130 Interview with Lord Whitty, 31 March 2014.

131 Milton, 'Knee Deep in Mush', p. 3.

132 G. Smyth, 'If You Lot Carry On Like This ...' Potted Plant, *New Statesman and Society*, 18 June 1993, p. 13.

133 Ibid.

134 Plant, 'Proportional Representation', p. 70.

135 Labour Party Archive, Press release, The Rt Hon. John Smith, 19 May 1993, Working Party on Electoral Reform, Labour History and Archive Study (LHASC).

136 Ibid.

137 Ibid.

138 John Smith's lecture, on 1 March 1993, was entitled 'A Citizens' Democracy' (Charter 88, 1993), *Guardian*, 3 March 1993.

139 Interview with Margaret Beckett MP, 26 March 2014.

140 *The Times*, 'One of My Women Colleagues Said to Me: They Buried You with John', 21 June 1994.

141 Minutes of the party meeting held on Wednesday, 12 May 1993 at 11.30 a.m. in Committee Room 14. Quoted in Stuart, *John Smith*, p. 295.

142 D. Butler, 'The Plant Report 1993: The Third Report of Labour's Working Party on Electoral Systems', *Representation*, vol. 31, no. 116 (1993), pp. 77–9.

143 *Guardian*, 'The Pros and Cons of Plant: A Fairer Way to Vote That Will Concentrate the Mind of the Punter', 2 April 1993.

144 M. Georghiou, 'Labour Responses to Plant', *Representation*, vol. 31, no. 116 (1993), p. 82.

145 R. Wainwright, 'Liberal Democrat Reaction to Plant', *Representation*, vol. 31, no. 116 (1993), p.79.

146 Interview with Margaret Beckett MP, 26 March 2014.

147 Interview with Lord Rosser, 28 March 2014.

148 Interview with Lord Whitty, 31 March 2014.

149 Gould, Personal correspondence, 26 February 2014.

4 Realigning the left and the Jenkins Commission

1 J. Bartle, 'Labour and Liberal Democrat Relations after 7th June 2001', *Representation*, vol. 38, no. 3 (2001), pp. 231–41.

2 *Financial Times*, 'Reform Leading to Effective Government', 15 August 1995.

3 P. Ashdown, *The Ashdown Diaries, Volume One, 1988–1997* (London: Allen Lane, The Penguin Press, 2000), p. 336, diary entry Tuesday, 1 August, 1995; p. 357, Monday, 6 November 1995; p. 522. Monday, 10 February 1996.

4 T. Blair, 'Electoral Reform Ain't the Answer', *New Statesman*, 4 September 1987, pp. 5–6.

5 P. Mandelson and R. Liddle, *The Blair Revolution, Can New Labour Deliver?* (London: Faber and Faber, 1996), p. 44.

6 Ibid., pp. 44–5.

7 Ibid., p. 45.

8 *New Statesman*, 5 July 1996, p. 15.

9 T. Blair, 'Blair on the Constitution', *The Economist*, 14 September 1996, pp. 35–6.

10 Ashdown, *Ashdown Diaries, Volume One*, pp. 507–8, diary entry Tuesday, 14 January 1997.

11 Interview with Lord Whitty, 31 March 2014; interview with Lord Lipsey, 21 January 2015. Lipsey affirms that Blair was pessimistic in subsequent elections (2001 and 2005).

12 Ashdown, *Ashdown Diaries, Volume One*, pp. 286–7, diary entry Wednesday, 12 October 1994.

13 *Observer*, 2 October 1994.

14 Interview with John Edmonds, 9 April 2015.

15 A. Campbell, *Volume One, Prelude to Power 1994–1997* (London: Arrow Books, 2010), p. 193, Wednesday, 3 May 1995. See Ashdown, *Ashdown Diaries, Volume One*, pp. 595–7, for the public statement on abandoning equidistance.

16 M. Foley, *The Politics of the British Constitution* (Manchester: Manchester University Press, 1999), pp. 210–11.

17 Interview with Lord Plant, 14 September 2016.

18 Report of the Joint (Labour Party – Liberal Democrats) Consultative Committee on Constitutional Reform (1997) quoted in Blackburn and Plant, *Constitutional Reform*, pp. 468–80.

19 Rawnsley, *Servants of the People*, pp. 193–4.

20 *Guardian*, 4 January 2001.

21 A. Campbell, *The Blair Years, Extracts from the Alastair Campbell Diaries* (London: Hutchinson, 2007), p. 179, Saturday, 26 April 1997 and p. 201, Thursday, 8 May 1997.

22 P. Ashdown, *The Ashdown Diaries, Volume Two, 1997–1999* (London: Allen Lane, The Penguin Press, 2001), p. 6, Tuesday, 6 May 1997 and p. 15, Thursday, 15 May 1997.

23 D. Draper, *Blair's Hundred Days* (London: Faber and Faber, 1997), pp. 113–16.

24 Ashdown, *Ashdown Diaries, Volume Two*, pp. 240–1, Tuesday, 18 August 1998.

25 Ibid., pp. 256–60, Friday, 11 September 1998. Blair suggested that if a change were to take place then the best option would be the Jenkins system, the strengthening of joint cooperation and private support for Lib Dem MPs most in danger of losing their seat. Italics in original.

26 Interview with Charles Clarke, 21 May 2014.

27 P. Mandelson, *The Third Man* (London: Harper Press, 2010), pp. 254–6.

28 T. Blair, *A Journey* (London: Hutchinson, 2010), pp. 117–22.

29 Oliver, 'The Progressive Coalition That Never Was', p. 47.

30 P. Cowley and M. Stuart, 'From Labour Love-In to Bona Fide Party of Opposition', *Journal of Liberal History*, vol. 43 (2004), pp. 18–19.

31 Ibid.

32 Campbell, *Volume One, Prelude to Power*, pp. 20–1, Thursday, 15 May 1997.

33 *Labour Party Manifesto 1997*, p. 33.

34 Quoted in Worcester and Mortimore, *Explaining Labour's Landslide*, p. 112.

35 M. Cole, 'Party Policy and Electoral Reform: A Survey of Developments, Motives and Prospects', in Fisher, *British Elections & Parties Review*, vol. 9, p. 79.

36 See Ashdown, *Ashdown Diaries, Volume Two*, p. 44, Thursday, 12 June 1997; A. Rawnsley, *Servants of the People: The Inside Story of New Labour* (London: Penguin Books, 2001), pp. 195–6.

37 Interview with John Edmonds, 9 April 2015.

38 Ashdown, *Ashdown Diaries, Volume Two*, p. 107, Tuesday, 21 October 1997 and P. 117, Friday, 31 October 1997.

39 *The Economist*, 'Jenkins' Ear', 6 December 1997, p. 39; *Guardian*, 'Poll Commission Leans to Reform', 2 December 1997.

40 Interview with Baroness Gould, 3 March 2015.

41 D. Lipsey, *In the Corridors of Power* (London: Biteback, 2012), p. 195.

42 *The Report of the Independent Commission on the Voting System* (London: The Stationery Office, 1998), p. 1.

43 P. Dunleavy and H. Margetts, 'Mixed Electoral Systems in Britain and the Jenkins Commission on Electoral Reform', *British Journal of Politics and International Relations*, vol. 1, no. 1 (1999), p. 17.

44 Lipsey, *In the Corridors of Power*, p. 193.

45 I. Mclean, 'The Jenkins Commission and the Implications of Electoral Reform for the UK Constitution', *Government and Opposition*, vol. 34, no. 2 (1999), p. 153.

46 Lord Jenkins in the LSE Democratic Audit Seminar, 20 November 1998, Quoted in H. Margetts and P. Dunleavy, 'Reforming the Westminster Electoral System: Evaluating the Jenkins Commission Proposals', in J. Fisher, *British Elections & Parties Review, Vol. 9*, p. 47.

47 Interview with Lord Lipsey, 21 January 2015.

48 Ibid.

49 *The Report of the Independent Commission on the Voting System.*

50 Lipsey, 'How We Made Up Our Minds', *The Economist*, pp. 30–1.

51 Labour Party Submission to the Commission on Voting System, 6 July 1998, Accessed LIPSEY/2/2, London School of Economics Special Collection, 5 January 2015.

52 Ibid.

53 Ibid.

54 Ibid.

55 Ibid.

56 Ibid.

57 Ibid.

58 Ibid.

59 *Guardian*, 'Labour Leaders Sceptical of PR', 10 August 1998.

60 *The Report of the Independent Commission on the Voting System*, pp. 24–8.

61 Ibid., p. 29.

62 Ibid.

63 Ibid., pp. 31–3.

64 Lipsey, *In the Corridors of Power*, pp. 197–8, 200.

65 *The Report of the Independent Commission on the Voting System*, p. 34.

66 Ibid., p. 38.

67 *Financial Times*, 'Jenkins Vote Reform Proposals Hit by Split', Monday, 26 October 1998; interview with Lord Lipsey, 21 January 2015.

68 *The Report of the Independent Commission on the Voting System*, p. 37.

69 Ibid.

70 Ibid.

71 Ibid., p. 45.

72 House of Commons Debates, 6th series, vol. 318, cols. 1068–9, 5 November 1998.

73 Interview with Lord Lipsey, 21 January 2015.

74 D. Lipsey, 'How We Made Up Our Minds', *The Economist*, 31 October 1998, p. 31.

75 Ashdown, *Ashdown Diaries, Volume Two*, pp. 230–1, Wednesday, 22 July 1998; p. 235, Thursday, 23 July 1998.

76 LIPSEY/2/1, 'Lunch with Pat McFadden', 4 March 1998, accessed London School of Economics Lipsey Collection, 5 January 2015.

77 Margetts and Dunleavy, 'Reforming the Westminster Electoral System', in Fisher, *British Elections & Parties Review, Vol. 9*, p. 51.

78 Lipsey, *In the Corridors of Power*, p. 198.

79 Ashdown, *The Ashdown Diaries, Volume Two*, p. 106, Tuesday, 21 October 1997.

80 Interview with Lord Lipsey, 21 January 2015.

81 *Financial Times*, 'Electoral Reform Move Will Anger Lib Dems', 27 April 1998.

82 See *Financial Times*, 'Blair Sanctions Support for Diluted PR Plan', 20 February 1998; 'Jockeying Starts in Race to Replace First Past the Post', 9 June 1998. For more details on 'Keep the Link', see M. Cole, 'Party Policy and Electoral Reform: A Survey of Developments, Motives and Prospects', in Fisher, *British Elections & Parties Review, Vol. 9*, pp. 79–80.

83 *Observer*, 'Union Declares War on Blair's Coalition Dream', 23 August 1998; *Financial Times*, 'Unions to Fund Move Opposing Electoral Reform', 11 September 1998.

84 *The Times*, 'PR Puts Pressure on Lib Dems', 25 September 1998.

85 *Financial Times*, 'Brown Salvo May Scupper Ashdown Pact', 30 July 1998; Ashdown, *The Ashdown Diaries, Volume One*, p. 426, Wednesday, 8 May 1996; p. 436, Wednesday, 6 June 1996; p. 484, Tuesday, 3 December 1996.

86 *Sunday Telegraph*, 'There's More to PR Than Public Relations', 27 July 1997.

87 Ashdown, *Ashdown Diaries, Volume Two*, pp. 168–9, Wednesday, 18 February 1998.

88 J. Prescott, *Prezza, My Story: Pulling No Punches* (London: Headline, 2008), p. 219

89 See *Guardian*, 'Row Over Scrapped PR Vote', 2 October 1998; *Daily Mail*, 'Paddy's PR Dream Is Shelved', 2 October 1998; *Financial Times*, 'Leaders Accused of "Shabby Deals" on PR Vote', 2 October 1998.

90 *Guardian*, 'PM Warning on Electoral Reform Delay Is Problem for Ashdown', 28 September 1998.

91 *Guardian*, 'Beckett Plays Down Early PR Referendum', 23 October 1998.

92 *Guardian*, 'Jenkins PR Plan Redraws Political Map', 30 October 1998; *Financial Times*, 'Blair Backs Radical Plan for Voting Overhaul', 30 October 1998.

93 Campbell, *Power and the Peoples*, p. 546, Thursday, 29 October 1999.

94 *Financial Times*, 'Foes of Change United in an Unlikely Alliance', 30 October 1998.

95 *Financial Times*, 'Foes of Change', 30 October 1998; *Daily Mail*, 'Blair Votes for a Delay on Ballot Box Shake-Up', 30 October 1998.

96 House of Commons Debates, 6 Series, Vol. 318, cols. 1036–7, 5 November 1998.

97 Ibid., cols. 1044–6, 5 November 1998. Elsewhere, Kaufman considered the PR enthusiasts in Labour should 'identify the hundred volunteers who would sacrifice their seats in order to achieve "fair voting"'. *Guardian*, 'Not So Fair, After All', 7 June 1999.

98 Ibid., cols. 1049–50, 5 November 1998.

99 Ibid., cols. 1057–9, 5 November 1998.

100 Ibid., cols. 1053–5, 5 November 1998. Benn is alleged to have told Neil Kinnock that he was opposed to PR because under such a system, he, Benn, would be 599th on the list, while Dennis Skinner would be 600th. Neil Kinnock is supposed to have replied 'Do you want that in writing?' See Vernon Bogdanor's submission to the Independent Commission on the Voting System, 1998.

101 Ibid., cols. 1061–2, 5 November 1998.

102 Ibid., cols. 1071–3, 5 November 1998.

103 Ibid., cols. 1064–6, 5 November 1998.

104 Ibid., cols. 1075–7, 5 November 1998.

105 Ibid., cols. 1083–5, 5 November 1998.

106 Ibid., cols. 1087–9, 5 November 1998.

107 Mandelson, *The Third Man*, p. 258.

108 Ibid.

109 Campbell, *The Blair Years*, p. 323, Sunday, 13 September 1998; p. 545, Thursday, 27 October 1998.

110 *Guardian*, 'Prescott Scorns Links with Lib Dems'; *Financial Times*, 'Prescott Urges Party to Ditch Lib-Lab Links and PR Plans'; *The Times*, 'Prescott Buries PR Project', 25 September 2000.

111 Ashdown, *Ashdown Diaries: Volume Two*, p. 120, for 3 November 1997.

112 Interview with Baroness Armstrong, 16 July 2014.

113 Interview with Lord Mandelson, 31 March 2015.

114 Campbell, *Power and the Peoples*, p. 638, Thursday, 21 January 1999.

115 Mandelson, *The Third Man*, pp. 258–9.

116 Ashdown, *Ashdown Diaries*, pp. 224–5, diary entry Tuesday, 7 July 1998; p. 265, diary entry Sunday, 13 September 1998; p. 269, diary entry Thursday, 17 September 1998.

117 *The Times*, 'High Cost of Reform', 19 September 2001.

118 A. Campbell, *Power and Responsibility, 1999–2001, The Alistair Campbell Diaries, Volume Three* (London: Arrow Books, 2012), p. 138.

119 Interview with Lord Mandelson, 31 March 2015.

120 *The Times*, 'Crisis for Kennedy as Blair Dumps PR', 10 August 1999; *The Times*, 'PR Reforms Languish in Absence of Leadership', 26 October 1999.

121 http://news.bbc.co.uk/1/hi/events/euros_99/news/368450.stm (accessed 27 January 2015).

122 *Financial Times*, 'Labour Party Rank-and-File Hostile to Poll Reform', 5 January 2000.

123 *Guardian*, 'Labour Rivals Row over Claims That Grassroots Reject PR', 6 January 2000.

124 *Financial Times*, 'Union Thwarts Progress on Electoral Reform', 14 June 2000.

125 'Ambitions for Britain', *Labour Party Manifesto 2001*.

126 T. Wright, 'Electoral Reform: A Challenge for New Labour', *Representation*, vol. 33, no. 2 (1995), pp. 31–3.

127 Interview with Baroness Gould, 3 March 2015.

128 K. Hickson, 'Callaghan's Conservatism', in K. Hickson and J. Miles (eds), *James Callaghan: An Underrated Prime Minister* (London: Biteback, 2020), pp. 36–7.

129 Tony Blair is wrong – Labour should have nothing to do with the Lib Dems – LabourList (accessed 18 December 2021).

5 The end of New Labour

1 'Britain Forward Not Back', *Labour Party Manifesto 2005*.

2 *Guardian*, 'There Are No Short Cuts in Democracy', 12 May 2005.

3 J. Straw, 'New Labour, Constitutional Change and Representative Democracy', *Parliamentary Affairs*, vol. 63, no. 2 (2010), pp. 356–68.

4 *Guardian*, 'Falconer Warns Against Switch to PR', 20 May 2005.

5 J. Mitchell and A. Henderson, 'Elections and Electoral Systems', in M. Keating, *The Oxford Handbook of Scottish Politics* (Oxford: Oxford University Press, 2018), pp. 215–17.

6 See 'Proportional Representation? Bad Tactics, Bad Strategy and Bad for Britain', LabourList, http://revolts.co.uk/?p=711 (accessed 30 September 2016); 'Deliver, Don't Dither. Labour Must Drop Its Obsession with Constitutional Issues', LabourList, http://labourlist.org/2010/01/our-strategy-is-quintessential-clas sic-new-labour-the-ed-balls-interview/ (accessed 30 September 2016).

7 Ministry of Justice, *Review of Voting Systems: The Experience of New Voting System in the United Kingdom since 1997*, CM 7304 (London: TSO, January 2008).

8 Quoted in P. Norton, 'Brown's New Constitutional Settlement? Constitutional Developments in 2007-08', in M. Rush and P. Giddings (eds), *When Gordon Took the Helm* (Hampshire: Palgrave Macmillan, 2008), pp. 30–1.

9 *Guardian*, 'King Tony's Courtier', 29 October 1998.

10 *Guardian*, 'Not So Fair, After All', 7 June 1999.

11 *Guardian*, 'Fighting the Soggy Centre', 10 January 2000.

12 *Guardian*, 'Maybe I Was Wrong After All', 2 June 2003.

13 Interview with Lord Hattersley, 17 November 2014.

14 *The Governance of Britain*, Cm. 7170 (London, The Stationery Office, 2007), p. 5.

15 M. Campbell, *My Autobiography* (Hodder and Stoughton, 2008), pp. 278, 284.

16 P. Ashdown, *A Fortunate Life* (London: Aurum Press, 2009), pp. 374–7.

17 House of Commons Debate, 10 June 2009, c798.

18 Labour Party Conference, 2009.

19 'Towards a New Politics', Speech by Gordon Brown to the IPPR, 2 February 2010.

20 C. Mullin, *Decline and Fall, Diaries 2005–2010* (London: Profile Books, 2010), p. 414, dairy entry, Monday, 18 January 2010.

21 L. Baston and K. Ritchie, *Don't Take No for an Answer* (London: Biteback, 2011), p. 15.

22 *Daily Politics*, BBC2, Thursday, 11 June 2009.

23 Quoted in *Independent*, 'Gordon Brown to Ditch First-Past-the-Post Voting System', 2 February 2010.

24 LabourList, 'Our Strategy Is Quintessential, Classic New Labour', http://labourl ist.org/2010/01/our-strategy-is-quintessential-classic-new-labour-the-ed-balls-interview/ (accessed 1 November 2015).

25 *The Times*, 'Special Vote to Block More Powers for MPs', Thursday, 28 January 2010.

26 *New Statesman*, 'I Urge Lib Dems to Bite Their Lip and Back Us', 4 May 2010.

27 *The Times*, Monday, 25 May 2009, Johnson reiterated the argument in the *Independent*, Wednesday 8 July 2009.

28 Interview with Alan Johnson MP, 23 October 2015.

29 Interview with Ben Bradshaw MP, 21 October 2015.

30 A. Seldon and G. Lodge, *Brown at 10* (London: Biteback, 2010), pp. 418–19.

31 Blunkett and Richards, 'Labour in and Out of Government', pp. 185–7.

32 *The Times*, 'Cabinet Support for Johnson Puts Plans for Voting Reform on Electoral Agenda', Tuesday, 26 May 2009.

33 *Guardian*, 'Cabinet Members Urge Gordon Brown to Back Electoral Reform Now', 22 January 2010.

34 *New Statesman*, 'It Would Be a Missed Opportunity Not to Have a Referendum on Election Day', 5 November 2009.

35 The letter which appeared in November 2009 is referenced on the following website: http://liberalconspiracy.org/2009/page/23/ (accessed 14 May 2015).

36 Compass, *The Last Labour Government, Why Only a Referendum on Electoral Reform Can Save the Party Now* (London: Compass, 2009).

37 J. Curtice, 'The Death of a Miserable Little Compromise: The Alternative Vote Referendum', *Political Insight* (September 2011), p. 14.

38 *New Statesman*, 'It Would Be a Missed Opportunity'.

39 Mullin, *Decline and Fall*, p. 341, dairy entry, Sunday, 7 June 2009.

40 Interview with Charles Clarke, 21 May 2014.

41 Interview with Lord Mandelson, 31 March 2015.

42 *Independent*, 22 April 2010. Conversely, Cameron refused to rule out discussions on electoral reform, inviting his interviewer to 'put the question in Serbo-Croat if you want, you're going to get the same (non) answer'. *Observer*, 'David Cameron Leaves Door Open for Poll Deal with Liberal Democrats', 25 April 2010.

43 N. Clegg, *The Liberal Moment* (London: Demos, 2009).

44 *Irish Times*, 'Clegg Open to Labour Coalition if Brown Steps Down', 27 April 2010.

45 *Independent*, 'Andrew Adonis: It's Madness to Split the Centre-Left Vote', 9 April 2010.

46 A. Boulton and J. Jones, *Hung Together: The Cameron-Clegg Coalition* (London: Simon & Schuster, 2012), p. 134.

47 'A Fair Future for All', *Labour Party Manifesto 2010*.

48 *BBC Daily Politics*, BBC2, 2 February 2010.

49 See N. Allen and J. Bartle, *Britain at the Polls 2010* (London: Sage, 2011), p. 212.

50 Quoted in P. Diamond and G. Radice, *Southern Discomfort Again* (Policy Network, 2010), p. 11.

51 McGuinness, *Alternative Vote Referendum 2011*, p. 9.

52 D. Sanders, H. D. Clarke, M. C. Stuart and P. Whiteley, 'Simulating the Effects of the Alternative Vote in the 2010 UK General election', *Parliamentary Affairs*, vol. 64, no. 1 (2010), pp. 5–23.

53 C. Rallings and M. Thrasher, 'Suppose UK Voters Accept the Alternative Vote in the May Referendum … but Then Don't Use AV to Single Multiple Party Preferences?', *British Politics and Policy at LSE* (blog), 2010; *Independent*, 'The Miserable Compromise with Modest Gains for Clegg', Monday, 21 February 2011.

54 Speech by Tom Harris, MP for Glasgow South (2001–15), to East Lothian Fabians, Thursday, 24 March 2011.

55 Quoted in A. Geddes and J. Tonge, *Britain Votes 2010* (Oxford: Oxford University Press, 2010), p. 27.

56 A. Adonis, *5 Days in May: The Coalition and Beyond* (London: Biteback, 2013), p. 156.

57 Ibid., p. 146.

58 M. Stuart, *The Cameron-Clegg Government, Coalition Politics in an Age of Austerity* (Hampshire: Palgrave Macmillan, 2011), p. 43.

59 D. Kavanagh and P. Cowley, *The British General Election of 2010* (Hampshire: Palgrave Macmillan, 2010), p. 210.

60 Interview with Baroness Armstrong, 16 July 2014.

61 D. Edgar, 'When Dave Met Nick', *Guardian Review*, 15 June 2013.

62 B. Jones, 'The Road Not Taken and the 'Bad Faith' Theses: Why a Liberal Democrat-Labour Coalition Never Happened in May 2010', *Political Quarterly*, vol. 84, no. 4 (October–December 2013), p. 460.

63 Adonis, *5 Days in May*, p. 144.

64 Ibid., p. 119.

65 Ibid., p. 92.

66 Ibid., p. 94.

67 Ibid., pp. 94–5.

68 Ibid., p. 95.

69 Ibid.

70 Ibid.

71 Ibid., p. 96

72 Ibid., p. 118.

73 Ibid., p. 95.

74 J. Straw, *Last Man Standing, Memoirs of a Political Survivor* (London: Macmillan, 2012), p. 530.

75 Seldon and Lodge, *Brown at 10*, p. 454.

76 Straw, *Last Man Standing*, p. 531.

77 A. Darling, *Back from the Brink* (London: Atlantic Books, 2011), p. 294.

78 Ibid., p. 303.

79 *Sky News*, 10 May 2010.

80 Interview with Ben Bradshaw MP, 21 October 2015.

81 http://www.politics.co.uk/news/2010/05/11/labour-heavyweights-come-out-against-lib-lab- (accessed 5 October 2015); *Irish Times*, 'Senior Labour MP's Sceptical on Coalition', 11 May 2010.

82 *Financial Times*, 'Brown to Quit in Effort to Woo Lib Dems', 11 May 2010.

83 BBC Radio 4, 11 October 2010.

84 Straw, *Last Man Standing*, p. 531.

85 Interview with Tom Harris, 2 October 2015.

86 http://www.politics.co.uk/news/2010/05/11/labour-heavyweights-come-out-against-lib-lab- (accessed 5 October 2015).

87 Interview with Ben Bradshaw MP, 21 October 2015.

88 Interview with Alan Johnson MP, 23 October 2015.

89 Mandelson, *The Third Man*, p. 564.

90 Quoted in V. Bogdanor, *The Coalition and the Constitution* (Oxford: Hart Publishing, 2011), pp. 30–1.

91 Interview with Lord Mandelson, 31 March 2015.

92 Quoted in Boulton and Jones, *Hung Together, The Cameron-Clegg Coalition*, p. 138.

93 See appendix in Adonis, *5 Days in May*, p. 181.

94 Ibid., p. 229.

95 M. Qvortrup, 'Voting on Electoral Reform: A Comparative Perspective on the Alternative Vote Referendum in the United Kingdom', *Political Quarterly*, vol. 83, no. 1 (Jan.–Mar. 2012), p. 109.

96 Adonis, *5 Days in May*, p. 97.

97 D. Laws, *22 Days In May* (London: Biteback, 2010), pp. 152–3.

98 Ibid., pp. 167–70.

99 Quoted in Boulton and Jones, *Hung Together*, pp. 229–30; *Newsnight*, BBC2, 29 July 2010.

100 Interview with Alan Johnson MP, 23 October 2015.

101 Seldon and Lodge, *Brown at 10*, p. 459.

102 House of Commons Debate, 7 June 2010, vol. 511, col. 29–30.

103 Ibid., vol. 511, col. 44.

104 *Five Days That Changed Britain*, BBC2, 29 July 2010.

105 *Newsnight*, BBC2, 29 July 2010.

106 *Financial Times*, 'Did the Lib Dems Eer Want a Coalition with Labour?', 14 October 2010.

6 Debating the electoral system in opposition, 2010–21

1 Quoted in D. Kavanagh and P. Cowley, *The British General Election of 2010* (Hampshire: Palgrave Macmillan, 2010), p. 226.

2 Electoral Commission, *May 2011 Polls: Campaign Spending Report* (London: Electoral Commission, 2012), p. 33, footnote 44 'campaign spending', quoted in D. Seawright, "Yes, the Census': The 2011 UK Referendum Campaign on the Alternative Vote', *British Politics*, vol. 8, no. 4 (2013), p. 467.

3 R. Johnston and C. Pattie, 'Parties and Crossbenchers Voting in the Post-2010 House of Lords: The Example of the Parliamentary Voting System and Constituencies Bill', *British Politics*, vol. 6, no. 4 (2011), pp. 434–5, 439.

4 Lipsey, *In the Corridors of Power*, pp. 206, 211.

5 Interview with Tom Harris, 2 October 2015.

6 *BBC Newsnight, AV Referendum Debate*, BBC 2, 26 April 2011.

7 *Guardian*, 'Voting Reform Ballot Planned for May', 20 May 2010.

8 *New Statesman*, 'Andy Burnham Interview', 22 July 2010.

9 Lipsey, *In the Corridors of Power*, p. 207.

10 *Guardian*, 'Labour Will Not Campaign for Alternative Vote, Says Andy Burnham', 5 November 2010.

11 *Guardian*, 'Labour in Last-Ditch Push on Both Sides of AV Debate', 1 May 2011.

12 *Financial Times*, 'Unions Campaign against Vote Reform', 9 March 2011, http://labouryes.org.uk/video-trade-unions-say-yes/ (accessed 3 October 2012).

13 *Guardian*, 8 December 2010. Notable Signatories included Ben Bradshaw, Alan Johnson, Sadiq Khan, Douglas Alexander, Ken Livingstone, John Denham, Peter Hain, Tessa Jowell, Hilary Benn, Liam Byrne, Jack Straw, Tom Watson, Jon Cruddas, Chris Bryant, David Lammy, Liz Kendall, Chuka Umunna, Anas Sarwar, Alison McGovern, Gloria de Piero, Stephen Timms, Helen Goodman, John McDonnell, Stephen Twigg, Susan Elan Jones, Richard Burden, Frank Field, Hugh Bayley, Ann Coffey, Willie Bain, Paul Blomfield, Joan Ruddock, Heidi Alexander, Stephen Pound, Kevin Brennan, Fiona Mactaggart, Malcolm Wicks, Fabian Hamilton, Alan Whitehead, Prof. Lord Plant, Lord Adonis, Lord Hattersley, Baroness King, Lord Mandelson, Lord Lipsey, Lord Beecham, Baroness Gould, Baroness Quinn, Lord Kinnock, Baroness Kinnock, Baroness Lister, Richard Howitt, Claude Moraes, Murad Queshi, Tony Benn, James Purnell, Nick Pearce (director, IPPR – personal capacity), Phil Collins, Gavin Kelly, Luke Akehurst (NEC), Chris Mullin.

14 *New Statesman*, 'It Would Be a Missed Opportunity Not to Have a Referendum on Election Day', 5 November 2009.

15 *Guardian*, 16 November 2010.

16 Interview with Alan Johnson MP, 23 October 2015.

17 Interview with Tom Harris, 2 October 2015.

18 Interview with Margaret Beckett MP, 26 March 2014.

19 *BBC Newsnight, AV Referendum Debate*, BBC 2, 26 April 2011.

20 http://www.bbc.co.uk/news/uk-politics-13082549 (accessed 21 October 2016).

21 *Guardian*, 'AV Referendum: Why Progressives Must Unite to Vote Yes', 1 May 2011.

22 Healey, *The Time of My Life*, pp. 582–3.

23 Harris, Speech to East Lothian Fabians.

24 Written evidence submitted by Rt Hon Denis MacShane MP, 15 July 2010, House of Commons Political and Constitutional Reform Committee, Parliamentary Voting System and Constituencies Bill, Third Report of Session 2010–11,

25 *BBC Daily Politics, AV Referendum Debate Special*, BBC 2, 6 April 2011.

26 Harris, Speech to East Lothian Fabians.

27 Ibid.

28 *BBC Daily Politics, AV Debate Special*, BBC 2, 6 April 2011.

29 *Campaign Broadcast by No to AV.*

30 David Cameron and John Reid Joint Statement, No to AV, Transport House, 18 April 2011.

31 D. Hodges, 'No We Can', The Inside Story of the No to AV Campaign', *New Statesman*, 11 May 2011.

32 *BBC Newsnight*, BBC 2, 2 December 2010; *BBC Daily Politics, AV Debate Special*, BBC 2, 6 April 2011.

33 Interview with Tom Harris, 2 October 2015.

34 *Guardian*, 'Why the Alternative Vote Gets My Vote', 16 February 2011.

35 Ed Miliband, Launch of Labour Yes, 16 March 2011.

36 *Financial Times*, 'Voters Set to Deliver Resounding No to AV', 5 May 2011.

37 *Financial Times*, 'Miliband Calls for Progressive Yes', 3 May 2011.

38 *Guardian*, 'Labour in Last-Ditch Push on Both Sides of AV Debate', 1 May 2011.

39 *Independent*, 15 March 2011.

40 M. D'Anconna, *In It Together: The Inside Story of the Coalition Government* (London: Penguin Books, 2013), p. 82.

41 Hodges, 'No We Can', 11 May 2011.

42 Interview with Baroness Armstrong, 16 July 2014.

43 Interview with Tom Harris, 2 October 2015.

44 Liberal Democrats, *Liberal Democrats Consultative Session: Election Review May 2011* (London: Liberal Democrats Policy Unit, 2011), p. 7.

45 Interview with Lord Whitty, 31 March 2014.

46 Interview with Tom Harris, 2 October 2015.

47 Baston and Ritchie, *Don't Take No for an Answer*, pp. 46–8.

48 Ibid., pp. 56–7.

49 Lipsey, *In the Corridors of Power*, pp. 208–10.

50 Quoted in Baston and Ritchie, *Don't Take No for an Answer*, pp. 51–2.

51 *Independent*, 'Andrew Adonis: It's Madness to Split the Centre-Left Vote', 9 April 2010.

52 A. Adonis, *5 Days in May: The Coalition and Beyond* (London: Biteback, 2013), p. 160.

53 Ibid., pp. 157–9.

54 Ibid., pp. 160, 164.

55 Interview with Ben Bradshaw MP, 21 October 2015.

56 Lipsey, *In the Corridors of Power*, p. 211.

57 *Independent*, 'No to AV Yes to PR, 12 March 2011.

58 Interview with Margaret Beckett MP, 26 March 2014.

59 K. Ghose, 'Embracing Electoral Reform', in L. Nandy, C. Lucas and C. Bowers (eds), *The Alternative: Towards a New Progressive Politics* (London: Biteback, 2016).

60 P. Blomfield, 'Beyond Tribalism', *Progress*, www.progressonline.org. uk/2012/11/30/beyond-tribalism (accessed 9 September 2015).

61 *Independent on Sunday*, 'Balls No Longer Sticking Point in Lib-Lab Coalition', 29 December 2013.

62 *Daily Telegraph*, 'What Is My Party Playing At? No One Wants Votes for 16-Year-Olds', 19 August 2013.

63 Quoted in G. Eaton, 'Ed Miliband Interview – on the Trade Unions, Party Funding and Arnie Graf', *New Statesman*, 24 February 2014.

64 *Independent*, 'Let's Reboot Democracy and Replace Our Broken Electoral System', 14 December 2015.

65 *Independent*, 'John McDonnell Calls on Labour to Back Proportional Representation', 7 May 2016.

66 PR Alliance Building Conference, St James the Less Centre, London, Monday, 8 February; *Independent*, 'Electoral Reform: Labour, SNP, UKIP and Lib Dems to Campaign for Proportional Representation', 7 February 2016.

67 See *Independent on Sunday*, 'Lib Dems and Labour in Secret Talks on Voting Reform', 24 January 2016; 'Party Leaders Call for a Left-of-Centre Pact to Secure Electoral Reform', 31 January 2016; John Spellar: The People Have Spoken. They Don't Want Electoral Reform', LabourList (accessed 16 December 2021).

68 L. Nandy, C. Lucas and C. Bowers (eds), *The Alternative: Towards a New Progressive Politics* (London: Biteback, 2016), pp. xi–xxviii.

69 N. Lawson, 'Building a Good Society: An Argument for Radical Hope', in *The Alternative*, pp. 3–15.

70 *Guardian*, 'Labour's Leadership Contest Will Be a Chance to Seal Electoral Reform in Britain', 13 January 2020.

71 *Guardian*, 'Labour Leadership Candidates Urged to Back Electoral Reform', 3 February 2020.

72 *Guardian*, 'Labour's Leadership Contest Will Be a Chance to Seal Electoral Reform in Britain', 13 January 2020.

73 N. Lawson, 'Labour and Electoral Reform: Rage against the Machine', *Prospect*, 15 October 2021.

74 See 'Proportional Representation Would Spell Disaster for Labour. Party Members Should Reject It', *Guardian*, 27 September 2021.

75 https://www.independent.co.uk/news/uk/politics/general-election-voting-electo ral-reform-proportional-representation-first-past-the-post-a9367546.html (accessed 21 April 2020); 'Proportional Representation? Bad Tactics, Bad Strategy and Bad for Britain', LabourList (accessed 16 December 2021).

Conclusion

1 See *Financial Times*, 'GMB Ready to Oppose Electoral Reform', 14 August 1995; *Financial Times*, 'Reform Leading to Effective Government', 15 August 1995.
2 'Tony Blair Is Wrong – Labour Should Have Nothing to Do with the Lib Dems' – LabourList, http://ukpollingreport.co.uk/historical-polls/voting-intent ion-1992-1997 (accessed 16 December 2021).
3 Interview with Lord Plant, 14 September 2016.
4 Healey, *The Time of My Life*, pp. 458 and 582–3.
5 Interview with Margaret Beckett MP, 26 March 2014.
6 Interview with Baroness Armstrong, 16 July 2014.
7 Interview with Lord Mandelson, 31 March 2015.
8 Interview with Lord Hattersley, 17 November 2014.

Bibliography

Primary sources

Pamphlets

Clegg, N. *The Liberal Moment* (London: Demos, 2009).

Compass, *The Last Labour Government, Why Only a Referendum on Electoral Reform Can Save the Party Now* (London: Compass, 2009).

Conservative Research Department Paper, 'Proportional Representation', *Politics Today*, no. 12, 19 September 1991.

Crosland, C. A. R. *Can Labour Win?*, Fabian Tract 324 (London: Fabian Society, 1960).

Dunleavy, P., Margetts, H. and Weir, S. *The Politico's Guide to Electoral Reform in Britain* (London: Politico's Publishing, 1998).

Ellis, T., Hughes, R., and Whitehead, P. *Electoral Reform*, Fabian Tract 483 (London: Fabian Society, 1982).

Finer, H. *The Case against Proportional Representation*, Fabian Tract 211 (London: Fabian Society, 1924).

Hanham, H. J. *The Reformed Electoral System in Great Britain, 1832–1914* (London: Historical Association, 1968).

Hunter, P. *Winning Back the 5 Million – Understanding the Fragmentation of Labour's Vote* (London: The Smith Institute, 2011).

Kuper, R. *Electing for Democracy, Proportional Representation and the Left* (London: Socialist Society, 1990).

Lawson, N. 'Labour and Electoral Reform: Rage against the Machine', *Prospect*, 15 October 2021.

Lawson, N., and Cox, J. *New Politics, Tactical Voting and How the Left Should Deal with the Governing Coalition* (London: Compass, 2010).

Linton, M. *Labour's Road to Electoral Reform* (Guildford: Labour Campaign for Electoral Reform, 1993).

Morrison, H. 'Our Parliament and How It Works', Labour Party Educational Series, no. 4, January 1953.

Radice, G. *Southern Discomfort*, Fabian Pamphlet 555 (London: Fabian Society, September 1992).

Radice, G., and Pollard, S. *Any Southern Comfort?*, Fabian Pamphlet 568
   (London: Fabian Society, September 1994).
Shaw, G. B. *Report on Fabian Policy and Resolutions*, Fabian Tract 70
   (London: Fabian Society, 1896).

Reports

Conference on Electoral Reform and Redistribution of Seats (Cmnd. 6543), 1943–4.
Conference on Electoral Law (Cmnd. 3202), 1966–7.
*Democracy, Representation and Elections, First Interim Report of the Labour Party
   Working Party on Electoral Systems* (London: Labour Party, 1991).
Democracy, Representation and Elections, Second Interim Report of the Labour
   Party Working Party on Electoral Systems (London: Labour Party, 1992).
Dunleavy, P., Margetts, H. and Weir, S. *Replaying the 1992 General Election* (LSE
   Public Policy Paper No. 3, 1992).
Electoral Commission. *May 2011 Polls: Campaign Spending Report* (London:
   Electoral Commission, 2012).
Electoral Reform Society. *Evidence to the Hansard Society Commission on Electoral
   Reform, 1976* (London: Electoral Reform Society, January 1976).
Gay, O. *Voting Systems: The Jenkins Report*, Research Paper 98/112 (London: Home
   Affairs Sections, House of Commons Library, 10 December 1998).
Her Majesty's Government. *The Governance of Britain*, Cmnd 7170 (London: The
   Stationery Office, 2007).
House of Commons Political and Constitutional Reform Committee. *Parliamentary
   Voting System and Constituencies Bill*, Third Report of Session 2010–11
   (London: The Stationery Office, 2010).
Labour Party Conference Report, 1909.
Labour Party Conference Report, 1910.
Labour Party Conference Report, 1911.
Labour Party Conference Report, 1913.
Labour Party Conference Report, 1919.
Labour Party Conference Report, 1926.
Labour Party Conference Report, 1962.
Labour Party Conference Report, 1987.
Labour Party Conference Report, 1989.
Labour Party Conference Report, 1990.
Labour Party Conference Report, 1995.

Labour Party Conference Report, 2009.

Labour Party Manifesto 1997.

Labour Party Manifesto 2001.

Labour Party Manifesto 2005.

Labour Party Manifesto 2010.

Liberal Democrats. *Liberal Democrats Consultative Session: Election Review May 2011* (London: Liberal Democrats Policy Unit, 2011).

MacDonald, J. R. M., Roberts, G. H. and Anderson, W. C. *The Labour Party and Electoral Reform: Proportional Representation and the Alternative Vote* (London: Labour Party, 1913).

McGuinness, F. 'Alternative Vote Referendum 2011, Analysis of Results', Research Paper 11/44 (London: House of Commons Library, 19 May 2011), p. 19.

Meet the Challenge, Make the Change: A New Agenda for Britain (London: Labour Party, 1989).

Ministry of Justice. *Review of Voting Systems: The Experience of New Voting System in the United Kingdom since 1997*, Cmnd. 7304 (London: TSO, January 2008).

Report of the Working Party on Electoral Systems (The Plant Report), Guardian Studies, London, 1993.

The Report of the Independent Commission on the Voting System (London: Stationery Office, 1998).

The Report of Hansard Society Commission on Electoral Reform (London: The Hansard Society, June 1976).

Trades Union Congress Annual Report, 1908.

Memoirs

Adonis, A. *5 Days in May: The Coalition and Beyond* (London: Biteback, 2013).

Ashdown, P. *A Fortunate Life* (London: Aurum Press, 2009).

Ashdown, P. *The Ashdown Diaries, Volume One, 1988–1997* (London: Allen Lane, Penguin Press, 2000).

Ashdown, P. *The Ashdown Diaries, Volume Two, 1997–1999* (London: Allen Lane, Penguin Press, 2001).

Benn, T. *The End of an Era – Diaries 1980–90* (London: Hutchinson, 1992).

Bevan, A. *In Place of Fear* (London: Quartet Books, 1990).

Blair, T. *A Journey* (London: Hutchinson, 2010).

Callaghan, J. *Time and Chance* (London: William Collins, Sons, 1987).

Campbell, A. *Volume One, Prelude to Power 1994–1997* (London: Arrow Books, 2010).

Campbell, A. *Volume Two, Power and the Peoples, 1997-1999* (London: Arrow Books, 2011).

Campbell, A. *Power and Responsibility, 1999-2001, The Alistair Campbell Diaries, Volume Three* (London: Arrow Books, 2012).

Campbell, A. *The Blair Years, Extracts from the Alastair Campbell Diaries* (London: Hutchinson, 2007).

Campbell, M. *My Autobiography* (London: Hodder and Stoughton, 2008).

Castle, B. *The Castle Diaries 1974-1976* (London: Weidenfield and Nicolson, 1980).

Dalton, H. *High Tide and After: Memoirs 1945-60* (London: Frederick Muller, 1962).

Darling, A. *Back from the Brink* (London: Atlantic Books, 2011).

Draper, D. *Blair's Hundred Days* (London: Faber and Faber, 1997).

Healey, D. *The Time of My Life* (London: Penguin Books, 1990).

Laws, D. *22 Days in May* (London: Biteback, 2010).

Lipsey, D. *In the Corridors of Power* (London: Biteback, 2012).

MacDonald, J. R. *Parliament and Democracy* (London: Leonard Parsons, 1920).

MacDonald, J. R. *Socialism & Government* (London: Independent Labour Party, 1909).

Mandelson, P. *The Third Man* (London: Harper Press, 2010).

Mitchell, A. *Confessions of a Political Maverick* (London: Biteback, 2019).

Mullin, C. *Decline and Fall, Diaries 2005-2010* (London: Profile Books, 2010).

Prescott, J. *Prezza, My Story: Pulling No Punches* (London: Headline, 2008).

Snowden, P. *An Autobiography Vol. 2* (London: Ivor Nicholson and Watson, 1934).

Straw, J. *Last Man Standing, Memoirs of a Political Survivor* (London: Macmillan, 2012).

Archives

LIPSEY, London School of Economics Special Collection.

PARKER, London School of Economics.

Working Party on Electoral Reform, Labour History and Archive Study (LHASC).

Newspapers

Daily Mail
Daily Telegraph
Financial Times
Guardian

Independent
Independent on Sunday
Irish Times
Manchester Guardian
Observer
The Sunday Times
Scotland on Sunday
Scotsman
The Times

Periodicals

Marxism Today

David, T., and Green, D. Labour's One Hope: Labour Cannot Win the Next Election', February 1989, pp. 12–13.
Marquand, D. 'Spot the Radical', July 1988, pp. 12–15.

New Statesman

'Andy Burnham Interview', 22 July 2010.
Blair, T. 'Electoral Reform Ain't the Answer', 4 September 1987, https://www.newst atesman.com/politics/2021/04/ns-archive-electoral-reform-aint-answer.
Eaton, G. 'Ed Miliband interview – on the trade unions, party funding and Arnie Graf', 24 February 2014.
Hasan, M. 'I Urge Lib Dems to Bite Their Lip and Back Us', vol. 139, no. 5000, 4 May 2010, p. 34.
Hasan, M. and Macintyre, J. 'An interview with the Culture Secretary Ben Bradshaw', vol. 137, no. 4949, 2009.

New Statesman and Society

Milton, C. 'Knee Deep in Mush', in Potted Plant: Your Guide to Labour's Great Vote Ddebate, *New Statesman and Society*, 18 June 1993, p. 3.
Samizdat, September/October 1990.
Smyth, G. 'If You Lot Carry On Like This ...', in Potted Plant: Your Guide to Labour's Great Vote Debate, *New Statesman and Society*, 18 June 1993, p. 13.

The Economist

Blair, T. 'Blair on the Constitution', 14 September 1996.
'How We Made Up Our Minds', vol. 349, no. 8092, 31 October 1998, p. 30.
'Jenkins' Ear', vol. 845, no. 8046, 6 December 1997, p. 34.

House of Commons Reports (Hansard)

House of Commons Debate, vol. 95, 28 March 1917, 4 July 1917.
House of Commons Debate, vol. 169, 12 February 1924.
House of Commons Debate, vol. 229, 2 July 1929.
House of Commons Debate, vol. 403, 10 October 1944.
House of Commons Debate, vol. 428, 28 October 1946.
House of Commons Debate, vol. 770, 14 October 1968, 11 December 1968.
House of Commons Debate, vol. 318, 5 November 1998.
House of Commons Debate, vol. 505, 9 February 2010.
House of Commons Debate, vol. 511, 7 June 2010.

Speeches

Bradshaw, B. Speech to Kings College London Think Tank Society, 24 March 2011.
Brown, G. 'Towards a New Politics', Speech to the IPPR, 2 February 2010.
Cameron, D., and Reid, J. Joint Statement, No to AV, Transport House, 18 April 2011.
Harris, T. MP for Glasgow South (2001–15), Speech to East Lothian Fabians,
    Thursday, 24 March 2011.
Jenkins, R. 'Home Thoughts from Abroad', Dimbleby Lecture, Royal Society of Arts,
    London, 22 November 1979.
Miliband, E. Launch of Labour Yes, 16 March 2011.

Television and Radio

BBC Radio 4, 11 October 2010.
Campaign Broadcast by NOtoAV.
Daily Politics, BBC 2, Thursday, 11 June 2009.
Daily Politics, BBC 2, 2 February 2010.
Daily Politics, AV Debate Special, BBC 2, 6 April 2011.
Five Days That Changed Britain, BBC 2, 29 July 2010.
Newsnight, BBC 2, 3 April 1992.

Newsnight, BBC 2, 29 July 2010.

Newsnight, BBC 2, 2 December 2010.

Newsnight, AV Referendum Debate, BBC 2, 26 April 2011.

Sky News, 10 May 2010.

Secondary literature

Books

Allen, N., and Bartle, J. *Britain at the Polls 2010* (London: Sage, 2011).

Anderson, P., and Mann, N. *Safety First: The Making of New Labour* (London: Granta, 1997).

Bagehot, W. *The English Constitution* (Glasgow: Fontana/Collins, 1963).

Barker, B. *Ramsay MacDonald's Political Writings* (London: Allen Lane, Penguin Press, 1972).

Barker, R. *Political Ideas in Modern Britain*, 2nd edn (London: Routledge, 1997).

Baston, L., and Ritchie, K. *Don't Take No for an Answer, the 2011 Referendum and the Future of Electoral Reform* (London: Biteback, 2011).

Beech, M., and Hickson, K. *Labour's Thinkers* (London: Taurus Academic Studies, 2007).

Beech, M., and Lee, S. *The Cameron-Clegg Government, Coalition Politics in an Age of Austerity* (Hampshire: Palgrave Macmillan, 2011).

Beech, M., and Lee, S. *Ten Years of New Labour* (Hampshire: Palgrave Macmillan, 2008).

Beer, S. *Modern British Politics* (London: Faber & Faber, 1982).

Benn, T. *Arguments for Democracy* (London: Jonathan Cape, 1981).

Benn, T. *Arguments for Socialism* (Middlesex: Penguin Books, 1980).

Bennie, L., et al. *British Elections & Parties Review, Vol. 12, The 2001 General Election* (London: Frank Cass, 2002).

Birch, A. H. *Representative and Responsible Government* (London: Allen & Unwin, 1964).

Blackburn, R. *The Electoral System in Britain* (Hampshire: Macmillan, 1995).

Blackburn, R., and Plant, R. *Constitutional Reform: The Labour Governments Constitutional Reform Agenda* (Harlow: Longman, 1999).

Blewett, N. *The Peers, the Parties and the People: The General Elections of 1910* (London: Macmillan, 1972).

Bogdanor, V. *Politics and the Constitution: Essays on British Government* (Aldershot: Dartmouth, 1996).

Bogdanor, V. *The British Constitution in the Twentieth Century* (Oxford: Oxford University Press, 2003).

Bogdanor, V. *The Coalition and the Constitution* (Oxford: Hart Publishing, 2011).

Bogdanor, V. *The New British Constitution* (Oxford: Hart Publishing, 2009).

Bogdanor, V. *The People and the Party System: The Referendum and Electoral Reform in British Politics* (Cambridge: Cambridge University Press, 1981).

Bogdanor, V. *What Is Proportional Representation?* (Oxford: Martin Robertson, 1984).

Boulton, A., and Jones, J. *Hung Together: The Cameron-Clegg Coalition* (London: Simon & Schuster, 2012).

Brivati, B., Buxton, J. and Seldon, A. *Contemporary History Handbook* (Manchester: Manchester University Press, 1996).

Bryman, A. *Quantity and Quality in Social Research* (London: Routledge, 1988).

Burch, M., and Moran, M. *British Politics: A Reader* (Manchester: Manchester University Press, 1987).

Butler, B., and Kavanagh, D. *The British General Election of 1992* (London: Macmillan Press, 1992).

Butler, B., and Kavanagh, D. *The British General Election of 1983* (London: Macmillan, 1983).

Butler, B., and Kavanagh, D. *The British General Election of 1997* (Basingstoke: Macmillan, 1997).

Butler, D., and King, A. *The General Election of 1966* (London: Macmillan, 1966).

Butler, D. *Coalition in British Politics* (London: Macmillan, 1978).

Butler, D. *The Electoral System in Britain 1918–1951* (Oxford: Oxford University Press, 1953).

Butler, D. *The Electoral System in Britain since 1918* (Oxford: Clarendon Press, 1963).

Callinicos, A. *The Revolutionary Road to Socialism: What the Socialist Workers Party Stands For* (London: Socialist Workers Party, 1983).

Campbell, J. *Lloyd George, the Goat in the Wilderness* (Chatham: W&J Mackay, 1977).

Catterall, P., Kaiser, W. and Walton-Jordan, U. *Reforming the Constitution Debates in Twentieth-Century Britain* (London: Frank Cass, 2000).

Cliff, T., and Gluckstein, D. *Marxism and Trade Union Struggle: The General Strike of 1926* (London: Bookmarks, 1986).

Cliff, T., and Gluckstein, D. *The Labour Party – A Marxist History* (London: Bookmarks, 1988).

The Coalition: Our Programme for Government (London: Cabinet Office: 2010).

Coates, D., and Lawler, P. (eds). *New Labour in Power* (Manchester: Manchester University Press, 2000).

Coates, D. *The Labour Party and the Struggle for Socialism* (Cambridge: Cambridge University Press, 1975).

Cole, G. D. H. *Self-Government and Industry* (London: G. Bell, 1917).

Cole, G. D. H. *Social Theory* (New York: Frederick A. Stokes, 1920).

Cook, C. *A Short History of the Liberal Party, 1900–2001* (Hampshire: Palgrave, 2002).

Cook, C., and Taylor, I. *The Labour Party: An Introduction to Its History, Structure and Politics* (London: Longman, 1980).

Cowley, P., et al. *British Elections & Parties Review, Vol. 10* (London: Frank Cass, 2000).

Cowling, M. *Conservative Essays* (London: Cassell, 1978).

Crines, A., and Hickson, K. *Harold Wilson: The Unprincipled Prime Minister?* (London: Biteback, 2016).

Crossman, R. *How Britain Is Governed* (London: Labour Book Service, 1939).

Crossman, R. *Inside View* (London: Jonathan Cape, 1972).

Crossman, R. *The Backbench Diaries of Richard Crossman*, ed. J. Morgan (New York: Hamish Hamilton and Jonathan Cape, 1981).

D'Anconna, M. *In It Together: The Inside Story of the Coalition Government* (London: Penguin Books, 2013).

Daniels, S. R. *The Case for Electoral Reform* (London: George Allen & Unwin, 1938).

De Wolf Howe, M. *Holmes-Laski Letters: The Correspondence of Mr Justice Holmes to Harold J Laski* (London: Oxford University Press, 1953).

Denver, D., et al. (eds). *British Elections & Parties Review, Vol. 8, The 1997 General Election* (London: Frank Cass, 1998).

Diamond, P., and Radice, R. *Southern Discomfort Again* (London: Policy Network, 2010).

Dorey, P. *The Labour Party and Constitutional Reform, A History of Constitutional Conservatism* (Hampshire: Palgrave Macmillan, 2008).

Downs, A. *An Economic Theory of Democracy* (New York: Harper & Row, 1957).

Drucker, H. *Doctrine and Ethos in the Labour Party* (London: George Allen & Unwin, 1979).

Duncan, G. *Democracy and the Capitalist State* (Cambridge: Cambridge University Press, 1989.

Duverger, M. *Political Parties*, 3rd edn (London: Methuen, 1992).

Evans, M. *Charter 88: A Successful Challenge to the British Political Tradition* (Hampshire: Dartmouth, 1995).

Evans, M. *Constitution-Making and the Labour Party* (Hampshire: Palgrave Macmillan, 2003).

Finer, S. *Adversary Politics and Electoral Reform* (London: Anthony Wigram, 1975).

Fisher, J., Cowley, P., Denver, D. and Russell, A. (eds). *British Elections & Parties Review, Vol. 9* (London: Frank Cass, 1999).

Foley, M. *The Politics of the British Constitution* (Manchester: Manchester University Press, 1999).

Foote, G. *The Labour Party's Political Thought: A History* (London: Croom Helm, 1986).

Gamble, A. *Britain in Decline* (Hampshire: Macmillan Education, 1981).

Geddes, A., and Tonge, J. *Labour's Landslide* (Manchester: Manchester University Press, 1997).

Geddes, A., and Tonge, J. *Britain Votes 2010* (Oxford: Oxford University Press, 2010).

Glasman, M., Rutherford, J. Stears, M. and White, S. (eds). *The Labour Tradition and the Politics of Paradox* (The Oxford London Seminars, 2010–11).

Gould, B. *A Future for Socialism* (London: Cape, 1989).

Gould, J. *The Witchfinder General* (London: Biteback, 2016).

Gould, P. *The Unfinished Revolution: How the Modernisers Saved the Labour Party* (London: Abacus, 1998).

Hain, P. *Proportional Misrepresentation: The Case Against PR in Britain* (Hampshire: Wildwood House, 1986).

Hart, J. *Proportional Representation, Critics of the British Electoral System 1820–1945* (Oxford: Clarendon Press, 1992).

Harvey, A. *Transforming Britain, Labour's Second Term* (London: Fabian Society, 2001).

Harvey, J., and Bather, L. *The British Constitution* (London: Macmillan, 1966).

Hattersley, R. *Choose Freedom: The Future for Democratic Socialism* (London: Penguin, 1987).

Heath, A., Jowell, R. and Curtice, J. 'Can Labour Win?', in A. Heath, R. Jowell, J. Curtice and B. Taylor (eds), *Labour's Last Chance? The 1992 Election and Beyond* (Aldershot: Dartmouth, 1994), p. 291.

Heath, A., Jowell, R. and Curtice, J. (eds), *Labour's Last Chance? The 1992 Election and Beyond* (Aldershort: Dartmouth, 1994).

Herman, V., and Hagger, M. (eds). *The Legislation of Direct Elections to the European Parliament* (Hampshire: Gower, 1980).

Hickson, K. *Britain's Conservative Right Since 1945* (Hampshire: Palgrave Macmillan, 2020).

Hickson, K. *The IMF Crisis of 1976 and British Politics* (London: Tauris Academic Studies, 2005).

Hickson, K., and Miles, J. *James Callaghan: An Underrated Prime Minister?* (London: Biteback, 2020).

Hickson, K., Miles, J., Taylor, H. *Peter Shore: Labour's Forgotten Patriot* (London: Biteback, 2020).

Hirst, P. *After Thatcher* (London: Collins, 1989).

Hirst, P. *From Statism to Pluralism* (London: UCL Press, 1997).

Hirst, P. *The Pluralist Theory of the State* (London: Routledge, 1989).

Hirst, P., and Khilnani, K. *Reinventing Democracy* (Oxford: Blackwell, 1996).

Hodgson, G. *Labour at the Crossroads* (Oxford: Martin Robertson, 1981).

Honeyman, V. *Richard Crossman* (London: I.B. Taurus, 2007).

Hutton, W. *The State We're In* (London: Jonathan Cape, 1995).

Hughes, C., and Wintour, P. *Labour Rebuilt* (London: Fourth Estate, 1990).

Johnston, R. J., Pattie, C. J. and Allsopp, J. G. *A Nation Dividing?* (London: Longman, 1988).

Jones, B., and Keating, M. *Labour and the British State* (Oxford: Clarendon Press, 1985).

Joyce, P. *Realignment of the Left?* (London: Macmillan, 1999).

Judge, D. *The Parliamentary State* (London: Sage, 1993).

Kavanagh, D. *The Reordering of British Politics* (Oxford: Oxford University Press, 1997).

Kavanagh, D., and Cowley, P. *The British General Election of 2010* (Hampshire: Palgrave Macmillan, 2010).

Keating, M. *The Oxford Handbook of Scottish Politics* (Oxford: Oxford University Press, 2018).

Laski, H. J. *Reflections on the Constitution* (Manchester: Manchester University Press, 1951).

Lassman, P., and Speirs, R. *Political Writings* (Cambridge: Cambridge University Press, 1994).

Linton, M., and Southcott, M. *Making Votes Count: The Case for Electoral Reform* (London: Profile Books, 1998).

Lowther, J. W. 1st Viscount Ullswater, *A Speaker's Commentaries Vol. II* (London: Edward Arnold, 1925).

Lyman, R. W. *The First Labour Government: 1924* (London: Chapman and Hall, 1957).

MacIver, D. *The Liberal Democrats* (Hemel Hempstead: Prentice Hall/Harvester Wheatsheaf, 1996).

Mackintosh, J. P. *People and Parliament* (Hampshire: Saxon House, 1978).

Mandelson, P., and Liddle, R. *The Blair Revolution: Can New Labour Deliver?* (London: Faber and Faber, 1996).

Marquand, D. *John P. Mackintosh on Parliament and Social Democracy* (London: Longmans, 1982).

Marquand, D. 'Populism or Pluralism? New Labour and the Constitution', Mishcon Lecture (London: Constitution Unit, 1999).

Marquand, D. *Ramsey MacDonald* (London: Jonathan Cape, 1977).

Marquand, D. *The Progressive Dilemma*, 2nd edn (London: Orion Books, 1999).

Marquand, D. *The Unprincipled Society* (London: Jonathan Cape, 1988).

Marsh, D., and Stoker, G. *Theory and Methods in Political Science*, 2nd edn (Hampshire: Palgrave Macmillan, 2002).

McKibbin, R. *Parties and People: England 1914–1951* (Oxford: Oxford University Press, 2010).

McKenzie, R. *Angels in Marble: Working Class Conservatives in Urban England* (London: Heinemann, 1968).

McSmith, A. *John Smith* (London: Verso, 1993).

Miliband, R. *Capitalist Democracy in Britain* (Oxford: Oxford University Press, 1982).

Miliband, R. *Parliamentary Socialism* (London: Merlin Press, 1961).

Miliband, R., and Saville, J. *Socialist Register* (London: Merlin Press, 1976).

Morgan, K. O. *Callaghan: A Life* (Oxford: Oxford University Press, 1997).

Morrison, H. *Government and Parliament* (Oxford: Oxford University Press, 1954).

Morrison, H. *Our Parliament and How It Works* (London: Labour Party, 1953).

Morrison, J. *Reforming Britain: New Labour, New Constitution?* (London: Reuters, 2001).

Nandy, L., Lucas, C. and Bowers, C. *The Alternative: Towards a New Progressive Politics* (London: Biteback, 2016).

Norton, P. *New Direction in British Politics?* (Aldershot: Edward Elgar, 1991).

Norton, P. *The Constitution in Flux* (Oxford: Martin Robertson, 1982).

Owen, F. *Tempestuous Journey: Lloyd George, His Life and Times* (London: Hutchinson, 1954).

Panitch, L. *Working-Class Politics in Crisis* (London: Verso, 1986)

Pelling, H., and Reid, A. J. *A Short History of the Labour Party*, 11th edn (Houndmills: MacMillan, 1996).

Pimlott, B. *Labour and the Left in the 1930's* (London: Allen & Unwin, 1977).

Poirier, P. P. *The Advent of the Labour Party* (London: Allen & Unwin, 1958).

Popper, K. *All Life Is Problem Solving* (Florence: Taylor and Francis, 2013).

Popper, K. *The Open Society and its Enemies*, vol. 1, 1st edn (London: Routledge & Kegan Paul, 1945).

Rawnsley, A. *Servants of the People: The Inside Story of New Labour* (London: Penguin Books, 2001).

Richards, D. *New Labour and the Civil Service: Reconstituting the Westminster Model* (Hampshire: Palgrave Macmillan, 2008).

Rose, R. *Do Parties Make A Difference* (London: Macmillan, 1980).

Ross, J. F. S, *Elections and Electors* (London: Eyre & Spottiswoode, 1955).

Rush, M., and Giddings, P. *When Gordon Took the Helm* (Hampshire: Palgrave Macmillan, 2008).

Rustin, M. *For a Pluralist Socialism* (London: Verso, 1985).

Schumpeter, J. *Capitalism, Socialism and Democracy* (London: George Allen & Unwin, 1976).

Seldon, A., and Lodge, G. *Brown at 10* (London: Biteback, 2010).

Shaw, G. B. *Fabian Essays* (London: George Allen & Unwin, 1962).

Skidelsky, R. *Politicians and the Slump: The Labour Government 1929–1931* (London: Macmillan, 1994).

Smyth, G. *Refreshing the Parts: Electoral Reform and British Politics* (London: Lawrence & Wishart, 1992).

Stuart, M. *John Smith: A Life* (London: Politico's Publishing, 2005).

Tanner, D., Thane, P. and Tiratsoo, N. *Labour's First Century* (Cambridge: Cambridge University Press, 2000).

Taylor, A. J. P. *English History 1914–1945* (London: Penguin, 1970).

Thorpe, A. *The British General Election of 1931* (Oxford: Clarendon Press, 1991).

Wainwright, H. *Labour: A Tale of Two Parties* (London: Hogarth Press, 1987).

Walkland, S. A., and Ryle, M. *The Commons in the Seventies* (Glasgow: Fontana, 1977).

Westlake, M. *Kinnock: The Biography* (London: Little, Brown, 2001).

Wilson, T. *Downfall of the Liberal Party 1914–1935* (London: Collins, 1966).

Wilson, T. *The Political Diaries of C. P. Scott, 1911–1928* (London: Collins, 1970).

Worcester, R., and Mortimore, R. *Explaining Labour's Landslide* (London: Politico's Publishing, 1999).

Wright, T. *Citizens and Subjects: An Essay on British Politics* (London: Routledge, 1994).

Ziegler, P. *Wilson: The Authorised Life* (London: Weidenfield & Nicolson, 1993).

Journal articles

Allsopp, S. 'An Inquest into the Treatment of the Proportional Representation Issue during the General Election', *Representation*, vol. 31, no. 113 (1992), pp. 12–14.

Bartle, J. 'Labour and Liberal Democrat Relations after 7th June 2001', *Representation*, vol. 38, no. 3 (2001), pp. 231–41.

Beetham, D. 'The Plant Report and the Theory of Political Representation', *Political Quarterly*, vol. 63, no. 4 (1992), pp. 460–7.

Best, K. 'Plant: A Conservative View', *Representation*, vol. 31, no. 116 (1993), pp. 80–1.

Blackburn, R. 'The Ruins of Westminster', *New Left Review*, vol. I, no. 191 (January–February 1992), pp. 5–35.

Blunkett, D., and Richards, D. 'Labour in and out of Government: Political Ideas, Political Practice and the British Political Tradition', *Political Studies Review*, vol. 9, no. 2 (2011), pp. 178–92.

Bogdanor, V. 'The Constitution and the Party System in the Twentieth Century', *Parliamentary Affairs*, vol. 5, no. 4 (2004), pp. 717–33.

Butler, D. 'The Plant Report 1993: The Third Report of Labour's Working Party on Electoral Systems', *Representation*, vol. 31, no. 116 (1993), pp. 77–9.

Catterall, P. 'The British Electoral System, 1885–1970', *Historical Research*, vol. 73 (June 2000), pp. 156–74.

Cole, M. 'The Fabian Society', *Political Quarterly*, vol. 15, no. 3 (July 1944), pp. 245–56.

Cowley, P., and Stuart, M. 'From Labour Love-In to Bona Fide Party of Opposition', *Journal of Liberal History*, vol. 43 (Summer 2004), pp. 18–19.

Curtice, J. 'The Death of a Miserable Little Compromise: The Alternative Vote Referendum', *Political Insight* (September 2011), pp. 14–17.

Curtice, J. 'Politicians, Voters and Democracy: The 2011 UK Referendum on the Alternative Vote', *Electoral Studies*, vol. 32 (2013), pp. 215–23.

Curtice, J. 'So What Went Wrong with the Electoral System? The 2010 Election Result and the Debate about Electoral Reform', *Parliamentary Affairs*, vol. 63, no. 4 (2010), pp. 623–38.

Diamond, P. 'Beyond the Westminster Model: The Labour Party and the Machinery of the British Parliamentary State', *Renewal*, vol. 19, no. 1 (2011), pp. 64–73.

Dummett, M. 'Toward a More Representative Voting System: *The Plant Report*', *New Left Review*, vol. 194 (July/August 1992), pp. 98–113.

Dunleavy, P., and Margetts, H. 'Mixed Electoral Systems in Britain and the Jenkins Commission on Electoral Reform', *British Journal of Politics and International Relations*, vol. 1, no. 1 (April 1999), pp. 12–38.

Eatwell, R., and Wright, A. 'Labour and the Lessons of 1931', *History*, vol. 63, no. 1 (1978), pp. 38–53.

Ellis, T. 'Dear Professor Plant', *Representation*, vol. 30, no. 112 (1991), pp. 59–60.

Ellis, T. 'The Plant Report: An Assessment', *Representation*, vol. 30, no. 112 (1991), pp. 63–5.

Emy, H. 'The Mandate and Responsible Government', *Australian Journal of Political Science*, vol. 32, no. 1 (1997), pp. 65–78.

Fair, J. D. 'The Second Labour Government and the Politics of Electoral Reform, 1929–1931', *Albion: A Quarterly Journal Concerned with British Studies*, vol. 13, no. 3 (Autumn 1981), pp. 276–301.

Gamble, A. 'The Progressive Dilemma Revisted', *Political Quarterly*, vol. 88, no. 1 (2017), pp. 136–43.

Georghiou, M. 'Labour Responses to Plant', *Representation*, vol. 31, no. 116 (1993), pp. 81–3.

Hanson, A. H. 'The Labour Party and House of Commons Reform – I', *Parliamentary Affairs*, vol. 10, no. 4 (1956), pp. 454–68.

Hanson, A. H. 'The Labour Party and House of Commons Reform – II', *Parliamentary Affairs*, vol. 11, no. 1 (1957), pp. 39–56.

Hennesy, P., and Coates, S. 'The Back of the Envelope: Hung Parliaments, the Queen and the Constitution', *Strathclyde Analysis Paper*, No. 5 (Glasgow: Department of Government, University of Strathclyde, 1991).

Hofferbert, R., and Budge, I. 'The Party Mandate and the Westminster Model: Election Programmes and Government Spending in Britain, 1945–85', *British Journal of Political Science*, vol. 22, no. 2 (April 1992), pp. 151–82.

Jones, B. 'The Road Not Taken and the 'Bad Faith' Theses: Why a Liberal Democrat-Labour Coalition Never Happened in May 2010', *Political Quarterly*, vol. 84, no. 4 (2013), pp. 460–9.

Johnston, R., and Pattie, C. 'Parties and Crossbenchers Voting in the Post-2010 House of Lords: The Example of the Parliamentary Voting System and Constituencies Bill', *British Politics*, vol. 6, no. 4 (2011), pp. 430–52.

Lamport, T. 'The Plant Report Two Years On – Some Reflections', *Representation*, vol. 33, no. 3 (1995), pp. 17–22.

Lipsey, D. 'Keeping the Plus in AV+', *Representation*, vol. 37, nos 3–4 (2000), pp. 231–6.

Marquand, D. 'Democracy in Britain', *Political Quarterly*, vol. 71, no. 3 (2000), pp. 268–76.

Mclean, I. 'The Jenkins Commission and the Implications of Electoral Reform for the UK Constitution', *Government and Opposition*, vol. 34, no. 2 (1999), pp. 143–60.

Morrison, H. 'British Parliamentary Democracy', *Parliamentary Affairs*, vol. 4, no. 2 (1949), pp. 349–60.

Norris, P. 'Anatomy of a Labour landslide', *Parliamentary Affairs*, vol. 50 (1997), pp. 509–32.

Norris, P. 'The Politics of Electoral Reform in Britain', *International Political Science Review*, vol. 16, no. 1 (1995), pp. 65–78.

Oliver, D. 'The Progressive Coalition That Never Was – Lessons from the Ashdown-Blair "Project"', *Journal of Liberal History*, vol. 83 (2014), pp. 45–7.

Plant, R. 'Criteria for Electoral Systems: The Labour Party and Electoral Reform', *Parliamentary Affairs*, vol. 44, no. 4 (1991), pp. 549–57.

Plant, R. 'The Plant Report: A Retrospective', *Representation*, vol. 33, no. 2 (1995), pp. 5–16.

Pugh, M. 'Political Parties and the Campaign for Proportional Representation 1905–1914', *Parliamentary Affairs*, vol. 33, no. 1 (1980), pp. 294–307.

Qvortrup, M. 'Voting on Electoral Reform: A Comparative Perspective on the Alternative Vote Referendum in the United Kingdom', *Political Quarterly*, vol. 83, no. 1 (2012), pp. 108–16.

Rallings, C., and Thrasher, M. 'Suppose UK Voters Accept the Alternative Vote in the May Referendum … but Then Don't Use AV to Single Multiple Party Preferences?' *British Politics and Policy at LSE* (blog), 2010.

Reilly, B. 'The Plant Report and the Supplementary Vote: Not So Unique After All', *Representation*, vol. 34, no. 2 (1997), pp. 95–102.

Sanders, D., Clarke, H. D., Stuart, M. C. and Whiteley, P. 'Simulating the Effects of the Alternative Vote in the 2010 UK General Election', *Parliamentary Affairs*, vol. 64, no. 1 (2011), pp. 5–23.

Scargill, A. 'Proportional Representation: A Socialist Concept', *New Left Review*, vol. 1, no. 158 (1986), pp. 76–80.

Seawright, D. ' "Yes, the Census": The 2011 UK Referendum Campaign on the Alternative Vote', *British Politics*, vol. 8, no. 4 (2013), pp. 457–75.

Straw, J. 'New Labour, Constitutional Change and Representative Democracy', *Parliamentary Affairs*, vol. 63, no. 2 (2010), pp. 356–68.

Utley, T. E. 'The Mandate', *Cambridge Journal*, vol. 3, no. 1 (1949), pp. 3–18.

Wainwright, R. 'Liberal Democrat Reaction to Plant', *Representation*, vol. 31, no. 116 (1993), p. 79.

Whiteley, P., Clarke, H. D., Sanders, D. and Stewart, M. 'Britain Says NO: Voting in the AV Ballot Referendum', *Parliamentary Affairs*, vol. 65 (2012), pp. 301–22.

Wright, A. 'British Socialists and the British Constitution', *Parliamentary Affairs*, vol. 43 (1990), pp. 322–40.

Wright, T. 'Electoral Reform: A Challenge for New Labour', *Representation*, vol. 33, no. 2 (1995), pp. 31–3.

Theses

Kirkup, J. 'The Parliamentary Agreement between the Labour Party and the Liberal Party 1977–1978 "The Lab-Lib Pact"', PhD Thesis, Cardiff University, United Kingdom, 2012.

Morris, A. 'Labour and Electoral Reform, 1900–1997', PhD Thesis, University of Essex, United Kingdom, 2005.

Pugh, M. 'The Background to the Representation of the People Act of 1918', PhD Thesis, University of Bristol, United Kingdom, 1974.

Online articles

Blomfield, P. 'Beyond Tribalism', *Progress*, www.progressonline.org.uk/2012/11/30/beyond-tribalism (accessed 9 September 2015).

'Deliver, Don't Dither. Labour Must Drop Its Obsession with Constitutional Issues', LabourList, http://labourlist.org/2010/01/our-strategy-is-quintessential-classic-new-labour-the-ed-balls-interview/ (accessed 30 September 2016).

http://labouryes.org.uk/video-trade-unions-say-yes/ (accessed 3 October 2012).

http://liberalconspiracy.org/2009/page/23/ (accessed 14 May 2015).

http://news.bbc.co.uk/1/hi/events/euros_99/news/368450.stm (accessed 27 January 2015).

http://www.bbc.co.uk/news/uk-politics-13082549 (accessed 21 October 2016).

http://www.newstatesman.com/uk-politics/2009/12/prescott-blair-interview.

http://www.politics.co.uk/news/2010/05/11/labour-heavyweights-come-out-against-lib-lab- (accessed 5 October 2015).

https://www.politicshome.com/news/uk/social-affairs/politics/news/69720/union-bosses-tell-ed-miliband-give-lib-dems-election (accessed 15 December 2016).

'John Spellar: The People Have Spoken. They Don't Want Electoral Reform', LabourList, https://labourlist.org/2016/07/the-people-have-spoken-they-dont-electoral-reform/.

'Proportional Representation? Bad Tactics, Bad Strategy and Bad for Britain', LabourList, http://revolts.co.uk/?p=711 (accessed 30 September 2016).

'Tony Blair Is Wrong – Labour Should Have Nothing to Do with the Lib Dems', LabourList, http://ukpollingreport.co.uk/historical-polls/voting-intent ion-1992-1997 (accessed 16 December 2021).

Interviews

- Dame Margaret Beckett MP, 26 March 2014, Houses of Parliament.
- Lord Elder, 27 March 2014, Houses of Parliament.
- Lord Rosser, 28 March 2014, Houses of Parliament.
- Lord Whitty, 31 March 2014, Houses of Parliament.
- Charles Clarke, 21 May 2014, St Ermins Hotel, London.
- Dr Tim Lamport, 14 July 2014, Personal Residence, Croydon.
- Baroness Armstrong, 16 July 2014, Houses of Parliament.
- Lord Hattersley, 17 November 2014, Houses of Parliament.
- Lord Lipsey, 21 January 2015, Houses of Parliament.
- Baroness Gould, 3 March 2015, Telephone Interview.
- Lord Mandelson, 31 March 2015, Telephone Interview.
- John Edmonds, 9 April 2015, Kings College London.
- Tom Harris, 2 October 2015, Café Gandolfi, Candleriggs, Glasgow.
- Ben Bradshaw MP, 21 October 2015, Telephone Interview.
- Alan Johnson MP, 23 October 2015, Telephone Interview.
- Lord Plant, 14 September 2016, Houses of Parliament.

Personal correspondence

- Bryan Gould, 26 February 2014.

Index